Comparative Encounte
Artaud, Michaux and The
Rationality, Cosmology and Ethics

LEGENDA

LEGENDA, founded in 1995 by the European Humanities Research Centre of the University of Oxford, is now a joint imprint of the Modern Humanities Research Association and Routledge. Titles range from medieval texts to contem-porary cinema and form a widely comparative view of the modern humanities, including works on Arabic, Catalan, Chinese, English, French, German, Greek, Italian, Portuguese, Russian, Spanish, and Yiddish literature. An Editorial Board of distinguished academic specialists works in collaboration with leading scholarly bodies such as the Society for French Studies, the British Comparative Literature Association and the Association of Hispanists of Great Britain & Ireland.

MHRA

The Modern Humanities Research Association (MHRA) encourages and promotes advanced study and research in the field of the modern humanities, especially modern European languages and literature, including English, and also cinema. It also aims to break down the barriers between scholars working in different disciplines and to maintain the unity of humanistic scholarship in the face of increasing specialization. The Association fulfils this purpose primarily through the publication of journals, bibliographies, monographs and other aids to research.

LONDON AND NEW YORK

Routledge is a global publisher of academic books, journals and online resources in the humanities and social sciences. Founded in 1836, it has published many of the greatest thinkers and scholars of the last hundred years, including Adorno, Einstein, Russell, Popper, Wittgenstein, Jung, Bohm, Hayek, McLuhan, Marcuse and Sartre. Today Routledge is one of the world's leading academic publishers in the Humanities and Social Sciences. It publishes thousands of books and journals each year, serving scholars, instructors, and professional communities worldwide.

www.routledge.com

TRANSCRIPT

Transcript publishes books about all kinds of imagining across languages, media and cultures: translations and versions, inter-cultural and multi-lingual writing, illustrations and musical settings, adaptation for theatre, film, TV and new media, creative and critical responses. We are open to studies of any combination of languages and media, in any historical moments, and are keen to reach beyond Legenda's traditional focus on modern European languages to embrace anglophone and world cultures and the classics. We are interested in innovative critical approaches: we welcome not only the most rigorous scholarship and sharpest theory, but modes of writing that stretch or cross the boundaries of those discourses.

www.legendabooks.com/series/transcript

TRANSCRIPT

1. *Adapting the Canon: Translation, Visualisation, Interpretation*, edited by Ann Lewis and Silke Arnold-de Simine
2. *Adapted Voices: Transpositions of Céline's Voyage au bout de la nuit and Queneau's Zazie dans le métro*, by Armelle Blin-Rolland
3. *Zola and the Art of Television: Adaptation, Recreation, Translation*, by Kate Griffiths
4. *Comparative Encounters between Artaud, Michaux and the* Zhuangzi*: Rationality, Cosmology and Ethics*, by Xiaofan Amy Li
5. *Minding Borders: Resilient Divisions in Literature, the Body and the Academy*, edited by Nicola Gardini, Adriana Jacobs, Ben Morgan, Mohamed-Salah Omri and Matthew Reynolds

Comparative Encounters between Artaud, Michaux and the *Zhuangzi*

Rationality, Cosmology and Ethics

Xiaofan Amy Li

LONDON AND NEW YORK

2015

First published 2015 by Modern Humanities Research Association and Routledge

2 Park Square, Milton Park, Abingdon, Oxfordshire OX14 4RN
52 Vanderbilt Avenue, New York, NY 10017

Routledge is an imprint of the Taylor & Francis Group, an informa business

First issued in paperback 2020

ISBN 978-1-909662-67-4 (hbk)
ISBN 978-0-367-60520-9 (pbk)

CONTENTS

ACKNOWLEDGEMENTS

I am especially indebted to Martin Crowley for his insightful and constructive discussions, and extremely encouraging guidance during my doctoral research, which laid the foundations for this book. I also thank in particular Professor Sir Geoffrey E. R. Lloyd for his enthusiasm, kindness, interest in my work and inspirational conversations, which have been and still are invaluable for thinking about my research. I also express my gratitude to Ian James and Timothy Mathews, who pointed out challenging questions and gave me excellent advice in regard to how to develop ideas for this book; Matthew Reynolds for his support for this book project and other aspects of my research life during my Junior Research Fellowship; John Moffett for sharing his massive knowledge on bibliography with me; Graham Nelson and Anna Davies for their prompt and extremely helpful guidance throughout the production of this book; as well as my two anonymous reviewers for their helpful and encouraging comments on the manuscript.

I would also like to extend thanks to the French department, MML Cambridge, and Queens' College, Cambridge, for providing me with such a warm and excellent academic environment during my doctoral research which led to this book; to the Needham Research Institute for providing research material and space for discussions; to St Anne's College, Oxford, for supporting me as a Junior Research Fellow since September 2013; and to the John Fell OUP Research Fund, which has provided funding for the research from which this publication arises. I am lucky to have resided in such welcoming and intellectually stimulating places.

I am also extremely grateful to my friends for conversations related to this book and general intellectual discussions that stimulated my research. Special thanks go to Minyan Sun, Shuangyi Li, and Yang Fu. And last but not least, big thanks and love to my parents, who have given me unwavering support throughout my research and life.

X.A.L., Oxford, March 2015

INTRODUCTION

The possibility of dialogue

Imagine Artaud and Michaux, both Francophone writers of the twentieth century and great admirers of Chinese culture, meeting with the ancient Chinese thinker Zhuangzi for a chat. What would such an encounter be like? Should not Artaud and Michaux be particularly interested in hearing what Zhuangzi has to say, since they have read about him and are fascinated by ancient Chinese thought? Would the three thinkers discover common interests and argue about differences in opinion? How would such a conversation transform their ways of thinking, and ours?

Such a scene of encounter between different minds and perspectives or across time and space should not be unfamiliar, for is it not the dream shared by many readers that the writers and thinkers they have read about would meet each other in dialogue? And such dialogues have indeed taken place, both in real life and literary space. We know of Bergson's heated debate with Einstein on relativity and time in 1922, the hilarious competition between the ghosts of Aeschylus and Euripides over the throne of tragedy as staged in Aristophanes's *Frogs*, or Dante's meeting with past famous figures in the *Inferno*. These encounters have never been inconsequential, nor left the encountering subjects unchanged. Despite the failure to agree on some mutual understanding between the philosopher's time and the physicist's time, Bergson went away to produce his much disputed *Durée et simultanéité* and insisted on the specificity of philosophical time, whereas Einstein increasingly took the stance of the physicist who thinks the philosopher's views on time say nothing more than psychological issues.[1] The debate itself also sparked much thought on intellectual changes in modernity, dubbed by Merleau-Ponty as the 'crisis of reason', and heralded the growing animosity between philosophy and science which radicalized later in the twentieth century. We also know that Aeschylus's triumph over Euripides by the end of the *Frogs* not only voices Aristophanes's deep desire to return to the good old ways and values which Aeschylus was seen to represent, but also shows how Euripidean tragedy reflected a major shift in intellectual tendencies and world-view in classical Athens.

Likewise, the fictional encounter between Artaud, Michaux and Zhuangzi would also be significant, as I will aim to show. First, let us continue to imagine that the three thinkers start their conversation with self-introductions, which then leads them to reflect on their posthumous images. Most likely, I believe, they would feel slightly frustrated and ruffled on this topic. Artaud, with his usual disdain for critics, would start off by protesting vehemently: 'I am so annoyed that when people think about me now, they first discuss some guy called Deleuze who stole my concept "the body without organs" ("corps sans organes"). In fact, people now think this idea is — indeed, that *I* am — Deleuzian! Also, I really wish people would read more of my other works rather than get fixated on my *Théâtre et son double.* Well of course, that is one of my own favourites. But I also wrote it with a deep hatred for theatre. I hated theatre so much that I wanted to destroy it by turning it into cosmology. On top of this, a bunch of theorists have insisted on my "mad language", or "schizophrenia", or "simulation of madness" — whatever they call it. But I cannot have stressed enough, on every possible occasion, that I am not mad, nor pretending to be so! Why does nobody understand that I highly appreciate lucid understanding and even mathematical thinking?'[2]

'Ah, I can sympathize with you', Michaux now chimes in, 'for similar things have happened to me too. I have been labelled "existentialist" and "solipsist" on various occasions — oh, the horror of these isms! Some people have also created numerous different ways to analyse the texture of my language, since they too eagerly understand my drug writings, my interest in magic and images as pure aesthetic and poetic concerns. Sometimes they even forget *what* I am saying by thinking that what I am saying is really simply *how* I am saying it. But I am not only a poet; in fact very often I'd rather be a sailor, a sage, an omniscient! This is one of the biggest reasons why China and India fascinated me, why I tried to travel as far as possible, even into the space of my own body and mind.'

At this point Zhuangzi sighs: 'All your grievances are as nothing compared to mine. My writings and those of my followers were chopped up into pieces, some lost or corrupted during tumultuous years of social unrest. Then in the second century BCE some careless historian classified the bunch of texts under my name into the Daoist school — actually I don't know what this school is about! Some 300 years later, these texts were further edited by someone who was so chock-full of himself that he had to use the opportunity of editing me to smuggle in his own philosophical system.[3] Since then many people tried to make sense of this hotchpotch of texts called the *Zhuangzi*, some trying to prove the connections between different sections, the meaning of a chapter, a passage, down to the most microscopic sentence and term. They are at loggerheads about what I mean, just like the Confucian and Mohist disputers I lampooned![4] Now I have all kinds of labels such as "relativist", "idealist", "joker", "mystic", "nihilist"... But! — this is not what bothers me most. For I was not writing for author copyright nor do I really care about how others label me. I said in the text (or was it I who said it? but that doesn't matter) that I speak with abandonment and my words are flights of enigmas (*diaogui* 弔詭), that my audience should hear them in abandonment too. Unfortunately most of the people who have tried to understand me have failed to do so. I would prefer people to be inspired by my texts so that they do something *interesting* with them.'

Now, after this mini-tirade of imaginary complaints, my reader may be feeling a mixture of amusement and indignation. Fair enough, even if these writers feel unhappy about their reception, why should readers' freedom of interpretation be restricted by authorial intentions and preferences? Anyway, we cannot approach texts as their authors do, just as it is impossible for the musician to hear herself playing music in the same way as her listeners. Moreover, this whole dialogue is not possible, for even if Artaud, Michaux and Zhuangzi could meet in a fictional space, what language would they speak to communicate with each other? And even if supplied with some magical means of communication, would they speak like this? Is this what they would really think about their reception? These questions are precisely relevant to the issues I address in this book, for the book itself will be a translatory and comparative medium between the personae that embody Artaud, Michaux and Zhuangzi's works and thought. Indeed, these personae can only speak in the way imagined above because I have put these words into their mouths, because I have understood and translated them thus. This is why they necessarily remain fictional personifications, for by being so they do not aim to reveal the 'true' Artaud, Michaux and Zhuangzi.

Translating and interpreting the voices of literary and philosophical personae is simultaneously an inevitability and an advantage. There is no way to hear these voices but through a medium, and by using different and multiple media their voices will sound different and say different things. This is what makes reading and thinking about them so much fun. By serving as the translatory medium between my three personae, this book will communicate their philosophical thought to each other and explore what happens when they start comparing and interacting. The study will also address the insufficiencies in reception my three personae pointed out, which are the current critical problems that I believe to exist — namely, that despite the corpus of existing studies on Artaud, Michaux and the *Zhuangzi* (the text), some of which are extremely important and interesting contributions, there is still much space for rethinking these texts, retrieving them from certain appropriations, and taking new interpretative approaches.

Consider now these questions: can Artaud and Michaux write rationally and didactically, and think cosmologically? Can the *Zhuangzi* be used as a generator of ideas and comparative perspective from which Artaud and Michaux will be seen in a new light? Are there ways of doing a philosophical rather than literary reading of these texts, treating what they say more propositionally than stylistically? These descriptions do not fit with their typical images as avant-garde *poètes maudits* and the *Zhuangzi* as an exemplary text that debunks all theory and systematization. But these anti-typical questions about these thinkers and texts (implied already in the fictional conversation above) are exactly those that I find most interesting and worthy of exploration. There is still much to ask about their philosophical status, especially the thesis of irrationality and epistemological nihilism that is habitually attributed to them, as well as the insufficiently-studied themes of philosophical cosmology, nature and corresponding ethics in their thought. Too much ink has been spilt on how iconoclastic, transgressive and aestheticist these thinkers are, so that the possibility that their works have rational and ethically transformative dimensions is easily overlooked. Seeing something from an unexpected viewpoint is one of the great delights of reading and re-understanding familiar literature, and it is especially enriching when you find that it can be justifiably done. This book sets out to argue that not only can we re-understand and use Artaud, Michaux and the *Zhuangzi* in this way, but also that the themes of rationality, cosmology and ethics are particularly pertinent to bridging a comparative dialogue between the three texts.

My discussion and arguments of this book will unfold in successive steps, each engaging with a major issue and leading to the next. Chapter 1 is a methodological prelude to the following chapters. It examines the very possibility of this book's comparative enterprise by discussing the challenges arising from questions about cross-cultural translation and comparison, and proposes new ways to think about comparative criticism that could overcome impasses such as incommensurability and the definition of comparability. Having established the methodological grounds, Chapters 2 to 5 proceed to engage with textual and thematic discussions. Chapter 2 examines the question of rationality, as well as its intimately related issue of knowledge. It considers the rational and non-rational methods of writing inherent in the form of Artaud's, Michaux's and the *Zhuangzi*'s texts, and well as their views on reason and knowledge. The problem of irrationality — one major thesis in existing criticisms — will be addressed first. Then the chapter goes on to demonstrate that logic, reason and knowledge are present in these writers' thought, as well as madness, scepticism and fantasy. Thus emerges the need for a non-reductive interpretative approach that does not impose consistency and systematization on the texts, so that these texts' non-rational but not *irrational* modes of thought can be established as the basis for their metaphysics.

Chapters 3 and 4 both engage with cosmology, but from two different aspects. Chapter 3 explores the cosmological dimensions of time and space. It relates back to chapter 2, for the indeterminate and sometimes paradoxical views on time and space expressed by Artaud, Michaux and the *Zhuangzi* can only be understood when the reader recognizes their non-rational modes of thought and challenge to systematic knowledge. The analysis centres upon two issues: the shape of time, where I argue that neither linear nor cyclical time well describes these texts' views; and infinity in space, particularly on how the infinite is both maximal and minimal, cosmic and personal. Chapter 4 then continues the theme of cosmology but considers it from the idea of nature, which is central to any understanding of the cosmos. It focuses on the themes of nature as fate, nature as *phusis* and transformation, and the nature-culture problem, and demonstrates nature's crucial importance to the systems of thought in Artaud, Michaux and the *Zhuangzi*. Nevertheless, 'nature' needs to be re-understood as a *multiplicity* not only in a non-dual relationship to man and culture but also *internal* to them.

Finally, from the non-rational, cosmological and nature-based views discussed in chapters 2 to 4, I move on to examine in chapter 5 how a concern for ethics is manifest in the texts, for their non-rational modes of thought, indeterminate cosmology and ambiguous articulations of nature all lead to the question of ethical action. The discussion first compares some key ideas about ethics in different cultures to question certain assumptions about ethics in European thought, and then explores three important concepts and debates in ethics that Artaud, Michaux and the *Zhuangzi* engage with: the gift, indifference, and agency. Through these conceptual dialogues between literature and philosophy, the texts will be revealed to point towards a non-normative, relational and embodied ethics that values spontaneous action without subjective agency.

We may now recall the primary questions triggered by the encounter of these three thinkers — namely, how would their ideas interact, and what change would such a conversation bring about? Employing broad philosophical themes to interlace, compare and put the thought of these three authors into dialogue, I take a two-layered approach to these questions. The first interpretative layer concerns these texts themselves, and seeks to examine how Artaud and Michaux can be rethought through the specific metaphysical issues that the *Zhuangzi* raises. Rationality, cosmology and ethics then act as conceptual frameworks that structure this examination, for they are common concerns of the texts as well as philosophical issues that are broad enough to be applicable not only to European culture and thought. The dialogue bridged between the texts then leads to the second interpretative layer: the less local and more abstract level of metaphysical thought beyond these texts, the understanding of which is nevertheless deepened by these texts' contribution. In other words, this book serves to point out the significance and consequences of the cross-cultural and cross-temporal encounter between these texts. By the end of this comparative dialogue, I hope it will have offered the reader a refreshed picture of Artaud, Michaux, and the *Zhuangzi,* painted in new perspectives. At the same time, this picture also illustrates the contemporary relevance of these writers' ideas for expanding our understanding of certain important metaphysical concepts, as well as offering new methods and possibilities for the comparative study of literature.

Notes to the Introduction

1. See Jimena Canales's 2005 article documenting Bergson and Einstein's debate.
2. This fictional account of how Artaud could speak is, however, based on Artaud's writings and preferences. Given that Artaud is someone who would accuse Lewis Carroll of plagiarizing his translation of Carroll, as well as writing a diatribe against the stereotype of the mad artist in his *Van Gogh, le suicidé de la société,* it would not be unreasonable to imagine him ranting against his critics.
3. This is the basic story of the transmission and reception of the *Zhuangzi.* Its classification in the Daoist school of thought by Sima Tan (ca. 165–110 BCE) and its edition by the philosopher Guo Xiang (ca. 300 CE) are the two significant instances that have given the *Zhuangzi* the label 'Daoist', and made the text what it is today.
4. This can be found in *ZZ,* 2.4.

CHAPTER 1

Variations on Perspective: Clearing the Methodological Grounds

Holding a cross-cultural dialogue between Artaud, Michaux and the *Zhuangzi* so far looks very promising. But a percipient reader may turn to the very basics of this interpretative enterprise and question its primary conditions: is it even possible to start such a dialogue? Can the *Zhuangzi*, a syncretist text dating from the fourth century BCE and fraught with uncertainties in meaning in every passage, be translated in a way that makes sense in the context of a comparison with two writers who are different in just about every aspect (language, culture, history...)? What does it take to translate different intellectual and cultural experiences into each other? And if we can, is it desirable to do so? Although the comparative method seems to offer a tempting perspective onto wider and more exotic horizons, on what grounds is it anchored? Can we simply pluck writers and texts from any context and 'do' comparative literature?

These doubts about translation and comparison reflect the fundamental problems in comparative criticism, but are particularly radicalized by the comparison that this book purports to construct. Though there is already no dearth of comparative studies between European literatures, or between writers and texts that share a certain cultural tradition or historical era, a comparison such as that between Artaud, Michaux and the *Zhuangzi* poses questions about translatability and comparability in a much starker way. And this is precisely the methodological aim and interest of this book, for it does not treat translation and comparison as simply methods that structurally support its discussions but which become obscured in the end result, submerged in the façade of interpretation. Rather, my architectural vision of the book is a clear glass building where its bolts and nuts are seen. Much as the methodological questions about comparison stem from my chosen texts and writers for comparison, this choice also stems from the questions I want to ask. To see is to see from a perspective, and the intercultural and comparative perspective is, alongside the other central themes, also one major topic of this study.

Variation one: Translation as interpretation and the comparative experience of other cultures

Translation — understood both linguistically and metaphorically — is one of the most familiar perspectives that we constantly employ in life. Nevertheless, our literary and cultural sensibility is also constantly haunted by the fear of the untranslatable. We know that the translation will never be faithful to the original, that it is always more or less an interpretation. In the case of the *Zhuangzi*, the interpretative element in translation is particularly significant, because there is no way to talk about the text in its own language: classical Chinese. Nor can we access its living context. Even translating the text into modern Chinese means interpreting and explaining the original textual ambiguities in a certain way, which explains why there is so much debate about which Chinese translation of the *Zhuangzi* is better, or whether there is a single satisfactory Chinese translation at all. In this study, all citations from the *Zhuangzi* are my own translations (or occasionally modified from an existing translation I like), which take classical Chinese grammar as the most important guiding principle. This means that the *Zhuangzi*'s words presented here are my reading of them, since not a little interpretation is required to render the text into readable English (in fact the original text itself is sometimes unreadable). This interpretational caveat about translating the *Zhuangzi* has to be borne in mind throughout the book, for I am only presenting one possible view of the text to explore how this particular view becomes the starting point of a dialogue with other thinkers and intellectual traditions. As mentioned above, the main novelty of this book's engagement with the *Zhuangzi* is not focusing on the excavation of meaning through the textual intricacies, but on how the text can be used to inspire new thought about Artaud and Michaux. The same goes for the French writers, for I am not primarily interested in what their works mean by themselves, but what they could mean when seen from the perspectives of different Zhuangzian ideas. In this sense, my emphasis is on operation rather than meaning, centrifugal inspiration from the *Zhuangzi* instead of centripetal exegesis within the text.

Besides the problem of translating the *Zhuangzi*, there is also the difficulty of how to treat the text. We know that the present edition of the text is a patchwork of different fragments of different authors assembled into thirty-three chapters. These chapters have been divided posthumously as the Inner chapters (1–7), Outer chapters (8–22), and Miscellaneous chapters (23–33), the Inner chapters being conventionally regarded as the most authentic or ancient parts of the whole *Zhuangzi*.[1] Any reader of the text would naturally wonder whose voice is speaking in a specific passage, or how to make sense of the plethora of different, sometimes contradictory ideas the whole corpus presents. My approach, however, does not endorse any partiality to more 'authentic' chapters, nor addresses the problem of attributing authorship. The *Zhuangzi* functions as a text for me and I do not need to access its authors' psychology, nor believe that a single author is always self-consistent, or that different authors cannot coincide. I treat the *Zhuangzi* as a textual entirety that offers a mine of different ideas scattered in different sections, but not an entirety that reflects *as a whole* any consistent views or theories. In other words, I say that certain views on rationality, for instance, can be found in the *Zhuangzi*, but not that the *Zhuangzi* endorses a particular stance towards rationality. This approach also works for Artaud and Michaux, who are highly inconsistent and 'messy' writers whose writings resist systematization and fixed intellectual positions.

But translation is always more than translation. Linguistic rendering into another sign system is only the peak of the iceberg, and especially so in the case of translating ideas into cultural dialogues that go well beyond the contextual specificities from which these ideas emerged. Comparatively reading Artaud, Michaux and the *Zhuangzi* is also an extended way of translating them into each other, into philosophical concepts and discourses about rationality, cosmology and ethics. Through this process, different cultural and intellectual experiences suddenly seem to be transferable; the medium of comparison as translation, at first an indirect way of experience, seems to become the interstitial space where one can experience different cultures most directly and simultaneously. Of course, there is much reason to rejoice if this is indeed the case, for this would almost be an ideal cultural eclecticism that opens up our epistemological and experiential horizons. On the other hand, do we really want this to happen? Do we not fear that too much is lost, especially cultural specificity and identity, in such a process? Isn't the very idea that cultural experiences — in fact, any experiences — are exchangeable and available to others to re-experience both terrifying and repugnant?

What is at stake in cultural translation and comparison almost always concerns what we lose and gain from this practice, and whether the gain is worth the loss. This is why so few critics have dealt well with Artaud's and Michaux's fascination with the Far East, for it can be so easily slipped into the clothes of the naïve exoticist who fantasizes about an Oriental alternative to life and thought. This also explains why for a long time, and sometimes even now, sinologists have persisted in upholding some kind of incommensurability or untranslatability when Chinese culture is compared with others. For instance, possible doubts about my approach to translating and using the *Zhuangzi* could be: should it be translated into this comparative context? Can we properly talk about concepts laden with baggage such as 'reason' and 'nature' in such a text, and relate Western theories to it? In my view, these questions reflect the fundamental dilemma between difference and sameness. Namely, it involves the argument that different cultures and languages are incommensurable and cannot be meaningfully discussed within one (usually Eurocentric) framework, versus the view that there are universally shared commonalities between all human civilizations and that cultures are not self-enclosed cocoons but can be translated into each other. The first view has found not a little support in sinology, as debates on whether Chinese philosophy is philosophy, whether Chinese modernity is modernity, or whether Chinese feminism is feminism show.[2] In resistance to an all-too-easy cross-cultural communication, sinologists have typically insisted upon historical context, commentatorial tradition, and refused to gel with the free-flowing pan-nutritional fluid of Western theory for fear of Eurocentricism. I believe, however, that comparison neither means decontextualization, nor judges one culture in terms of another.[3] In fact, sinology has always been inherently cross-cultural, since it denotes Chinese studies in a non-Chinese — especially Western — cultural context. There is no sinologist who is not aware of her non-Chineseness, and the vast majority of Western scholarship on China has always emphasized how *different* Chinese culture is from Indo-European cultures, and how inappropriate it is to use Western terms and conceptual schemata to understand China. These views can only be conceived when a comparative logic is already at work. The very possibility of studying a foreign culture is already founded upon an awareness of how this foreign culture compares with one's own. In regard to understanding ancient Chinese culture, in particular, the real problem is not about using non-contextual language and methods, but about how impossible it is to *not* use non-contextual language and methods in any analysis or interpretation. Classical Chinese is not the means of expression of modern Chinese people; the context in which classical Chinese texts were written is also no longer accessible. To make sense of these ancient texts, we have to use our contemporary mindsets and non-contextual language and ideas. I remember reading in an art newsletter a few years ago about an archaeological museum displaying the catchphrase 'All art is contemporary'. That said a lot about the conditions for the living production of culture and our reception of culture from the past.

Assertions of incommensurable differences are often essentialist pitfalls, for they require the bearers of difference or sameness to be in some way *absolutely* different or identical. Such absoluteness does not enrich the multiplicity of cultures but becomes just another version of totalization. As the comparatist Zhang has argued (1998: 12), nothing is really 'identical', yet most things have 'widely shared' aspects. Certainly one culture should not be judged by another culture's standards, but should we deny that certain similarities do exist between these cultures, that one can achieve a deep understanding of another culture, simply because of the fear of appropriation? Some critics of Artaud and Michaux are so wary of colonial Orientalism that they unconsciously adopt an Occidentalist attitude, and insist on the Other's ultimate incomprehensibility. For instance, the typical claim is that Artaud and Michaux never accessed the 'real' Far East but dreamed it as a spiritual therapy, remaining enclosed within their cultural tradition despite their self-exile. Susan Sontag declared that Artaud's attitude 'is an ultimate refinement of the colonialist outlook: an imaginative exploitation of non-white cultures [...] whose wisdom it plunders and parodies' (Sontag in Artaud 1976: xl); and Dina Hamdan argued that for Michaux, the Orient is really about the self, an 'egotisme' that loves an 'Orient féminisé' because it suits Michaux's 'idealist' exoticism (Hamdan 2002: 194). But they are mistaken. We do not understand intercultural practices and intellectual exchanges well enough — not even those involving ourselves — to pass any judgments on Artaud and Michaux, who spent most of their lives battling against identity, against the monolithic and self-enclosed understanding of Western culture and the colonial insistence that non-Western cultures must be essentially different and un-understood.

By considering Artaud and Michaux together with the *Zhuangzi*, I challenge these reductionist views about the European avant-garde's engagement with the supposedly 'Other' and argue for a much more positive intellectual relationship between them. Although admittedly, Artaud and Michaux were introduced to Chinese culture partly via colonialist exhibitions and exoticist journalistic accounts, this by no means leads automatically to the conclusion that they were spoon-fed by the racist and appropriating ideology. As Segalen showed in his *Essai sur l'exotisme* (*Essay on exoticism*, 1911) which revolutionized the 'exotic' into an ethical instead of colonial (i.e. unethical) position, one can love the difference of the Other without appropriating it, and understand difference aesthetically and philosophically, leaving behind the political struggle between cultures for power domination. The Segalenian version of 'exoticism' affirms the Other, to the extent that the exoticist ultimately becomes the Other, then finds that the Other is always already part of the Self as well as part of the Others of the Other, thus resulting in the evaporation of the monolithic and dichotomist conceptualizations of Self and Other. I believe that Artaud and Michaux are 'exoticists' in this Segalenian sense rather than naïve Orientalists. A cursory glance at their lives and intellectual tendencies is already very telling in terms of their cultural hybridity and complexity. Firstly, Artaud and Michaux were never firmly situated in one culture nor even mildly sympathetic to the idea of cultural identity — in fact, any identity *tout court*. Artaud's family was from Smyrna and he grew up speaking Greek, Turkish, Italian and French.[4] So Artaud is only problematically 'French', this being a cultural belonging that Artaud neither asserted nor even preferred. For example, he states that his favourite painter is Delacroix, 'parce que le moins français dans l'essence' ('because he is the least French in spirit') (II: 263). Michaux, on the other hand, seems to have an inborn abhorrence of being Belgian and European in general, embedded in an expressed hatred for his lineage and tradition (2003: 94): 'J'ai vécu contre mon père (et contre ma mère et contre mon grand-père, ma grand-mère, mes arrière-grands-parents)' ('I have lived against my father (and against my mother and against my grandfather, my grandmother, my great-grandparents)'). He left his native town — or rather, escaped from it — in his youth and spent most of his life travelling or living in Paris, existing between rather than in cultures.[5] Secondly, Artaud and Michaux most consciously embraced cultural self-exile by learning about non-European cultures, travelling to distant lands, vehemently tearing down all constructions of identity or fluctuating between fictional identities so that any notion of identity ends up liquidated. Significantly, they also wrote against their own language and culture — although as mentioned, French has always been foreign to them to a certain extent. As Casanova remarked in her *La République mondiale des lettres* (1999), the cult of language is a refusal to acknowledge the inherent comparison and interaction with other languages and cultures. This is why thoughtful writers have never been willing to perpetuate their linguistic heritage. Such writers' literary career is one of expatriation, a flight from the grips of one's mother tongue:

> C'est à partir [...] d'inventer leur propre liberté, c'est-à-dire de transformer, ou de refuser [...] leur héritage littéraire national qu'on pourra comprendre tout le trajet des écrivains et leur projet littéraire' (Casanova 1999: 65).
>
> [Only by taking as the point of departure [...] the invention of their own freedom, namely, transforming or refusing their national literary heritage, can the entire itinerary of these writers and their literary project be understood.]

Therefore, Artaud and Michaux cannot be seen as simply 'European' writers but are much more culturally hybrid. Thirdly, there is no Other strictly speaking for Artaud and Michaux, because they have no privileged position of the Self to occupy, nor see the Other as other (and for a truly non-culturally-centric mentality, the very concepts of Self and Other would evaporate). In the manner of the ultimate exoticist (à la Segalen, that is), they feel at home in foreign environments but alienated and othered in their own culture. Artaud describes how close to nature and life he felt when staying with the Tarahumaras (IX: 85); and Michaux is deeply moved by Indian strawhuts but shocked by European architecture (1977: 76): 'Grandes surfaces de coffres-forts, coffres-forts cimentés [...] coffres-forts à compartiments' ('Vast surfaces of strong-boxes, cemented strong-boxes, [...] compartmentalized strong-boxes'). After having 'exiled' themselves and engaged so persistently with other cultures, Artaud and Michaux become the Other only to discover that there never was an absolute or unified Self or Other to start with. The truly non-discriminating attitude sees mutual dissolution between the Self and Other rather than attempt to overcome their opposition, since 'overcoming' already implicitly affirms the dichotomy. Artaud's and Michaux's thought does not need to be always fundamentally or distinctly different from any non-European thought, such as that of the *Zhuangzi*.

In fact, the translation of Artaud and Michaux into intercultural experiences that this book seeks to undertake is what Artaud and Michaux have always already done. We need new ways to approach their practice of translating and metamorphosizing other cultures into their own knowledge structures and experiences, as well as themselves into other cultures — new ways that avoid thinking of translating and comparing cultures as another way of making culture into a product of exchange value, or as a tug of war between cultural incommensurability and loss of identity. After all, have Artaud's and Michaux's works become any the less rich and thought-provoking because of their interculturality? Certainly, the perspectives of translation and comparison will always involve loss and gain, just as *any* perspective would (except the omni-perspectival one).[6] But if the epistemological and experiential horizons are not opened up through them, we will not even be aware of what losses and gains are at stake.

Variation two: Different comparabilities and comparative grounds

In the National Gallery in London hangs a painting entitled *The Ambassadors*, probably the most famous work of Hans Holbein the Younger (Fig. 1). What makes the painting particularly interesting is the distorted baguette-shaped object in the bottom-centre of the composition. When approached from the left extreme angle of the painting, this unidentifiable object appears in its proper perspective as a skull (Fig. 2). Some critics have hypothesized that Holbein painted the picture for it to be hung on the walls of a staircase, so people approaching it from the slanting perspective of the stairs will see correctly the anamorphic skull. This is a brilliant example of how perspective changes the reality of our perception. Certain things can only be seen from a particular viewpoint that is situated in a particular context. In my case, this involves seeing new dimensions in Artaud, Michaux and the *Zhuangzi* from a comparative viewpoint that stems from its own site-specificity.

With the rising trend of comparative studies and interdisciplinarity, the term 'comparison' has become so nebulous that it no longer denotes a single method specific to any field of study. But this methodological fluidity seems to be particularly diffuse in comparative literature, for even now the debates about why

FIG. 1. Hans Holbein the Younger, *The Ambassadors*, 1533.

FIG. 2. Anamorphic skull seen from the left angle

we do comparative literature, what precise role it gives to comparison, and what interpretative approaches count as 'comparative' are still ongoing.[7] This study both exploits the extreme elasticity of the comparative field in literature and seeks to define a more particular sense of comparison that can hold together my unusual pairing of Artaud, Michaux and the *Zhuangzi*. On the first aspect, I believe that the multiplex state of comparative literature introduces many new possibilities for constructing different hybridities of methods. Thus I would like to understand and use comparison as potentially *any* perspective, theory, or methodology that can deepen or extend the understanding of a text or issue. This is not advocating a methodological nihilism of 'anything goes', but arguing that we would benefit from an open-minded, non-hierarchizing approach to different ways of understanding literature. As William Righter said (cited in Glicksberg 1970: 162): 'There is almost no point of view from which something illuminating about literature cannot be said, and the most perverse can produce valuable insights'. After the heyday of theory in the 1980s, it is safe to say that a text can be well interpreted by not only the most frequently used methods in literary criticism or even exclusively literary criticism itself, but also by other means such as linguistics, sociological context analysis, or psychoanalytic diagnosis. There is no universally preferable method, although there certainly are more pertinent and insightful methods. I would like to term this view the 'anthropological' view of hermeneutic methods, since in anthropology, from the time of Franz Boas's cultural relativism that levelled the hierarchizing perception that 'culture' denotes music and advanced technologies rather than cooking utensils and slang, anthropological perception acknowledged that everything related to human activities can say something about humans and their environment, and is worth studying. Likewise, an anthropological perception of literary criticism means that all perspectives and approaches are equally possible and potentially valid for revealing something about literature. For this reason, my comparative method is not restricted to methods and arguments conceived within the literary discipline but freely draws upon other disciplines such as anthropology, art theory, linguistics, philosophy of science and logic, provided that they shed light on the questions which the primary literary texts pose. As for my second concern about simultaneously using comparison in a particular sense, it denotes rethinking comparison in terms of *site-specificity* instead of comparability. To explain this shift away from the notion of comparability, which has typically featured in theoretical debates in comparative literature and philosophy, it is necessary first to consider the major understandings of comparability and their problems.

Comparability seems to loom in the background of any comparative study, for it is usually understood as the very raison d'être of the comparison itself. The question of comparability involves the basic problems of what comparability consists of and how to establish it. In existing comparative literature, which is approximately a century old, three kinds of comparabilities dominate: the genealogical, temporal, and generic comparabilities, each justified by literary influence, contemporaneous periods, and the same genre of texts. These factors have become assumed common grounds that justify comparison, and each of them poses a different kind of question from the comparison I attempt to make here: Can Artaud and Michaux count in the history of reception of the *Zhuangzi* and be seen to have been influenced by it? How can the huge historical difference between the French writers and the Chinese text be bridged? What difficulties do these different genres of texts pose for the discussion of common themes such as rationality?

Before answering these questions, an examination of the common grounds supporting the three comparabilities is necessary. To begin with, genealogical comparability is based upon the question of influence, and can as well as usually does sidestep the limitations of temporal and generic frameworks. It gives concrete evidence of cross-cultural contact such as textual transmission and translation, as in the case of Western writers like T. S. Eliot and W. B. Yeats who read (about) and were inspired by the *Bhagavad-Gītā*. Some excellent comparative studies have also been based upon genealogy, such as J. J. Clarke's *The Tao of the West* (2000), Shu-mei Shih's *The Lure of the Modern* (2001), and Zhaoming Qian's *Ezra Pound & China* (2003). That the cross-cultural contact between a modern writer A and an ancient text B of some foreign culture should make a strong case for comparing the thought of A and B was something taken for granted in the early phases of comparative studies. In early twentieth-century France, the 'rapports des faits' — i.e. genealogical influence — were the *sine qua non* for doing comparative literature. Nevertheless, the step from cross-cultural contact to determinable influence — such as saying that because writer A read text B, and because the former's idea C is similar to the latter's idea D, we can conclude that C is the result of D's influence and can be genealogically traced back to D — is too risky. All literary and artistic ideas are hybrid, since the writers and intellectuals who conceived them have fused different ideas and influences and become so eclectic and complex in intellectual structure that to pinpoint an influence — unless the author clearly states or cites it — is too speculative. The causal model of genealogical influence reads intellectual history in a too rigid way of action-and-reaction.[8] Although solid facts such as cross-cultural contact form a favourable background for carrying out a comparative study, they are neither guarantors of comparability nor the focus of comparison. It is the ideas and issues in writer A and text B that are compared, not the contact between writer A and text B that are important. Thus comparative focus is actually on conceptual affinities between A and B, or how they present different versions and/or solutions to the same problem, and so forth. The contact between them simply serves as an argumentative means to contextually support the findings of comparison. In this case, would it not be more appropriate to say that conceptual affinity and the comparatist's chosen point of departure — for instance, choosing the framework of the concept of knowledge to compare Artaud, Michaux and the *Zhuangzi* — say more about comparability than influence? Moreover, contact and influence are easily overrated, just as causality is usually assumed to be more meaningful than coincidence. Can two thinkers never hit upon the same idea or say similar things although they have never read each other? And is it not more interesting if they do have the same or similar ideas, despite never having read each other? A coincidental encounter of complementary ideas and issues requires a more probing and complex exegesis than simply giving the causal reason of contact and influence, and may reveal how the sameness of thought can be produced through difference rather than reduplication. In fact, the Surrealist techniques of *bricolage* and *collage*, which disorientatingly juxtapose incongruous ideas and objects to create new perspectives and effects, precisely celebrate coincidence and show its non-triviality. My emphasis is therefore on encounter rather than influence.

Now the objection to anachronism may arise, since the argument for literary influence is essentially based upon a historicist approach that manifests the critical desire for a more authentic context where the text we are left with now can be correctly and objectively situated. But refuting that genealogy is a condition for justifiable comparison does not deny historicism, but points out that although learning as much as possible about the origins of a text is both necessary and important, this knowledge does not hinder the text from moving through time and remaining contemporary, simply because we as contemporary readers cannot help but see the text with contemporary eyes. Our starting point is always already ahistorical, but this is not necessarily a negative thing. There can be an appropriate use of ahistoricism, given that it says something new and insightful about historical texts, and shows how their meaning extends from their origins up until now through mutating readings, how we contemporary readers differ from our predecessors in understanding and what this difference tells us about our own era. Moreover, anachronism suits Artaud, Michaux and the *Zhuangzi,* and actually stems from them, since they are explicitly and confidently anachronistic thinkers. Artaud does not distinguish myth from history and when Jean Paulhan asks him whether his *Héliogabale* is true to history, he is exceedingly annoyed by the superficiality of the question (Artaud 2004: 476); Michaux discards the linear model of time and often expresses sensations of displacement through time and space and cyclical reincarnation; and the *Zhuangzi* shows a typical disregard for historical context and factuality by attributing fictional dialogues to historical figures such as Confucius and mixing dreams and myths with historical anecdotes.

As for the question of Artaud and Michaux's knowledge of the *Zhuangzi*, indeed they knew about the text to some extent, but this is no longer a crucial issue, because my comparison does not depend on their direct contact with the *Zhuangzi* to exist. In fact, the less genealogical influence the better, for there is nothing so slippery and haunting as influence. Artaud and Michaux certainly instructed themselves about ancient Chinese culture by befriending sinological scholars and artists, reading academic publications and translations of Chinese texts, probably even some translations of the *Zhuangzi* available at that time.[9] And Michaux had some first-hand experience of China through travelling, which he wrote about in his *Un Barbare en Asie* (*A Barbarian in Asia*, 1933).[10] But they knew very little Chinese, nor had any precise knowledge of Chinese literature and thought. Moreover, both of them took a syncretist approach to the ancient cultures, myths and mysticisms they learned about. If they read the *Zhuangzi*, no doubt they would have found it appealing to their aesthetic sensibilities, but they would also have freely assimilated its ideas into their own systems of thought.

Although some 'rapports des faits' do exist between Artaud, Michaux, and the *Zhuangzi*, they do not suffice to point out any substantial connection but rather lay out a broad background for interculturality. The whole happening of intercultural experience — and not its precise contents — of Artaud's and Michaux's fascination with China offers a favourable opportunity for critically creating a comparative structure between the three texts that furthers this aspect of interculturality. This means that the choice of compared elements, namely, the *structure* of comparison, is neither random nor unreflective, for it is not that *all* comparisons are equally insightful and worth the effort (not 'everything goes', as I mentioned). But the *contents* of comparison, such as this book's arguments about the thought modes shared between the three texts — e.g. the absurdly imaginative and non-logical, a vehement antinomianism accompanied by a contemplative *amor fati* — do not depend on any evidence of causal influence but on conceptual analogies and dialogues. My comparison thus moves away from genealogical comparability and historical interpretation, but reflects upon the idea of 'confluence' that emerged from more recent cross-cultural studies. As Eugene Eoyang expounds (2007):

> Confluence may be detected in shared literary experiences; it may involve influence, or it may not. [...] Defined as the coming together of two or more sources into one stream, [it] precludes the fallacy of [...] trying to distinguish between what is derivative and what is original. [...] Furthermore, one can identify confluences without the need to establish intentionality on the part of either the author or the text (pp. 15–16).
>
> [Most importantly,] the warrant for [confluence] is not historical verifiability, but the gain of intellectual insight. (p. 11)

The notion of confluence therefore better shows the huge flexibility and diversity of the ways in which different thinkers, texts and cultures can relate to each other.

Turning to temporal comparability, if one browses existing comparative studies involving different cultures, one finds that the vast majority tend to choose more or less contemporaneous periods as the comparative time scope. Contemporaneity seems to be an obvious standard of comparability, the common assumption being that comparison is more justifiable and telling when carried out across contemporaneous periods between different cultures. But this anchorage on temporality is not so straightforward as it seems.[11] To begin with, there is the problem of how to understand and justify the ideas of time and history. Given that different cultures have different stages of development and understandings of what is considered 'development' and whether it is desirable at all, what does a specific time measurement alone such as contemporaneity say of any two cultures? It does not seem to say much more than that these two cultures co-existed simultaneously. Moreover, if these two cultures had little or no awareness and knowledge of each other, can they be said to be 'contemporaneous', even though our globalized calendrical system puts them on the same time scale? For instance, a considerable number of studies compare ancient Greece with Warring-States China within the timeframe of fifth to the third century BCE (such as Lisa Raphals 1992, Shankman and Durrant 2000, Jean-Paul Reding 2004). There is certainly nothing objectionable about the choice of this historical period as long as the comparison offers insight into the issues of study. But the view that the Greek states of the fifth to the third century BCE are contemporaneous to the Chinese states of fifth to the third century BCE is simplistic and misleading, because every culture has its own time and measurement of time (such as historical records). What we call the fifth century BCE can be seen as such only in one particular time measurement system, i.e. the Roman solar calendar that has become standardized and globalized. Moreover, this uniform time view essentially reflects a time model that is linear, irreversible, and universal, so that five o'clock on the earth means also five o'clock on the sun. But after the revolutions in modern physics such as relativity and the recognition of non-Western paradigms of time in anthropology, nobody can unquestioningly accept such a mechanical and totalizing time view.[12] After all, the establishment of this universal calendrical time that systematically and uniformly dates the totality of recorded human existence is a recent phenomenon, and time itself has a history too — histories rather, since different cultures have different conceptions of time. Before our global temporal norm, different peoples lived on their own time scales, situated themselves in relationship to their own perceptions and experiences of history, and were unaware of or relatively uninfluenced by other time scales and histories. Therefore, given that the ancient Chinese and ancient Greeks had little or no knowledge of each other, nor had a common measurement or conception of time and history to relate to, the simultaneously existing Warring-States China and ancient Greece can be understood as *dyssynchronous*. For instance, to tell a Chinese man living in 460 BCE that somebody in a city called Athens about which he had no notion was engaging at that time in a certain activity makes little more sense to this Chinese man than telling him that somebody else in a city called Sparta (about which he had equally no notion) was doing something else two hundred years earlier. Because, although 460 BCE Athens is different from 660 BCE Sparta, they do not relate historically, culturally, or geographically to any known experience of this Chinese man, and therefore cannot hold significance for him as they would for us living in 2015, with our global map and calendar implanted in our minds. In contrast, we can relate the ancient Greeks to the ancient Chinese much more easily than they could to each other. This is because the mutual awareness that cultures have of one other, the contact between them, sometimes even the one-sided knowledge of one culture about another are more important than their simultaneous existence. In this sense, it is not absurd to say that the Warring States are more vivid, more meaningful and contemporaneous to *us* — in the field of knowledge that encompasses different times and spaces — than to the Greeks of the same period. Historical periods dated as 'contemporaneous' may have nothing temporally in common with each other; whereas periods dated as 'disparate' may, on the contrary, be 'contemporaneous' to each other in the sense that each of these periods have reached within their own time-frames the stages of development that manifest the levels of sophistication or concerns that are comparable and similar to those in another historical era of another culture. In fact, Ernst Bloch's argument (1990) that the unevenness of different cultural developments produces a 'contemporary non-contemporaneousness' (*Gleichzeitligkeit der Ungleichzeitigen*) can conversely show how a non-contemporary contemporaneity is also possible. Homogeneous time and culture do not guarantee a justifiable comparability, nor do disparate times and cultures necessarily pose problems for comparison.

This misconception about supposedly 'contemporaneous' historical periods is probably one of the most important and least addressed issues in comparative literature. Since my study conjoins texts that are from widely disparate periods and cultures, I choose to highlight rather than avoid this problem of time-frame to show that the very understandings of cross-temporality and contemporaneity should be contested before any justification or refutation based upon them can be made. The non-contemporaneity of Artaud, Michaux and the *Zhuangzi* is not a drawback, for affinities across different temporal contexts can be as telling as those within the same context. Again, this putting-into-the-background of the temporal concern finds support in the thought of these writers themselves, for they all disregard linear and historical time. If literary methodology should be appropriate for its 'object' i.e. the texts it studies, then the method should be as much transformed by its object of study as it transforms the texts themselves by producing new readings and approaches. The methodology can naturally grow from or have recourse to the views found in the texts. Taking an approach that does not depend upon temporal restrictions to study texts that deny temporal restrictions is reasonable.

Finally, generic comparability is based upon classifications of genre and discipline. Comparison within the same field of study is usually assumed to be more justifiable than across different fields. For example, the *Zhuangzi* has been compared to Nietzsche and Heidegger[13] — whose texts are considered philosophical, but not to Tzara, who is primarily a literary and artistic figure; Artaud has been compared to Brecht and Adamov but never to Schopenhauer. But do thinkers and texts grouped in the same discipline and genre necessarily share more in common with each other? Moreover, who decided that certain texts are of the same genre? And does not every taxonomical system depend upon certain principles that are more or less challengeable? For instance, is Artaud's *Héliogabale* a rewriting of myth, or a treatise on his metaphysics of the *coincidentia oppositorum* of cosmic forces? Is Michaux writing travel reports or pure fiction in his *Ecuador* and *Un barbare en Asie*? Is the *Zhuangzi* philosophy, religious literature, poetry and fiction, myth and fables? Is it Daoist (since it was posthumously classified so)? All the critics who have touched upon this thorny issue of classifying these writings have remarked that they are so heterogeneous and fluid in composition and style that the notions of genre, the distinctions between poetry and philosophy, and the labels of 'artist', 'poet', 'avant-garde', or 'philosophical Daoism' do not really apply. Yet, to take Zhuangzi studies as an example, if one looks up the entries for comparative studies on the *Zhuangzi*, one finds that scholarship still pre-dominantly focuses on the conventional taxonomy of genres and disciplines, the major two of which are philosophy and religion.[14] The choices of comparison show how critical views are still restricted — often at the subconscious level — by artificial categorizations. Why not a study comparing the eccentric poetic language and startling images of the *Zhuangzi* and the Tang poet Li He? Why not a comparative exploration of the issues of imagination and iconoclasm in the *Zhuangzi* and Dada? The Dadaists were by no means ignorant of the text; Tzara even said that Zhuangzi the thinker was in spirit a Dadaist (1978: 140): 'Dchouang-Dsi était aussi dada que nous' ('Zhuangzi was as dada as we are'). Although comparative literature is probably the literary field that is most open-minded in regard to interdisciplinarity, cross-cultural, cross-temporal and cross-spatial explorations, it has not been so efficient in breaking down rigid categorical boundaries, nor so radical in challenging the established norms of literary and historical criticisms as it purports to do. Maybe the fear of being attacked on the grounds of establishing a commonly accepted 'comparability' — such as shared conceptual or linguistic frameworks, pin-downable influence, contemporaneity and genre, which are bubbles that easily burst upon some serious poking — has stunted the ideas of many a comparatist, resulting in comparative literary studies being often less radical, innovative or interesting than they could have been.

As it turns out, neither genealogy, temporality, nor genre provide a firm foundation for establishing comparability. But is comparability indeed the necessary *condition* for making an argument in a comparative study, rather than part of the argument itself? Firstly, to think that comparability must set up some a priori frameworks or notions upon which a comparative project can rest is a misconception. Of course, the very choice of, say, comparing Spinoza and the *Daodejing* on nature already shows a pre-existing concept and application of comparability, since nobody starts with a zero ideological apparatus, and any comparatist's existing modes and structures of thought would influence his choice. The presence of some prerequisite criteria for a comparative study — well, for any study in fact — has always already taken place, and often subconsciously. But it does not seem very interesting or important to focus on figuring out what this pre-existing idea of comparability is, or how to establish a consensus about what this comparability should be. The very idea that comparability is the pre-existing condition for a comparative project is idealistic, since it implicitly abstracts the similarities, differences, and dialogical correspondences of the inter-relationships between the texts and issues of comparison as something existing independently of and externally to these texts and issues. Rather than the starting point or precondition, comparability is the end goal of a comparative project. In other words, comparability is *the argument that needs to be made*, including the viewpoints that can only be established after analysing the specific connections between the problems of comparison. For example, the notions of nature and fate are often interchangeable in Artaud and the *Zhuangzi*, so I decided to discuss nature by relying on various related ideas about numinosity, which involves fate as something naturally given — such as the mandate from heaven *(tianming* 天命), and fate as organic growth in a certain direction — such as the Nietzschean 'become what you are' that well illustrates Artaud's view. But if I were to compare, say, Nicholas de Cusa and the *Zhuangzi*, then I would not make nature and fate my main topic but rather the idea of infinity and the understanding of paradoxes such as *coincidentia oppositorum* and ignorant knowledge or knowledgeable ignorance. As well as changing the issues of comparison, I could approach Cusanus and the *Zhuangzi* from the viewpoints of the history and philosophy of cosmological science rather than from subversions of rationality and cosmologically-determined ethics as I will do for Artaud and the *Zhuangzi*. These different approaches and foci of examination show that each comparative study deals with different texts and issues that have their own characteristics and particular contexts to be considered. It is reductive and universalizing to think that there should be standards of comparability such as 'common ground' or 'basic biological facts' that can justify every comparative study. Comparability as the a priori condition is very much a chimera.

Instead of comparability, the notion of 'site-specificity' is much more helpful. 'Site-specificity' first emerged as an idea and practice in contemporary art, referring to an artwork conceived according to the characteristics (and their internal relationships) of the environment where it is supposed to be, and which can only exist *qua* this artwork on that very spot and/or during that specific time. This artwork is therefore 'site-specific'. Thus, transporting a site-specific artwork elsewhere, such as to a museum (or even to a less controversial site), or drastically changing its environment, such as erecting a new building, simply destroys it. Famous examples are Richard Serra's *Tilted Arc* (1981) in Federal Plaza, New York, which was eventually dismantled; or Robert Smithson's land art projects on beaches where the tide would eventually wash away the sand-and-stone artworks. This idea of site-specificity in art theory is transposable to the field of comparative literature (ironically, the concept of site-specificity itself is not site-specific), in that every comparative project is necessarily 'site-specific'. This means the comparatist needs to conceive of the comparative project by considering what internal relationships two texts or issues have, and by discovering the comparable issues that are pertinent to and revealing of them. In this way, the site-specific comparatist does not begin with the idea of a common standard of comparability — just as the site-specific artist does not begin with the assumption that his artwork can be displayed in or moved to any museum at any time — but adopts an approach tailored to his project. If this site-specificity is made clear to the reader from the start, then the comparatist could pay more attention to the concrete problems under examination and the arguments that stem therefrom, rather than go through the preliminary labour of battling for a certain definition of comparability. In fact, comparative methodologies are constantly expanded and created in the process of each new comparative study, so each 'site-specific' study would need to create a framework most appropriate to itself. There is no need to insist upon an overall justificatory criterion before exploring what exactly is at stake in the study in question. Therefore, by suggesting the idea of site-specificity, I argue that comparability is not very important to comparative projects, at least less important than conceptual relationships and interactions, shedding light cross-textually or revealing some bigger issue. The focus on comparability in comparative studies could well be shifted to site-specificity. The specific thematic concerns and ideas that dialogue with each other in this book will be concrete examples of how site-specificity operates in a particular comparison.

Shifting from comparability to site-specificity reveals another issue: that of understanding what 'comparison' does in comparative literature. The term 'comparison' misleadingly suggests tracing out similarities, and then differences (albeit typically with less emphasis), usually in a parallel rather than intersecting form. But comparisons in literature and thought are much more than that. It is not enough to state how ideas, styles and pragmatics are similar to or different from each other; what is more important is what these similarities and differences say about the texts or issues in question that cannot be revealed without comparing them. In other words, what the compared elements *do* to each other — be it shedding light on some obscurity, complementing our understanding of each element, revealing some larger problem, expanding our ways of thinking — is far more interesting and important than simply pointing out their resemblances and discrepancies. This is why terms like 'interaction' and 'dialogue' that are significantly less bogged down by expectations of non-contiguous and self-sufficient poles of analogy are better than 'comparison'. To hold a dialogue and to interact with one other already imply the crucial notion of transformation that is much less evident in 'comparison'. Someone who has read, say, Kant on ethics together with Lucretius's *De rerum natura* would usually have a different and more heterogeneous concept of morality than someone who has only read Kant. However different the texts, historical backgrounds and languages may be, once they are juxtaposed within the reader's mind, they can no longer remain autonomous and impermeable spheres but will more or less penetrate and transform each other. This process is precisely analogical to a comparative study in literature, i.e. juxtaposition and comparison of different texts so they elucidate each other and are better understood in themselves. To simply map out points of similarities and contrasts under thematic frameworks such as cosmology and ethics between Artaud, Michaux and the *Zhuangzi* is neither sufficiently convincing nor meaningful, and leaves the texts relatively disconnected to each other. It is far more interesting to explore how to establish a contiguous relationship between these texts. For example, how does the complex and syncretist composition of the *Zhuangzi* — which frustrates the critical attempt to thread out an overall consistency and construct a system of arguments — make us rethink the rationalist demands that criticism makes on an author's works? Consider Artaud's case: his writings span some twenty years and are notably hybrid and 'messy', with his later works written in psychiatric hospitals often contradicting his earlier views. The heterogeneity of Artaud's œuvre is similar to the *Zhuangzi*'s, except that we still have one single name 'Artaud' to label these writings with. But individual authorship itself is very much a fiction in terms of the inner coherence of views, since almost every author changes and not all of her ideas develop continuously or at all. Therefore, having learned from the approach of reading the *Zhuangzi* without demanding authorial consistency and overall relevance between internal parts, we may understand that to explain away the incoherencies and fragmentation of Artaud's œuvre, however cleverly, would not really do justice to Artaud. This kind of relating different texts by analogical borrowing and transposing of methods or of conceptual complementarity is precisely what many comparative studies have been doing. But they are still labelled as 'comparative' — a term that misleadingly does not emphasize the crucial aspect of mutual transformation of the compared elements — rather than as 'interactive' or 'dialogical' studies.

Variation three: Reading literature comparatively and literature's self-theorization

After these questions about the methods, structure and nature of comparison, there still remains an essential concern: how will the texts themselves be read, especially when they are made to meet in a space that does not belong to their original contexts? There has to be an interpretation of what Michaux's or the *Zhuangzi*'s ideas are about before a comparison can take place. And on this matter I believe that the self-theorization of the texts can help explain the texts to us readers.

It has been mentioned that some methods of this study, such as intercultural translation and non-historicism, stem from and cohere with the texts themselves. This is because the relationship between criticism and text can be rethought by prioritizing the text as a system that self-reflexively generates theory over theories external to and independent of the text. Certainly, the use of particular theoretical systems to reinterpret literary texts is not a new practice; and since the explosion of a constellation of different theories in literary criticism heralded by Barthes's 'La mort de l'auteur', contemporary theories that are posthumous and unrelated to the texts they aim to study are often freely applied as interpretive prisms. This approach has the advantage of increasing critical freedom and creativity. Nevertheless, uncritically and arbitrarily 'applying theory' can be totalizing if it substitutes the author with the critic as the God-figure who makes the text say whatever he wants it to say, or makes a Procrustes's bed out of theory upon which the richness of literature is reduced. Here, the question emerges as that of deciding what kind of theory and what application are appropriate, or as some more radical critics such as Knapp and Michaels have asked, whether theory is necessary at all for understanding literature.[15] In fact, much of post-60s theory — such as deconstruction and psychoanalysis — has bent back upon itself to show that theory and philosophy overlap to a great extent with literature and do not occupy an objective and neutral standpoint in language. In Thiher's words (1988: 338–39), 'semiotic and poststructural analyses [...] are literary fabulations that operate as a second-degree homologous construct with regard to the literary texts that they purport to explain. [...] Literature and theory are in this view much the same activity'. In this case, maybe we can also say that vice versa, literature is not essentially different from theory in that it can explain itself just as well as, or maybe even better than, theory can explain it? This is already shown by Barbara Johnson's review of Barthes's reading of Balzac's *Sarrasine*. The literary text 'itself demystifies the logocentric blindness inherent in Sarrasine's reading of the Zambinellian text', and thus 'has already worked out the same type of deconstruction of the readerly ideal as that which Barthes is trying to accomplish' (Johnson 1978: 8). That a text can have 'self-knowledge' is another way of saying that the complex of ideas in a text can be read into each other in meaningful ways, that when authors write, they explain themselves to themselves as well as to others. Indeed, any text does posit more or less its own 'critical terms' and they can be duly recognized and employed by the reader and critic. But not all texts have an equal degree of self-theorization, nor do a text's intrinsic critical terms make it a self-enclosed system only relevant to itself. In other words, some texts explain themselves better than others and it is more appropriate to emphasize the dimension of self-theorization in these texts. Moreover, literature is not only self-theory, but can also be *used as* theory to explain other texts and issues.

Now, in particular, Artaud, Michaux and the *Zhuangzi* are texts that manifest a high degree of theoretical self-awareness and on many occasions provide self-exegetical means. For instance, volume V of Artaud's *Oeuvres complètes* is fundamentally a more analytical and abstract explanation of the ideas in volume IV, *Le Théâtre et son double*; or, in the *Zhuangzi*'s case, the text fictionalizes itself by referring to its own words as 'flights of enigmas' (*diaogui* 弔詭, *ZZ*, 2.12) which, even when used to point out that everyone is dreaming, are nonetheless dreams themselves. Thus the *Zhuangzi*'s ideas become 'the set of all sets that can also be a member of that set' (Thiher 1988: 344), i.e. fiction as literature, theory and meta-literature-and-theory, which makes the *Zhuangzi* particularly appropriate for creative critical uses. Therefore, textual self-theorization enables treating the text itself as the first-hand interpretative context. This is how Artaud, Michaux and the *Zhuangzi* will be initially read: first extrapolating their self-reflexive explanations and theories, which will be then compared or used to examine one another. For instance, I will use the *Zhuangzi*'s theorization of infinity as the infinitely divisible smallness and infinitely multipliable bigness in order to understand Artaud's self-contradiction about limited and limitless space repeating each other as a reference to the infinite divisibility of both the limited and limitless. This is how textually-generated ideas can talk about these texts themselves, function as interpretative prisms between the texts, and even help to clarify ideas beyond the texts.

Concretely speaking, the format of the textual discussions in the following chapters is first to examine the *Zhuangzi,* and second to consider Artaud and Michaux. This sequence of analysis is necessary since the *Zhuangzi* will be a perspective and theory-generator through which new readings of Artaud and Michaux can emerge. As these new readings need to be understood in a conceptual field that includes both Western and non-Occidental thought modes and traditions, I choose to start with the *Zhuangzi* because its marginal status as a text — philosophical but simultaneously fictional, Chinese but radically atypical of dominant Chinese thought trends — makes it the optimal text to open up this conceptual field. This format of exposition does not mean, however, that Artaud and Michaux are simply reflecting the *Zhuangzi*, or that my reading of the *Zhuangzi* is unaffected by bringing the French thinkers into consideration. What I will demonstrate is that Artaud and Michaux can, when considered in the light of ideas that are revealed by the *Zhuangzi*, further elucidate these ideas and the field of thought where these ideas are situated; and that on the other hand, the very choice of theoretical concerns that frame my discussion of the *Zhuangzi* is already the result of comparing the three texts, for these concerns are identified as these texts' shared concerns. In this way, there are three layers of theorizing processes at work: the self-theorization of texts, the inter-theorization of texts, and the theorization of bigger conceptual fields that are present in these texts but also go beyond them. These layers of analysis, however, are not distinct from each other but are simultaneously interactive processes of reading. Certainly, these processes will not be confined to the texts' self-reflexive theorization but will also branch out to related theories and perspectives external to the primary texts. The recognition and use of literature as self-theory does not invalidate the relevance of theories external to textual self-criticism, as long as these external perspectives provide insight.

At this point, the question about treating the literary status of these texts may arise. In other words, if my interpretative methods focus on the ideas and theories of the texts, how do I take into account their textual materiality and rhetorical status? Typically, a philosophical reading considers the language of a text for its propositional value, whereas a literary reading usually concentrates upon the expressionist and stylistic value of language. It can be said, however, that the ideas in texts of such striking texture as those of Artaud, Michaux and the *Zhuangzi* are, to a great extent, effects of the performativity of their language. Because of this view, Artaud and Michaux have been more often than not read in terms of textual performance: the performance of madness, of the self-referentiality of language, or of poetry as an act of writing. The *Zhuangzi* has also been questioned as concerns whether it is really serious about its views, since its language is so playful and paradoxical.[16] While linguistic form deserves much critical attention, we should be wary of carrying formalist interpretation to the extent that form becomes 'a solipsistic category of self-reflection' where 'referential meaning is said to be extrinsic' (De Man 1979: 4). Although ideas and theories are products of language, this does not mean that they are less than linguistic form, or that the exegesis of literature must predominantly involve stylistic analysis. For example, it can be said that Plato's use of the dialogue form to present a 'full-scale' philosophy does not confirm a literary reading of Plato as more justified but demands a 'comprehensive interpretation' including both formalist and metaphysical dimensions (Kahn 1999: xviii-xiv). Since Artaud, Michaux and the *Zhuangzi* also exemplify the uncategorizable writing that intersects philosophy with literature, I will read them both propositionally and stylistically in different degrees at different points of my arguments. But given the themes and frameworks of this book, and the abundant literary readings that already exist, I will present a mainly philosophical reading to emphasize the philosophical significance of these writers in transforming thought.

Notes to Chapter 1

1. Scholars such as Angus Graham and Liu Xiaogan have written about attributing date and authorship to different parts of the *Zhuangzi*. Generally speaking, the first seven chapters are considered to be the earliest and most 'authentic'. More recently, however, scholars have taken a more fragmented approach to understanding the text, focusing on explaining specific sections rather than discussing them in the bigger framework of the whole text or the more 'genuine' parts.
2. See debates in Qiao 2006, Defoort and Zhaoguang 2005, and counter-arguments made by Palumbo-Liu 1992.
3. The sinologist's critical fear of Eurocentrism and of violating difference is evidenced in Chan 2009, MacIntyre 1991, but criticized by Wang 1997 and Carrier 1995.
4. See Grossman's biographical notes in Artaud (2004: 1707).
5. See Bréchon 1959: 21.
6. I will say more about omniperspectivism in Chapter 2.
7. In contrast, other comparative disciplines such as comparative linguistics and comparative history have purposes and methods that are much better defined.

8. There are already a fair number of critics who argue against genealogical comparison; see Eoyang 2007, Cai 2002, and Routh 2005.
9. Regarding Artaud, from his references to Chinese medicine, to Daoist classics such as the *I-jing* and *Daodejing* — which he admires for their 'sagesse' and accordance with cosmic order (VIII: 133–34), to Daoist masters and their rituals (XXIV: 268), and his associations with erudites about China such as Soulié de Mourant (a pioneer in translating Chinese literature and introducing acupuncture into Europe), evidently his knowledge of intellectual and religious traditions of ancient China was by no means meagre. He also mentions various scholars who studied China such as René Guénon and Marcel Granet, one of the most influential twentieth-century sinologists. Granet's best-known book, *La Pensée chinoise* (1934) (of which a substantial part is dedicated to Daoist thought and the *Zhuangzi*) is mentioned by Artaud (1977: 55–56): 'Il y a dans un livre extrêmement savant et pertinent de Marcel Granet intitulé "La Pensée chinoise" un long exposé de la Théorie des *Trigrammes* qui est incompréhensible si l'on s'en tient à la logique ordinaire de la Pensée Européenne.' Therefore, although Artaud does not mention the name 'Zhuangzi', it is highly probable that he was aware of the text. Besides, as the quotation above shows, what strikes Artaud is the non-logical thinking in certain Chinese texts that offers a significant alternative to European logical rationality.
10. Concerning Michaux, we can talk with more certainty about how precise his knowledge of the *Zhuangzi* and Chinese culture was. He travelled to China, thus having the opportunity to experience the culture directly, in addition to reading about it. He learned about the Chinese language and its traditional arts such as calligraphy, which relates notably to Daoist ideas. Therefore Michaux was more aware of historical context than Artaud, as well as more consciously following the aesthetics or lifestyle of a Chinese sage. For example, he states (1967b: 156–57) his preference for Chinese people's accepting attitude towards life and death over the peace-destroying violent metaphysics of the West. In his *Un barbare en Asie*, Michaux notably mentions the *Zhuangzi* when expressing his admiration for the poetic style of Chinese writers (1967b: 185): 'Lao-tseu, Chuang-tsu, dans leur philosophie [...] ont ce style extraordinaire. Ce style où l'on épargne les mots.' From the romanised 'Chuang-tsu' for 'Zhuangzi', used in English translations rather than 'Tchouang-tseu' in the French, Tamogami infers (1996) that Michaux read the 1923 English translation by the Cambridge sinologist Herbert Giles. Michaux's concrete contact with the *Zhuangzi* is further confirmed by Graziani (2006: 35), who notes that 'le *Tchouang-tseu* était l'un de ses [i.e. Michaux's] livres de chevet'. Michaux's mentioning of the *Zhuangzi* is therefore not a passing remark but reveals an enduring interest, evidenced not least by his note of thanks (in Trotet 1992: 330) to Trotet for writing *Henri Michaux ou La sagesse du vide*: 'La lecture "Daoïste" vaut mieux que la lecture psychanalytique ou linguistique. Elle apprend davantage de ce qui compte'.
11. For a more extensive discussion, please see Li (2015), 'Temporality in the Construction of Comparative Interpretation', *Comparative Critical Studies,* 12, Edinburgh University Press.
12. See studies on rethinking time: Dainton 2010, Westfahl et al. 2002.
13. See Shang (2006) on Nietzsche and Zhuangzi, and Froese (2012) on Heidegger and Zhuangzi.
14. The *Zhuangzi* has been compared to Kierkegaard on mystic (anti-)rationality (Carr and Ivanhoe 2010), to Aristotle on ethics (Jullien 2007), and to Buddhist theories about meditation (Wang 2003).
15. See Knapp 1982.
16. 'The *Zhuangzi* as joke' idea has been suggested by Watson (1968) and Wu Kuang-ming (1982).

CHAPTER 2

Rationality and Knowledge: Order and Chaos, the Sage and the Child

It is now a truism to say that Artaud, Michaux and the *Zhuangzi* challenge norms of rationality and knowledge. Indeed, they include extensive discussions of views expressing anti-rationalism and epistemological scepticism, especially in the aspects of depreciating the reductive use of logic and linguistic distinctions, preferring a non-logical way of describing and experiencing the world, and endorsing a flexibility in adopting different viewpoints so that no universal standards for value and knowledge systems are imposed. Moreover, these texts' formal aspects also embody this heterodox understanding of rationality: stylistically speaking, where logical forms of reasoning are subverted by linguistic strategies such as the parodic use of logic, paradoxes and wordplay; and in physical format, namely, their syncretist, non-systematic and indefinite form as texts. Nevertheless, is the transgression of simply challenging rational and epistemological norms all that these texts can offer in terms of thinking about the concepts of reason and knowledge? Can there be a constructive side too? Such as an attempt to suggest alternative forms of reason and knowledge, as well as a re-understanding of their definitions? This is what this chapter sets out to explore.

An uneasy relationship

The very notions of reason and knowledge jar with the images of Artaud, Michaux and the *Zhuangzi* which their reception has constructed. To start with, Artaud has been, alongside transgressive and anti-rational writers like Sade and Nietzsche, championed by post-war critics for 'irrationality' and anti-epistemology. In Philippe Sollers's words, Artaud's works belong to the

> textes limites, [...] dont la lecture réelle serait susceptible de changer les conditions mêmes de notre pensée: ceux de Dante, Sade, Lautréamont, Mallarmé, Artaud et Bataille. [...] Ces limites sont communément nommées 'mystique, folie, littérature, inconscient' (Sollers 1971: prolegomenon).
>
> [liminal texts, [...] the genuine reading of which would be capable of changing the very conditions of our thought: those of Dante, Sade, Lautréamont, Mallarmé, Artaud and Bataille. [...] These limits are commonly called 'mysticism, madness, literature, the unconscious'.]

In the post-war context of French thought, one of the most urgent questions was how Enlightenment rationalism could have led to disastrous ideologies such as Fascism or reinforced social power systems by establishing categories of deviancy such as madness, hysteria, and homosexuality. Thinkers like Artaud, Bataille and Blanchot who turned away from conventional understandings of reason and epistemological positivism and whose works defied stylistic coherence were seen as particularly relevant to the critique and subversion of Enlightenment rationalism. For example, Artaud is seen by Deleuze (1969) to explode rationalist language into schizophrenic 'désarroi'. In his 'La Parole soufflée' (1965), Derrida aligns Artaud with *poètes maudits* like Hölderlin and Nietzsche, only that Artaud has out-done both in his attempt to kill all metaphors in both language and life. Artaud's œuvre and thought become breaths of dispossessed speech 'spirited away' through their rage against 'grammatical security', the exemplary endeavour to realize the *dépassement* of language, but which always remains in the eternal suspense of a question. Certainly, the post-war thinkers who have extensively engaged with Artaud — Foucault, Deleuze and Guattari, Derrida, Blanchot, Kristeva — have recognized that Artaud is much more complex than the pathological madman, and embodies, rather, a performativity of madness, a process of simulation where madness becomes both real and fictional. Nevertheless, as a simulacrum of madness itself, Artaud does not end up being perceived as any the more rational than a madman, and Artaud's voice is often submerged in the canonical post-structuralist scholarship on him.

Although there is much deconstructive value in deploying the figure of the madman to explode the very ideology that constructed it, this method ambiguously both resists and perpetuates the accusation of pathological irrationality in Artaud and therefore always undermines itself to a certain extent. Entrenched in the category of 'madness', Artaud seems to be one of the exemplary literary figures who hold an anti-Enlightenment intellectual stance. Consequently, later criticisms seldom examine seriously what kinds of rationality are at stake in Artaud's use of language, so that Artaud is always more somatic and material than intellectual and abstract: 'Artaud had dispensed with the question of having ideas in his poetry. He was preoccupied with gestural violence and the body' (Barber 1993: 26); and he 'suffers' instead of 'thinks' (Watteau 2011). To take an alternative approach to this problem, it would be refreshing to abandon altogether this framework of 'madness' and try to see Artaud's thought in and by itself, without the debilitating dialectic of reason versus madness. Rather than taking up the notion of 'irrationality' to frame Artaud's writings, more attention can be paid to their use of *both* logical and non-logical language, and how they — when seen from certain perspectives that the *Zhuangzi* offers — articulate heterogeneous forms of reason and knowledge that cannot be reduced to distinct oppositional categories of the rational and irrational. I believe that the extraordinary complexity and fluidity of Artaudian thought can be brought out most forcefully not when it raves against or negates reason, but when it understands reason in ways that reason has not been understood before. Through this chapter's discussion, therefore, we may increasingly see that although Artaud does sometimes express anti-Enlightenment and anti-rationalist views, he does not really hold an anti-Enlightenment *stance* because his flux of thinking cannot petrify into *any* stance.

Like Artaud, Michaux clearly has an important place in the twentieth-century French debate about the crisis of reason. Although the label of 'madman' is rarely associated with him, Michaux's use of parodic logic, analytical language and his epistemological views remain insufficiently examined. Existing criticism has pointed out Michaux's refusal of logic and reason in his use of language (Dessons 1993), his surpassing of dichotomies by aphoristic paradoxes (Trotet 1992), and his mockery of epistemological certainty in coining nonsensical and fictional names (Séris 1999). But these analyses usually either emphasize how Michaux subverts reductive rationalism without examining what precisely is the alternative rationality he seeks, or take recourse to an idealized alternative of Far-Eastern 'sagesse' in opposition to Western 'rationalism', subsuming the rational in Michaux under a general notion of 'spirituality' or 'mysticism'.[1] Michaux's anti-intellectualist attitude, preference for ignorance, and his self-contradictory obsession with self-exploration have been well noted,[2] but much of the critical focus is on how Michauldian knowledge is primarily and ultimately self-knowledge, resulting in the perpetuation of Michaux as the solipsistic and introverted poet who extends the Baudelairean tradition of narcissistic self-reflexivity. This chapter fills in some of these critical gaps by considering how Michaux's specific methods of reasoning can lead to redefinitions of rationality, how his self-contradictory aphorisms mean more than mere defiance of logical reductionism when read through the *Zhuangzi*'s theories of reason, and how his epistemological reflections concern not only the self but more importantly, a maximal understanding of the cosmos.

Finally, as for the *Zhuangzi*'s relationship to rationality, there is no shortage of discussion about its views on reason and knowledge. Owing to the text's self-contradictions, most commentators have tried to explain away these inconsistencies, either by limiting the scope of examination to a few 'authentic' chapters, as Graham (1985) does; or by providing a reading that seems to solve the problem of inconsistency, e.g. Hansen (1983a), who argues that a thoroughly relativist view would liquidate all contradictions, since each view would be perspective-specific and therefore irrelevant for mutual evaluation. But is textual inconsistency a problem that needs to be resolved? Suppose, instead of trying to use interpretation to iron out textual discrepancies, we could let the text transform our reading process into one that accepts textual incoherence as it is rather than solves it? Trying to make sense of the entire *Zhuangzi* does not necessarily mean making different parts — however small the scope — work together. Each textual fragment can tell us something independently (as in zoom-in mode) as well as collaboratively (when read with other passages, in zoom-out mode). Both zoom-in and zoom-out readings are valid readings of the text, and an understanding of the whole text may include infinite readings, depending on how much one zooms in or out. Many of the major arguments about the *Zhuangzi*'s articulations of reason and knowledge, however, have tried to do too much because they scrutinize the text with questions based upon certain rational categories, such as whether it is anti-rationalist or devoid of the notion of reason, mystic and esoteric or clear-thinking, epistemologically nihilist or scepticist.[3] The overall impression of the *Zhuangzi* built by these criticisms is that reason and knowledge are depreciated for supposedly superior actions or states such as intuition, esoteric insight, and direct experience. Moreover, the vast majority of these readings take recourse to the notion of the *dao* as an all-explaining justification for anti-rationalist, mystic, or scepticist views, so that whatever forms of rationality and knowledge in the *Zhuangzi* are seen as orientated towards grasping and embodying the *dao*, although what precisely the *dao* is and why it is the supreme value remain formidably unclear. I propose, however, that we do not need to over-rely on key terms like *dao* to read the *Zhuangzi*, but can focus on its specific methods of reasoning and epistemological views in particular passages.[4] In this way, the complexities of the *Zhuangzi*'s heterodox rationalities may be further articulated, and a reading that accommodates the mystic flights of fantasy as well as rigorously technical argumentation, the calculated as well as intuitional, the rational and non-rational may emerge. As will be shown, this reading is different from relativism (as Hansen argued) because it takes place through recognizing a meta-perspectivism. This reading will also provide viewpoints through which Artaud and Michaux can be re-viewed in a light different from that produced through the prisms of post-war critiques of Western rationalism and dualism.

Probing boundaries of definition

What are the issues at stake when the terms 'rationality' and 'knowledge' are used to examine Artaud, Michaux and the *Zhuangzi*? Firstly, the *Zhuangzi*'s intellectual context should be considered because the very applicability of the concepts of 'reason' and knowledge' to the *Zhuangzi* cannot be taken for granted. In Artaud and Michaux's cultural context, however, although they had very heterodox understandings of rationality and knowledge, these notions had already been long established in Western metaphysics and pose no issues about their interpretative applicability. The *Zhuangzi* differs in this aspect because in its time, reason and knowledge were not yet established philosophical categories, nor had definite terms of reference. For this reason, some have argued that Zhuangzi 'does not have the concept of logic or any rationalist theory to kick around' (Hansen in Rosemont 1991: 203). Moreover, Hansen (1983b) maintains that the very ideas of rationality and logic are based upon Euclidean geometry, where mathematical deduction and formal language dominate, and consequently, ancient Chinese thinkers could not have any concept of propositional knowledge. Insightful as this argument is, it understands reason and knowledge too rigidly, for one need not examine Chinese thought by focusing only on whether certain concepts were used in the same way as in Western philosophy. Logic does not exclusively denote Aristotelian syllogism and its developed mathematical forms, but can be widely understood as 'a structure of subjects and predicates and their separation within [...] grammar' (Lenk 1993: 1). Moreover, that there is no term or fixed conception of rationality does not mean that ancient Chinese thinkers had no concept of reason or knowledge in *any* form. A term does not equal the existence of a concept; for instance, most people have an idea of the metal tip wrapped around the end of the shoelace, but very few know it is called 'aglet'. Philosophical discussion around the *Zhuangzi*'s time shows that many thinkers already had different conceptualizations, idea clusters, and various related terms about rationality and knowledge. Thinkers like Confucius and Xunzi emphasized the importance of cultivating the knowledge of ancient texts and rites to learn from one's ancestors the proper code of conduct. For them, knowledge was therefore similar to the 'recognition (*shi* 識) of the structural principles' of moral action (Rosker 2008: 10). Other prominent thinkers who engaged with questions of language, reason and knowledge were the Mohists (fifth to the third century BCE), who for the first time in Chinese intellectual history seriously developed and advocated a formal logic and mechanistic language which included the principle of the excluded middle, and are seen by some critics to parallel Greek logic or evidence that a universal rationality exists.[5] Influential rhetoricians such as Hui Shi (reputedly Zhuangzi's close friend) and Gongsun Long (c. 325–250 BCE) debated extensively about the rational use of language for analysing reality into different classifications and the acquisition of abstract knowledge (*zhi* 知) through correct reasoning. Besides this mechanical and instrumental approach to reason and knowledge, there was another cluster of texts including the *Daodejing, Heguanzi* and possibly the *Liezi* that represent thinkers who prefer an organismic approach, prioritizing spontaneous action, intuitional and introverted knowledge obtained through intimate experiences of one's body and the world over linguistic differentiation and argumentation. All these different debates and understandings of how language relates to thinking and what is meant by knowledge around the *Zhuangzi*'s time show that although there were no definite terms nor consensus about definitions and uses of rationality and knowledge, they already existed in a broad semantic field. The *Zhuangzi,* moreover, engages actively with these debates and draws from various branches of thought on the topic. Therefore, although reason and knowledge did not exist as metaphysical categories in ancient Chinese thought, they can still be applied as conceptual frameworks to read the *Zhuangzi*.

But how are rationality and knowledge relevant concepts to Artaud, Michaux and the *Zhuangzi*? Are these specific kinds of reason and knowledge, or do they remain indeterminate? Firstly, as regards defining reason, I start from a most basic — and therefore least exclusive — understanding: that rationality is 'a condition of having thoughts at all' (Davidson 2004: 196). Nevertheless, when we say somebody acts 'rationally' it does not simply mean that he acts upon whatever thoughts or emotions he has in the moment, but that either from the logical viewpoint, he acts consistently with his beliefs, or from the conventional viewpoint, he acts in a socially acceptable and appropriate way. Perfectly rational self-consistency can nevertheless be seen as socially 'mad', since someone can act according to beliefs that do not agree with common perceptions of normality. This is important for Artaud, Michaux and the *Zhuangzi*, since their 'transgressions' of reason are, more often than not, violations of social norms. Coming back to rationality as a relationship between thought and action, we see that it functions to organize one's thoughts and feelings, guide one's choice of actions and beliefs, justify the state of things, and usually involves arbitration or differentiation 'in the light of what is known' (Aaron 1971: 182). These different functions of reason are indeed present in Artaud, Michaux and the *Zhuangzi*, although the ways in which these thinkers organize their thought processes, justify and differentiate things are often beyond conventional acceptability.

Secondly, knowledge may include all possible kinds of knowledge, for instance, propositional knowledge i.e. 'knowing that'; practical knowledge: 'knowing how', involving actions such as technical and artisanal skills; and experiential knowledge: knowing by acquaintance or being and acting in certain ways, which primarily involves empirical experience, memory, and recognition. Of course, these various forms of knowledge overlap and interact with each other, thus covering a wide field of experiences and cognitive structures and capacities. There is, therefore, no reason to prioritize the 'certain' propositional knowledge of 'truth' based upon logical reasoning as in continental rationalism, e.g. Kant, who expounds that knowledge is 'the holding of something [...] true both subjectively and objectively' (cited in Aaron 1971: 7). This is only a partial understanding of what knowledge encompasses. Usually, the statement 'I know that something is the case' is more performative than descriptive. Though it does imply certainty, it is 'not so much to vouch for the truth of whatever it may be as to report my state of mind' (Austin cited in Ayer 1956: 13). Knowing can be understood as relating to and interacting with other things rather than confirming from a judgmental standpoint the absolute truth about anything. Thus there can be an 'expansion of one's being' in having any kind of knowledge at all and in exercising the ability to know (Kuçuradi 1995: 62), so that knowledge could become an always open and indefinitely extending field of understanding, perception, experiences and *savoir-faire*.

These broad understandings of rationality and knowledge become relevant to Artaud, Michaux and the *Zhuangzi*, since by throwing these concepts into the open and purging them of restrictive norms, we draw closer to the views on the maximal expansion of thinking, being and epistemic non-exclusivity in the texts. In this textual context, 'rationality' does not need to exclusively mean rationalism and logic, 'knowledge' is not only propositional knowledge, and different modes of reason and knowledge need not be distinctly categorized or hierarchized.

Although reason and knowledge are meaningful notions for all three texts, it does not mean presuming that one universal rationality is shared by humanity regardless of time and space. Just as there are different cultures and histories, it can be said that there are plural rationalities and epistemologies. Artaud, Michaux and the *Zhuangzi* each has particular conceptions and forms of reason and knowledge. Nevertheless, if rationality and knowledge are understood as fundamentals of thought processes, as the relationship between actions and beliefs and the expansion of being, then there does exist a large structure in which different thoughts can be categorized as reason and knowledge. The commonality is in the scheme of classification, i.e. the viewpoint, which is not invariable, of course, but is established as such here because of its particular relevance to the three texts. Moreover, a common viewpoint does not impose any homogeneity of content in the thoughts it classifies, especially since the extreme relativist view that different rationalities and epistemologies have no overlap and are immeasurably incompatible has been proved fallacious. The anthropologist Evans-Pritchard has famously demonstrated that the oracles of the African Azande show a form of reasoning that is identical to logical deduction in the West, thus proving that 'rationality can be both particular and universal' (D'Avray 2010: 57). There is therefore no need to dichotomize universal rationality and plural rationalities.

After relaxing the boundaries of definitions of rationality and knowledge, the problem of irrationality or non-rationality still remains, especially for texts like Artaud's and the *Zhuangzi*. One way to think about it is offered by the thesis that rationality paradoxically includes the irrational because it is always necessarily *ab origine* irrational. This is because, firstly, considering something as 'irrational' is more often than not an arbitrary judgement. Here, irrationality is confirmed on the grounds of an inner inconsistency within a belief system. But 'why must *inconsistency* be considered irrational? (Alternatively, or perhaps equivalently, one could ask: who is to decide what consistency demands?) Isn't this just one more evaluative judgement, and one that an agent might reject' (Davidson 2004: 192)? Secondly, the very choice of exercising reason over one's thoughts and actions cannot be justified by anything other than reason itself, which is to say that the rational method is self-circular. Reason has an inherent 'radical irrationality' since it 'imposes standards of justification upon everything but cannot itself justify itself. [...] While judging and justifying everything else, reason cannot support its own use. Reason's irrationality lies in its absolutely arbitrary nature. That is, there is ultimately no "reason" for its use at all' (Garelick 1971: 90). So if there are no certain standards of what constitutes irrationality, if the rationalizing process is fundamentally inexplicable, and if reason is ultimately arbitrary, then rationality and irrationality do not so much oppose as enfold each other. The totality of any thought process — even the most calculated and reflected — will always be more or less irrational, since it is the sum of rationality and irrationality. I will call this sum of thought 'non-rationality', and the knowledge derived therefrom 'non-knowledge'. In this sense, non-rationality neither minimizes the irrational and inexplicable nor prioritizes logic and systematization, but includes all thought processes that are available, employing them flexibly without partiality. Just as rationality surpasses rationalism, non-rationality surpasses rationality. This surpassing, however, does not mean a clear demarcation of what is outside and inside rationality and knowledge, because every instance of excess changes what was previously perceived as their limits, and constitutes 'the opening of reason [and knowledge] to the infinite' (Marks and Ames 1995: 98). As we shall see, this dimension of opening to infinity is notably present in Artaud, Michaux and the *Zhuangzi*.

Here a note about the question of limits of reason is necessary. Although we may understand the notions of non-rationality and non-knowledge as that which includes, surpasses, and is alternative to rationality and knowledge, it does not follow that the latter two are definitely limited scopes of thought. Many post-Enlightenment thinkers usually champion anti-mechanistic or anti-rationalist ideas such as *l'élan vital* (Bergson), *la part maudite* (Bataille), or *l'impensée* (Blanchot, Derrida, Lyotard) as the outside of reason and knowledge. But this *dépassement* of limits is, however, as restricting as it is liberating, since its very transgression affirms the existence of limits. If the limit becomes the liminal space that signifies the furthermost stretch of knowledge, then it seems that anything that is beyond the limit is both non-knowledge and ultimate absolute knowledge. Nevertheless, two mutually exclusive and spatially distinct fields are delineated in this process: knowledge and non-knowledge, reason and non-reason. This delineation is, however, very problematic because 'to talk about reason's "boundaries" is to reduce reason by a spatial metaphor to an object in space. [...] [But] reason [...] is not a boundary; reason is reason, that is, *sui generis*' (Garelick 1971: 37). This shows the fundamental problem of positing any 'limits' to rationality and knowledge — what is in flux and in grey areas of half-certitude such as ideas in formation and the accumulating process of learning — is conceived of in geometrical terms as distinct spaces of what is thinkable and unthinkable. Although when thinking about 'limits' one has to, as Wittgenstein pointed out, think both sides of the limit, thus making the unthinkable somehow thinkable in the very realization of its unthinkability, the initial application of a spatial metaphor already restricts one's understanding by imposing an image on what is not always visually representable. Moreover, there is no certainty about any rational limit that is exceeded by non-rationality, since every excess enlarges any previous boundary but does not have the final say on determining a new boundary. Therefore, rationality and knowledge in Artaud, Michaux and the *Zhuangzi* will be understood as infinitely approaching non-rationality and non-knowledge instead of being circumbound by them.

Formal characteristics of the texts: embodying forms of rationality and knowledge

The way in which the texts of Artaud, Michaux and the *Zhuangzi* are composed reflects upon issues of reason and knowledge. To begin with, the physical form of these texts already resists rationalizing demands for internal coherence of style and content. For the *Zhuangzi*, it is constituted of different pieces of writings by different authors on various and often disconnected themes, grouped together posthumously into relatively self-contained chapters. It is not surprising, therefore, that there are not a few contradictions in the text. For example, in one passage one may find a vehement attack on Confucianism, yet another passage may be preaching those very Confucian ideals; although on many occasions the acceptance of fate and death seems to be recommended, creatures who have escaped harm and attained immortality are nevertheless seen to be ideal.[6] In addition to the compositional syncretism of the whole text, we often find in the very same chapter an indifference to making overall arguments or connecting neighbouring passages thematically. This absence of authorial intention to convince the reader or to write in continuously consistent style may be explained by two main reasons that complement each other: Firstly, the author writes for self-expression rather than persuasion. In Graham's view (2001: 9), sometimes one has the 'sensation' of an author writing for no particular aim other than 'thinking aloud' to himself, without assuming a particular audience. The text would then be a material manifestation of thought processes instead of systematically constructed arguments. Secondly, writing material at that time (fourth to the third century BCE) — mainly bamboo or wood strips and possibly pieces of silk — greatly influenced the writing style and content. The restricted space provided by the writing material, and the very difficulty in the writing act itself — namely, carving and inking characters onto bamboo — demanded extreme concision and may partly explain the aphoristic style of texts like the *Zhuangzi*. Also, authors would have had a different conception of the 'book' from our modern idea of a book with a beginning and an end connected by interrelevant discussions that culminate in a conclusion. Disconnected bamboo or silk strips discourage long continuous prose and it is much more likely authors composed relatively independent passages over intervals, thus allowing stylistic fragmentation and more time for the change of opinions. Therefore, in the *Zhuangzi*'s case, we understand not only that the search for a coherent thought system among different authorships is idealistic, but also that even the same author can produce self-contradictory writings, since his views and concerns can change or stop developing continuously.

Artaud's and Michaux's writings involve similar issues of unsystematic form and non-argument-orientated style. Although there is no multiple authorship in Artaud and Michaux, both corpora of their works are made up of miscellaneous pieces of writings of different genres and widely disparate themes, composed at irregular intervals over a few decades. We find in Artaud's *Œuvres* short poems and stories, dramatic pieces (e.g. *Les Cenci*), fictions (e.g. *Héliogabale*), adaptations (e.g. *Le moine*, *L'arve et l'aume* (Artaud's title for a translation of Lewis Carroll's *Humpty Dumpty*)), theoretical essays and art/literary criticism (e.g. *Le Théâtre et son double*, *À propos de la littérature et les arts plastiques*), personal letters, (pseudo-)auto-biographical accounts *(e.g. Histoire vécue d'Artaud-Mômo),* and the notoriously unreadable and disorientating scribblings and drawings made during Artaud's internment in psychiatric hospitals. Crossing over genres and different styles and manifesting great changes in opinion, these literary and artistic creations form an ensemble of a '*désœuvre*' rather than an œuvre (Foucault 1972: 555). Likewise, Michaux's works also span a range of different genres and are highly diverse in style and theme. They include fictions (e.g. *Au pays de la magie (In the land of magic)*), travelogues (e.g. *Ecuador*), poetry, stream-of-consciousness writings such as his drug notes (e.g. *L'Infini turbulent*), loosely theoretical essays on philosophical topics (e.g. *Façons d'endormi, façons d'éveillé* (*Ways of sleep, ways of vigilance*)), paintings and calligraphic pieces. The overall form, or rather, formlessness, of Artaud's and Michaux's œuvres is therefore very close to the *Zhuangzi*'s syncretism. In fact, from this similarity with the multiple-authored *Zhuangzi*, we could think of many Artauds and Michauxs in the writing process instead of a single unchanging author. Michaux himself declares at the end of *Plume* (1978b: 217) that anyone could have written it, for there is no one Michaux, the identity of 'moi' is only 'une entre mille autres continuellement possibles et toujours prêtes, [...] un mouvement de foule' ('one among thousands of others that are continuously possible and always ready, [...] a movement in swarms'). Moreover, even when we focus on one particular self-contained work rather than the entire corpus, we still find internally inconsistent views and irrelevant sections. For instance, in *Suppôts et suppliciations,* Artaud first declares that 'il n'y a pas de choses/ elles n'ont pas de constitution' ('things do not exist/they have no constitution'), then asserts the materiality of the world: 'Il n'y a que des corps ou objets' ('Only bodies or objects exist') (XIVii: 11, 77); in *Un barbare en Asie,* Michaux inserts a section 'Histoire naturelle' on animal ethnography — which is totally unrelated to the rest of the book — between his travelogues on Ceylon and China. Despite various critical attempts to explain it,[7] 'Histoire naturelle' still stands out disconcertingly as a deliberate incongruity. As mentioned in the *Zhuangzi*'s case, a text can be an expression of thoughts rather than a construction of arguments, so the reader should not — especially with Artaud and Michaux — always take their writings as propositions to be tested against each other. In particular, their psychotic and drug writings written in an ad hoc style, such as the *Cahiers de Rodez* and *Misérable miracle*, are much more likely to be records of random thoughts and feelings than texts aiming to convince any assumed readership about some kind of truth. In this case, inconsistency is a 'natural outcome' and 'consistency has to be fought for' (Priest 2006: 28). Propositions and arguments are the critic's rather than the literary writer's task. Finally, the question of whether Artaud and Michaux were influenced by material conditions of writing should also be asked. Artaud's supply of paper in psychiatric hospitals was limited and irregular, and the way he wrote, i.e. sprawling over the page in frequently disconnected sentences with word-image interplay shows anything but a consistent style directed towards producing a monolithic book. Michaux's drug writings and paintings were mostly produced in the form of notes and ink washes, during and between the unpredictable periods of intense drug effects. Thus the same factors of restricted material and disconnected writing times that led to stylistic fragmentation in the *Zhuangzi* are also relevant to Artaud and Michaux. The question of the notion of the book which is raised by the *Zhuangzi* leads us in turn to wonder about how far Artaud and Michaux conceptualized their literary creations as 'books', despite the fact their writings are now printed and bound in volumes.

The diffuse way in which Artaud and Michaux wrote thus contests the Romantic relationship between the book and author that highlights the author's distinct style and his figure as the artist-creator. This confirms the 'absence de livre' and 'désœuvrement' that Blanchot (1969) and Foucault (1972) see in Artaud, but shows simultaneously that this absence does not necessarily connect to Romanticism and madness.

Thus, despite the wide disparity between the *Zhuangzi*'s writing context and conditions and those of Artaud's and Michaux's works, the issues about authorship, the propositional value of literary texts and the non-book-orientated concept of writing that the *Zhuangzi* raises help us to better understand Artaud and Michaux. The texts' formal 'messiness' does not reflect so much an absence of reason as different ways and conditions of textual production, which should be taken into account by an interpretative method that does not constantly demand authorial consistency, systematic arguments, logical connections and clear explanations. Although this approach is not rationalizing, it is nevertheless rational because it suits the particular characteristics of the texts.

The next aspect of the texts' formal characteristics are their stylistics. Both logical and non-logical linguistic forms and techniques in the texts show that although Artaud, Michaux and the *Zhuangzi*'s authors refuse simplistic forms of rationality, they do not exclude rational language from their own reasoning but, on the contrary, employ it extensively. To begin with the *Zhuangzi*, one of its most important dimensions is the subversion of argumentation by adopting the very argumentative pattern that it aims to subvert. This shows that although the truism is that the *Zhuangzi* paradigmatically refuses to see language as capable of articulating the multiplicity of the world's 'myriad things' and their changes and operations, the text is far from a straightforward dismissal of the analytical and epistemological functions of language. The *Zhuangzi* in fact contains some of the most sophisticated arguments about the rational use of language in Chinese philosophical literature, showing that its authors not only engaged with contemporaneous logicians' debates on the topic but also fully mastered the relevant rhetorical patterns and techniques, employed them ingeniously and surpassed them. This is well demonstrated by an exemplary passage on the mathematical logic of classification (*ZZ*, 2.9):

> There is something, there is nothing, there is the state before the state of 'there is nothing'. [...] Suddenly there is nothing, but I do not know whether this 'there being nothing' really exists or not.
>
> [...]
>
> Heaven and earth are born together with me; the myriad things and I are one. Now that we are already one, how can I still say anything? Now that I have already said that we are one, how can I have said nothing? One and my saying 'it's one' make two, two and one make three; and going on from here not even a skilful mathematician could tell the final sum, much less the ordinary men! Thus if going from nothing to something you end up with three, then how much more would you get if you go from something to something! Take no step at all, then that by which you move will cease.

This passage is commonly seen as a parody of speaking about the world in monistic terms, especially directed at the logician Hui Shi's thesis that 'heaven and earth are one body' (*ZZ*, 33.7).[8] The very assertion of oneness turns out to be a schism, since it creates the situation where we have the world and the statement about it, i.e. the order of things versus the order of language. There is, however, more going on here, especially in the intriguing mathematical addition of 'from nothing to something you end up with three'. 'Nothing' refers to the time before things were born: the state of 'there being nothing', which has the numerical value of zero. Then there is the oneness of heaven, earth, the myriad things and I, which has the value of one. But this very saying that we are one becomes still another thing apart from the world's oneness, and is added to the world, thus making two. Here, if the author was simply refuting monism, he could have stopped the enumeration since he already shows a fundamental duality. But he goes on to add two to one, which is adding the sum of the world and the statement about it to the world again, and thereby obtains three. Following this curious logic, zero entails one, which entails two, which entails three and so on ad infinitum. Still, how this way of addition comes about remains formidably obscure unless we consider a contemporaneous text by the logician Gongsun Long, who presents a mathematical addition that uses exactly the same method. This is Gongsun's famously absurd argument that a chicken has three legs (*Gongsunlongzi*, 4.26): 'If you call chicken legs "one", then count the legs and get two, two plus one, that makes three. [...] Therefore a chicken has three legs'. The logic of these additions goes thus: classify chicken legs as one category, then count a chicken's legs — which make two; then the classification of chicken legs as one + the number of legs on any one chicken = three. Compared with the addition in the *Zhuangzi* passage, where the statement of the world's oneness is added to the world itself, we see that both additions share the same basic formula of adding the classification of something as one class to the things that are classified. This seems to be an obvious logical mistake, as Trauzettel remarks (1999: 22), since 'the elements of [a] class' are added 'to the class itself, [which] means that the term for the class chicken leg becomes a self-element of its own class'. From this Trauzettel argues (1999: 24) — returning to the well-noted monist paradox again — that both the *Zhuangzi*'s and *Gongsunlongzi*'s additions are philosophical jokes with the serious intent of showing that in monism 'the meta-basis of the speaking about things is added to the basis where the individual things that had been discussed are settled, and is considered to be part of it'.

Here I propose a different approach to the 'wrong logic' of this addition which Trauzettel has insightfully identified but explained in a way less thorough than desirable. In Gongsun's argument, the use of the conditional makes it clear that the necessary condition for counting a chicken's two legs *as* 'chicken legs' is the classification of them as sub-elements of the one set 'chicken legs'. But first to define something A as B, then use this definition to prove that B is A, is perfectly self-circular, and makes the classification and the classified — which should differ from each other as the order of language and abstraction differs from the order of concrete things — identical. To give a less confusing example than Gongsun's: I first call all deer 'horses', then count two deer and conclude that I have two 'horses'. But this conclusion does not tell us anything about what the two animals really are but only about what I classify them to be. This is to say that what appears as counting things is in fact the self-circular counting of their classificatory reference. Therefore, Gongsun seems to add two chicken legs to their classification as 'chicken legs' but in fact counts the same classification three times repeatedly. Thus understood, the addition would be a demonstration of the inevitable self-referentiality of classifications and taxinomical use of language rather than a logical error. Coming back to the *Zhuangzi* passage (which should be written with the knowledge of Gongsun's chicken legs argument, since a neighbouring section (*ZZ*, 2.6) specifically refers to the *Gongsunlongzi*), we see that the author not only fully understands and employs Gongsun's argument about self-circular language, but also carries the additive logic to its extreme as in a parodic *extension* ad absurdum: from zero to three to infinity. How does this happen? First, heaven, earth, the myriad things and I (referred to as a whole as X) are concrete existences and not a classification; their value as a classification is therefore zero. Second, saying that 'X are one', however, is a classification. This statement, i.e. this classification itself (referred to as Y), is neither the sum of X nor a member of X, and is therefore separate from X. But if Y is separate, then there is no longer oneness but twoness, namely: X and Y. Once we come to this, we then see that this twoness (referred to as Z) is again separate from X and Y, because it is neither X nor Y but a set containing them both. Thus Z is a *sui generis* thing, and we now have three different things. Then this threeness is another *sui generis* thing W, so we have four things W, X, Y, Z. This can go on ad infinitum, entailing the endless proliferation of sets each enfolding its precedents. This addition differs from Gongsun's in that it does not simply repeat the classification but also reduplicates the concrete reality that is classified (i.e. X). The *Zhuangzi* here implies that although language is self-referential, it is not totally divorced from concrete things but can on the contrary change something in the world and our experience of it. In this sense language is both one and not one with the world, just as the author feels that he is caught between speaking and not speaking: 'How can I still say anything? [...] How can I have said nothing?' The rational language of naming and classifying reality can infinitely tend towards grasping the world in its entirety, as well as undermine itself and monumentally miss the point that the world already is one without the assertion that it is one. Although this passage ends with an advocation for pure experience and co-existence with the world without discourse, this realization that discourse is unnecessary only happens after one has fully discoursed about the world. Ultimately the author neither asserts nor negates rational language, or says everything is one or plural, but shows that the process of reasoning itself can never be non-paradoxical or straightforward.

Thus, this *Zhuangzi* passage adopts Gongsun's argumentative language and logic, stretches them to the very limits where they begin to collapse into chaos, then criticizes them for their self-defeating nature, thereby pointing towards an understanding that is greater than exclusively linguistic rationality. What is important to note, however, is that this critique is not written in mystic enigmata but in highly technical and rhetorical language. In other words, the Zhuangzian form of language is effective, especially when reasoning about its own limitations. The greater understanding that this language reveals is therefore a rationality that transcends itself.

Turning to Artaud's stylistics, we find that Artaud not only can write in a dionysiac and disorderly style, but also in a rigorously analytical and reflective one. This is well demonstrated in his correspondence with Jacques Rivière, who declined to publish Artaud's poems because he considered them incoherent and disconcerting. In a penetratingly meticulous dissection of his thought processes, Artaud explains why he cannot but write in this way:

> le 5 juin 1923:
> Mots, formes de phrases, directions intérieures de la pensée, réactions simples de l'esprit, je suis à la poursuite constante de mon être intellectuel (I: 20).
>
> [5 June 1923:
> Words, shapes of sentences, interior directions of thought, simple reactions of the mind, I am in constant quest for my intellectual state of being.]
>
> le 29 janvier 1924:
> Ces vices de forme, de fléchissement constant de ma pensée, il faut l'attribuer non pas à un manque d'exercice, de possession de l'instrument que je maniais, de *développement intellectuel*; mais à un effondrement central de l'âme, à une espèce d'érosion [...] de la pensée, à la non possession passagère des bénéfices matériels de mon développement, à la séparation anormale des éléments de la pensée (l'impulsion à penser, à chacune des stratifications terminales de la pensée, en passant par tous les états, toutes les bifurcations, toutes les localisations de la pensée et de la forme).
>
> Il y a donc un quelque chose qui détruit ma pensée (*Ibid.* 25).

> [29 January 1924:
> These imperfections of form, of the constant enfeebling of my thought — indeed they are not due to a lack of control or of the means which I was employing, or *intellectual development*; but due to a crucial collapse of the soul, to a certain corrosion [...] of thought, to the transitory non-possession of the tangible advantages of my development, to the abnormal separation of elements of thought (the impulse to think, at each of the terminal stratifications of thought, by passing through all the states, all the bifurcations, all the positionings of thought and form.
> There is therefore a certain thing that destroys my thought.]

Artaud makes an important clarification here: the confusion of form and expression in his poems is not due to an incapacity of exercising reason but to the frustrating dispossession of his thought caused by a certain corrosive power. This corrosion makes Artaud acutely aware of the difficulty in the linguistic formation of thought, the whimsical and fragmented ideas that constantly diverge from each other, and the pulsating swarm of different mental processes that thwart any localization of thought. If we consider Artaud's poems of this period, we see that they do embody this chaotic 'multiforme de la pensée' (Artaud 2004: 107) that Artaud professes:

Et voici la vierge-au-marteau,
pour broyer les caves de terre
dont la crâne du chien stellaire
sent monter l'horrible niveau.
L'Ombilic des limbes (2004: 106)

[And here is the hammer-swinging virgin,
to grind the caverns of earth[9]
whose skull of the stellar dog
feels the horrible level rising.]

Les orages artificiels, j'en vends;
comme la foudre des faux mamtrams.[10]
Et je n'y vais pas à coups de langue, tastée, gonflée et masturbée[11]
mais à coups de nerfs bien pesés.
Adresse au Dalaï-Lama (*Ibid.* 138)

[Artificial thunderstorms, I sell them;
like the lightning of false mamtrams.
And I do not go in with blows of the tongue, savoured, swollen and masturbated
but with well-weighted blows of nerves.]

The disorientating and obscure style of these poems contrasts strongly with Artaud's clear and argumentative self-analysis to Rivière. In the first poem, although rhyme is kept, the words that rhyme seem to be nonsensical in their context. The second poem does not retain any definite form and the assonance in 'tast*ée*', 'gonfl*ée*', 'masturb*ée*', 'pes*és*' hammers these adjectives forcibly onto unsuitable nouns (for instance, how are nerves 'weighed'?). Along the lines of Surrealist juxtaposition but arguably exceeding the poetic innovation of the period by their inaesthetic unpleasantness, the poems give the impression of an orgy of words, which seems to express the freedom of sputtering any thought or word, but ends up communicating no substantial meaning. Coming back to Artaud's letters to Rivière, what is remarkable is that although Artaud repeatedly emphasizes that he cannot express himself articulately and is not in control of the thinking flux, he nevertheless articulates very well this impossibility of articulation and identifies precisely where and how his mental processes escape his grasp. Artaud's clarity in self-analysis is striking and deserves more attention, since critics such as Blanchot (1969) and Grossman (in Artaud 2004: 65) have typically focused on Artaud's revelation of his poems' chaotic dimension that bleeds through the channels of institutionalized reason like a 'haemorrhage'. In fact, Rivière was the first person to recognize the intensely rational nature of Artaud's introspection, as he replies:

> le 25 juin 1923:
> Il y a dans vos poèmes [...] des maladresses et surtout des étrangetés déconcertantes. Mais elles me paraissent correspondre à une certaine recherche de votre part plutôt qu'à un manque de commandement sur vos pensées. (in Artaud 2004: 71)

> [25 June 1923:
> In your poems there are [...] clumsy expressions and above all disconcerting bizarries. But they seem to me to correspond to a certain quest of yours rather than a lack of control over your thoughts.]

> le 25 mars 1924:
> Une chose me frappe: le contraste entre l'extraordinaire précision de votre diagnostic sur vous-même et le vague, ou, tout au moins, l'informité des réalisations que vous tentez.
>
> [...]
>
> Faut-il croire que l'angoisse vous donne cette force et cette lucidité qui vous manquent quand vous n'êtes pas vous-même en cause? [...] vous arrivez, dans l'analyse de votre propre esprit, à des réussites complètes, remarquables (*Ibid.* 75).

> [25 March 1924:
> I am struck by one thing: the contrast between the extraordinary precision of your self-diagnosis and the confusion, or, at least, the formlessness of the actual poems that you endeavour to execute.
>
> [...]
>
> Could it be that your anguish gives you this power and this clarity that fail you when you yourself are no longer called into question? [...] in analysing your own mind, you succeed completely and remarkably.]

Terms such as 'commandement', 'précision', 'lucidité' show that Rivière firmly acknowledges Artaud's ability to think clearly and use rational language, so much that he then offers to have their correspondence published. Contrary to his poems, Artaud's letters here are 'communicables' and 'accessibles' (Rivière in Artaud 2004: 75) rather than obscure. Why is there this difference? Blanchot identifies suffering with 'la raison poétique' itself (1969: 432), and Atteberry argues that Artaud points to the 'paralyzing effects of the linguistic principle' (2000: 723). But these explanations shed light on the metaphysical source and aliterary style of Artaud's poems, rather than on why this very same linguistically 'paralysed' Artaud can analyse the turmoil of his mental activities so rationally. Artaud in fact already provides some clues by indicating a liminal position in thought (2004: 149):

> Il y a dans le grouillement immédiat de l'esprit une insertion multiforme et brillante de bêtes. Ce poudroiement insensible et *pensant* s'ordonne suivant des lois qu'il tire de l'intérieur de lui-même, en marge de la raison claire et de la conscience ou raison *traversée.*
>
> [In the instant swarming of the spirit there is a multiform and brilliant engrafting of beasts. This ungraspable and *thinking* dust-haze arranges itself by following the principles that it derives from its own interiority, in the margins of clear reason and of consciousness or *deflected* reason.]

Artaud declares that the 'esprit' — precisely what Western thought characterizes as immaterial and principled by reason — is ingrafted with a multitude of 'bêtes', which supposedly pertain to brute materiality and non-rational animality. This multitude is simultaneously incomprehensible, subtle or hard to perceive, indifferent to external forces, as the ambiguity of 'insensible' implies, as well as *thinking.* It is not outside thought but situated 'en marge': in the periphery of and/or outside two forms of reason: the articulate and logical, and the 'traversée', which points to a rationality that deflects upon itself like a difficult path, and is adverse to 'la raison claire'. It is therefore impossible to determine whether this 'poudroiement' is a third form of rationality, or not rationality at all, or a mixture of both forms of rationality and non-rationality. Artaud thus identifies a lacuna that reason cannot seize. Could this be that corrosive 'effondrement' that destroys his thought? And how does this reflect upon his chaotic and orderly forms of language? Here we may refer back to the *Zhuangzi*'s use and subversion of logical argumentation for some ideas that are helpful for better understanding Artaud. First, as the *Zhuangzi* shows, language reflects both the logical and non-logical since it can classify everything as one and fail simultaneously to classify itself. Language's reverse effect on itself thus corresponds to a thinking that is not straightforward or transparent, which would in Artaud's case be the 'raison traversée'. Its deviant and obfuscated form is then embodied by Artaud's poems. Likewise, logical language correlates with 'la raison claire', which is reflected in Artaud's letters to Rivière. Thus, if logical and 'adverse' forms of reason both exist in Artaud's thought, naturally he can write in both clear and obscure language. This view also shows that Artaud's poems do not so much reflect the absence of reason as a self-deflectional form of rationality. As for the third thought-element, the lacuna, we can understand it as the state between speaking and not speaking shown by the *Zhuangzi.* Consequently, it cannot be expressed except through linguistic failure, since neither form of language nor reason is adequate to it. On the other hand, such failed expressions already say something about this third space of thought, and are therefore *negatively* effective and necessary.

Similar to the *Zhuangzi* passage, Artaud's letters to Rivière adopt a rational form of language to discuss something that escapes rationality. By anatomically analysing the impossibility of logically expressing the 'animality' in thought, Artaud shows that rational and irrational language are not so oppositional as complementary: they both reflect the complexity and ambiguity of thought. In fact, if rational language contains its own contradiction, as the *Zhuangzi* demonstrates, then vice versa, the supposedly irrational language can reflect back upon the rational, so that we recognize a 'raison traversée' rather than 'déraison' or pathological disorder in Artaud's poems. The mutual enfolding of both deflectional and logical rationalities shows that for Artaud, intellectual entirety is ultimately beyond them both and includes a terrain of thought that cannot be precisely mapped. Nevertheless, the ungraspability of this *terra incognita* can be indicated by both analytical and poetic language, which is precisely what Artaud endeavours to do. In this way, Artaud not only breaks down institutional literature and thought by unbridled self-expression, but also employs rational and detached language to explain what is typically expressed in mystic, poetic and subjective terms: the inexplicable, unknown and intimate dimensions of the mind.

If in the *Zhuangzi* and Artaud, rationalizing forms of language such as logical argumentation and detached self-analysis are simultaneously employed and subverted, in Michaux's case we find a similar self-undermining of linguistic form, but from the reverse direction: a highly random and automatic style, namely, what is supposedly irrational language is adopted and then shown to work against itself. Michaux's drug writings, the most representative of his stream-of-consciousness writing and which seem to manifest the process of going mad, in fact liquidate the notion of madness by their mad linguistic form. To begin with, Michaux's relationship to drugs and hallucinogens was very peculiar because he did not take them owing to medical need or addiction but to experiment with his body and psyche. As he states in *Les Grandes épreuves de l'esprit (The Major Ordeals of the mind)* (1966b: 12–14), drugs reveal the inner and normally imperceptible mechanisms of the mind and senses:

> La drogue prend en traître, découvre, démasque des opérations mentales.
> [...]
> Ce sont les perturbations de l'esprit, ses dysfonctionnements qui seront mes enseignants. Plus que le trop excellent 'savoir-penser' des métaphysiciens, se sont les démences, les arriérations, les délires, les extases, les agonies, le 'ne-plus-savoir-penser', qui véritablement sont appelés à 'nous découvrir'.
>
> [Drugs catch you unawares; they discover and unmask the operations of the mind.
> [...]
> It is the disturbances of the mind, its dysfunctionings that will be my teachers. More than the all-too-good 'knowing-how-to-think' of metaphysicists, it is precisely insanities, mental deficiencies, deliriums, ecstasies, agonies, and the 'no-longer-knowing-how-to-think', that are summoned to 'discover ourselves'.]

Michaux declares that drugs are a means to dissect the thinking process, so that he can observe his own psychological disturbances and gain knowledge therefrom. The extraordinary experiences such as delirium and agony are not appreciated for their sensational or aesthetic value but rather for their epistemic value: they give information about human thought. Clearly, Michaux breaks radically away from the Romantic tradition of the *poète maudit* who, in the constant pursuit of more heightened sensations, drugs himself to indulge in his subjectivity and narcissistically contemplate his sensitive soul. Michaux's drug writings therefore do not, as Bowie believes (1973: 96), extend the Romantic 'myth of absolute subjectivity' but are rather, as Parish asserts (2007: 72), an 'intellectual' project 'to acquire knowledge'. Paradoxically, these psychedelic and paranormal experiences are in fact intentionally and rationally planned instead of spontaneously produced, and the writing that reflects them is more akin to clinical records than self-expression. For example, in *L'Infini turbulent* (*Turbulent Infinity*), Michaux describes his feelings after having taken mescaline (1964: 11):

> Il y a une extrême accélération, une accélération en flèche des passages d'images, des passages d'idées, des passages d'envies, des passages d'impulsions. On est haché de ces passages. On est entraîné par ces passages, on est malheureux et las de ces passages. On devient fou par ces passages. On est saoul et somnolent parfois de ces passages.
>
> [There is an extreme acceleration, an arrow-swift acceleration of the passing of images, the passing of ideas, the passing of desires, the passing of impulses. You are hacked to pieces by them. You are carried away by them, you are unhappy, and weary of them. They make you mad. Sometimes they make you drunk and lethargic.]

The style of this passage with the recurring present tense implies that Michaux was tracking his altered perceptions and thoughts and simultaneously recording them. The sentences, each stating a different aspect or state of consciousness, are not logically connected and present the experience of contradictory feelings: mad and agitated at one moment, lethargic and sad at another. Michaux becomes a field of moving energies, thoughts and impulses, an impersonal 'on' instead of the subjective 'je'. Although these experiences are extremely personal and intimate, the subject of experience is absent. There seems to be only uncontrolled fluxes of sensations and ideas but no agent doing the sensing and thinking. Moreover, when the 'je' does appear in the narrative, it only appears sporadically and creates more delirium and chaos (1972: 24, 143):

> *J'étais et je n'étais pas*, j'étais pris, j'étais perdu, j'étais dans la plus grande ubiquité. Les mille et mille bruissements étaient mes mille déchiquetages.
>
> [...]
>
> Je pouvais faire mille choses insensées, me couper le doigt, briser les carreaux, brûler les chaises, les tentures, m'ouvrir les veines avec le rasoir, fracasser les glaces. Le contraire de l'acte normal se présentait tentateur.
>
> [*I was and I was not*, I was caught, I was lost, I was in the greatest ubiquity.
>
> The thousands and thousands of murmurs were my thousand fragmentations.
>
> [...]
>
> I could do a thousand absurd things, cutting my own finger, breaking window panes, burning chairs, or curtains, opening my veins with the razor, smashing mirrors. The opposite of normal action seemed so tempting.]

The frenetically short phrases used rhythmically in these descriptions reflect the repeated fragmentation of the 'je' and its total loss of self-control. The moment when anything like a subject of thought emerges, it is shattered by incomprehensible desires and conflictory impulsions and loses all agential power. As Michaux says, the 'moi' is only a matter of balance (1978b: 217): '*MOI n'est qu'une position d'équilibre*' ('The *I is nothing more than a situation of balance*'), and is temporary (1964: 183): 'l'idéal de perversité, [...] pensées et désirs groupés, devenu momentanément "moi"' ('the ideal of perverseness, [...] thoughts and desires grouped together, temporarily becoming "I".'). Thus Michaux's drug writings, which are produced by a writing subject, reflect the act of constant positioning that slips in and out of imbalance. This question of position is even demonstrated physically in the textual format: the main text on a page is often juxtaposed with some short notes printed in the margins, which disrupts the continuity of the reading experience and forces the reader to reposition his gaze repeatedly. For instance in *Misérable miracle* we have in the margin of page 147 a definition of perversion: 'changement de direction'; or on page 164: 'toutes les drogues sont des modificatrices [...] de la vitesse mentale' ('all drugs are modifiers [...] of mental speed'). The reader's gaze oscillates between the main text and the marginal notes, and is literally changing direction and speed in doing so. We realize that although these texts seem random and disorientating, Michaux has taken care that the textual form should echo the content, and that the reader's experience should simulate the fragmentation and search for balance in Michaux's drug experience. It is therefore doubtful that the apparent stream-of-consciousness style and outbursts of disconnected and irrational language were indeed composed on the spot and not retrospectively and with revisions. In fact, before or after a section describing delirium and hallucinations Michaux usually adds some comments that summarize or explain these abnormalities. For example, immediately following the above passage about the 'mille choses insensées', we read: 'Tout objet est bientôt capable de tout, quand une pensée à dramatiser la vie arrive à s'en saisir' (1972: 143); ('Every object will soon be capable of anything, when a thought that makes life more dramatic succeeds in understanding this'); or in *Connaissances par les gouffres*, Michaux explains that the metaphysical alienation which artists and madmen often profess to experience can be simply induced by a drug concoction (1961: 181, 184):

> Après l'injection de mescaline, de L.S.D. 25, de psilocybine, l'homme, jusque-là sain, sent son corps rapidement se retirer de lui [...]. Il dit aussi qu'il est vide, qu'il est changé en poupée, qu'il n'a plus d'organes, [...] qu'il est artificiel.
>
> [After injections of mescaline, L.S.D. 25, and psilocybin, the man, until then still sane, feels his body rapidly withdrawing from himself [...]. He also says that he is empty, that he has turned into a mannequin, that he no longer has any organs, [...] that he is artificial.]

These explanatory parts have a rationalizing and philosophizing effect and make Michaux's psychedelic experiences more comprehensible and metaphysical. This further confirms that these drug writings are constructed rather than spontaneous, thereby revealing Michaux's rationality rather than irrationality.

Despite their schizophrenic language and focus on irrational experiences, Michaux's drug writings have a fundamentally rational dimension because they originate from the rational intention of exploring the mind, and are constructed in a meditated way. What does this reveal about Michaux's views on thought and reason? Michaux's method of using irrational language and then subverting it can be understood through the *Zhuangzi*'s ideas analysed above, which see language as a constant process of flitting between the rational and irrational, since any excess on one side will turn the balance over to the other, as the attempt to use the simplest classification of one to include the whole world shows. Language can thus be visualized as a movement along a circle, the two halves of the circumference of which are reason and areason. The meeting points of these semicircles would be the extreme of reason and areason as well as the liquidation of both. Michaux's drug writings can be understood as starting from the irrational side and becoming increasingly irrational as repeated descriptions of psychosis proliferate, finally arriving at the point where the very excess of language shows itself to be a deliberate construction rather than genuinely mad scribbling. This has the same logic as the excess of repeated pornographic language in Sade and Guyotat, the perversion of which is 'paradoxically, rationalist in construction, even hyperrationalist' (Lingis in Klossowski 1992: introduction). The crossing-over from excessive areason to reason, however, does not return language to a conventionally rational state but challenges the distinction between rationality and madness. In Michaux's case, the question would be whether someone who decides to go mad periodically in order to observe himself going mad is mad or not. The very decision and attempt to spy impersonally on one's own subjectivity carry the exercise of reason to an extreme, but also undermine reason, since a normally rational person would not decide to be mad, and a genuine madman could not even make such a decision. It would take, rather, a '*sur*rational' person — as in Bachelard's view (1936: 1–4) that 'surrationalism is the self-conscious examination of the rational' — to carry out this enterprise. The forms of thought in Michaux can be called 'surrationality' and 'deflectional' irrationality.

In sum, the linguistic forms and strategies in Artaud, Michaux and the *Zhuangzi* show that all three texts adopt a discursive mode that is exemplary of rational or irrational language — which is logical argumentation in the *Zhuangzi*, analytical introspection in Artaud, and automatic drug writing in Michaux — and then flip the discourse over to its reverse side to show that language is like a door hinge that enables thought to swing flexibly between both reason and areason. By using the *Zhuangzi*'s demonstration of the mutual enfolding of rationality and irrationality to explore the deeper implications of Artaud's and Michaux's use of language, the two French thinkers' writing methods are shown to trace out a realm of thought where both rationality and irrationality, personal and impersonal knowledge exist in the same way that different concentrations of water exist in the same pool. This fundamental view on reason and knowledge, evidenced and supported by the formal and stylistic aspects of the three texts, finds further elaboration in the textual content. On many occasions, besides reflecting ideas about reason and knowledge through their form, the texts also make these ideas the topic of discussion and exegesis. So we will now turn from how the texts say things to what they say.

Textual content: Views on reason and knowledge

The issue of anti-rationalism is a good starting point, since an important strand of criticism identifies Artaud, Michaux and the *Zhuangzi* as 'anti-rationalist'.[12] I argue, however, that instead of a definitive stance of opposing specific forms of reason, such as logical differentiation in the *Zhuangzi*'s case or Enlightenment rationalism in Artaud and Michaux's, these texts present critiques of reductive thinking in a broad sense but do not categorically reject any particular view. This is better clarified upon close examination of passages that demonstrate this critique of reductionism. For instance, in the *Zhuangzi,* a recurrent theme of discussion is the use of argumentation to make distinctions and determine values. Zhuangzi criticism so far has established the conventional view that the text mocks at the logician's approach to the world — i.e. carving up living reality into distinct categories and hierarchizing them by value judgements — and advocates experiencing the world in a holistic and undifferentiating way. Nevertheless, the *Zhuangzi*'s repeated criticisms of differentiation and evaluation in fact show an intense interest in the rationalist manipulation of language. More accurately, the *Zhuangzi* neither always asserts non-differentiation, nor depreciates rational calculation, but relates each to an appropriate context of use. It is the exclusive use of or overabundant faith in any one mode of thought that is depreciated as narrow-spirited and reductive. Thus two kinds of rationalities emerge: the small and the great, as in the *Zhuangzi*'s words (2.2): 'Great understanding is spacious and leisurely, petty understanding is cramped and flustered; great words are ardent and powerful, petty words are chatter and trivial'.

The *Zhuangzi* contains various passages that illustrate the difference between reductive reason and all-encompassing, impartial reason, as well as the latter's flexibility in different contexts of use. Firstly, there is the criticism of using argumentation and logical differentiation as the sole means to exercise rationality, as well as the narrow-mindedness of taking this differentiating reason as the only valid or primary method to attain knowledge:

> Words are not just wind. Words say something, but what they say is in particular unfixed. So do words indeed say something? Or have they said nothing? [...] Words are obscured in proliferation and showiness. This is why there are the rights and wrongs of the Confucians and Mohists, what one calls right the other calls wrong, what one calls wrong the other calls right (*ZZ*, 2.4).
>
> [...]
>
> 'That' comes from 'this', 'this' also depends on 'that'. This is the view of 'that' and 'this' arising simultaneously. Nevertheless, with birth there is simultaneously death, with death there is simultaneously birth; with the allowable there is simultaneously the unallowable, with the unallowable there is simultaneously the allowable. Going by 'this' [or 'right'] is simultaneous with going by 'not this' [or 'wrong'], going by 'not this' is simultaneous with going by 'this' (*ZZ*, 2.5).

In passage 2.4, the Confucian and Mohist thinkers are criticised for their verbose disputes over value judgements. The author considers these disputes superficial and not knowledge-revealing because the disputers do not realize that the meaning of words is fundamentally uncertain and cannot constitute absolute standards. In fact, these disputes are themselves the proof that distinctions made by language are relative, since opposite values such as right and wrong can be attributed to the same thing. From this fluctuation of language use, the author proceeds to argue in passage 2.5 that opposites do not distinguish against each other but depend upon and transform into each other, in the sense that living is the process of dying, or that nothing is right except when there is the possibility that it can be wrong. The classical Chinese term for 'right', 是 *shi*, also means 'this', while the negation of 'this' is 非 *fei*, meaning 'wrong'. The last sentence in 2.5 thus uses this ambiguity to switch from the demonstrative 'this' and 'that' to the axiological 'right' and 'wrong', showing that the Confucian and Mohist perspectives only see half of the entire picture and are narrow forms of reason. Great understanding, however, includes both 'right' and 'wrong', which does not self-contradictorily mean seeing everything as 'X and non-X', but rather, to use Ziporyn's words (2000: 86), shows that 'in one respect the thing in question is X, but in other respects it is non-X, and in fact these are not really contradictory, since actually both X and non-X are types of Y'.

Thus, great understanding enables people to shift flexibly between different perspectives such as X and non-X and see beyond each of them by recognizing their interdependence rather than mutual exclusivity within a larger perspective Y. In other words, great understanding sees both difference and sameness in each other rather than exclude 'this' or 'that' perspective as small understanding does. Great understanding therefore includes both perspectivist and meta-perspectivist modes of rationality, which are specifically illustrated in the following (*ZZ*, 2.11):

> Gaptooth asked Wang Ni: 'Do you know if there is something which everything asserts as "That's it"?'
>
> 'How would I know that?'
>
> 'Do you know that you do not know?'
>
> 'How would I know that?'
>
> 'Then does nothing know anything?'
>
> 'How would I know that? Nevertheless, let me try to say it. How do I know if what I call knowledge is not ignorance? How do I know if what I call ignorance is not knowledge? Moreover, when humans sleep in dampness their waist hurts and becomes half paralysed; is that so of the loach? [...] Which of these knows the right place to live? [...] From my perspective, [...] the paths of right and wrong are inextricably entangled. How can I know the distinctions between them?'

This passage has been interpreted by Coutinho as the view that '*all* claims to objective judgement are really just claims from a particular point of view, and more significantly that *all* conflicting claims are *equally valid* since no judgement can be made between them' (2004: 64). This assertion of the incommensurability of different perspectives shows that knowledge is always contextual and the form of rationality used to attain this knowledge is rational only within this particular perspective. For instance, it would not be rational for humans to decide to sleep in marshes because loaches thrive in them. But Wang Ni's problem is not how one makes a contextual knowledge claim, but how one can make any meta-perspectival claim about reason or knowledge. The question 'How would I know?' shows a fundamental scepticism, even nihilism, about the notion of knowledge itself. Wang Ni realises that he cannot even begin to speak about knowing or not knowing because once he makes a meta-perspectival knowledge claim, even a negative one, he will be caught in self-defeat. If he says he knows, then there will always be a perspective from which his knowledge and reason can be negated; if he says he does not know, he falls into the self-undermining language of the Socratic paradox 'I know that I do not know', or the illogical tautology of 'I do not know whether I know or not' — since the confirmation of 'not knowing' already contradicts the uncertain state of 'whether knowing or not'. Thus knowledge as a concept in itself independent of any contextual determinations can only remain a question. Judging by this view, we can say that the *Zhuangzi* presents a perspectivism that can be understood in the Nietzschean sense as the 'strong' perspectivist view that 'every statement is true in some perspective, yet untrue in another' (Hales and Welshon 2000: 19).

Nevertheless, the *Zhuangzi* does not simply embrace a thorough relativism of perspectivist and incommensurable difference (as Hansen suggests). We also find meta-claims about reason and knowledge made with 'invulnerable confidence' (Graham 2001: 4), and assertions of sameness across heterogeneous things rather than difference. If the passage above shows that the disparity between multiple perspectives makes it impossible to distinguish or rationalize them by any universal standard, it does not mean that different perspectives absolutely cannot overlap with each other. For example, we find passages affirming that there are bigger and smaller perspectives, as when a sage discusses the difference between life and death and the heterogeneity of the myriad things (*ZZ*, 5.1):

> If you look at them from the viewpoint of their disparities, from liver to gall is as far as from Chu to Yue [two Chinese states]; if you look at them from the viewpoint of their sharedness, the myriad things are all one.

In addition, there is the idea that the more encompassing perspectives are better than the narrow ones, as in 17.2:

> You cannot talk to the well-frog about the sea, for it is limited by the hole where it lives; you cannot talk to summer bugs about ice, for they are restricted by the time of their season. [...] We say the number of things is a myriad, and mankind is one of them. [...] Compared to the myriad things, is not mankind like a tip of a hair on a horse's body?

In passage 5.1, the perspective of absolute difference between things is affirmed, as well as the perspective of the sharedness between things that annuls all differences and unites everything. The perspective of commonality is, however, bigger than that of difference, because it encompasses different things and surpasses the limitations of particular contexts. The logic of difference is therefore exclusivity, whereas the logic of commonality is inclusivity. In passage 17.2, we are given a grading of different perspectives where the bigger and more inclusive perspective is always preferred to the smaller and exclusive. Although the well-frog is recognized as a viewpoint per se, it is a narrow viewpoint from which only the patch of sky visible from the well's bottom constitutes the frog's world. Likewise, the anthropocentric perspective is depreciated for its pettiness in comparison to the perspective that embraces the myriad things. Measured against the vast cosmic entirety, mankind — as well as every other particular thing — is next to zero. Thus despite the recognition that every perspective is valid and has some rational and epistemic value, the *Zhuangzi* presents a hierarchy of perspectives in which the holistic and all-encompassing viewpoint of cosmic totality is on top and leads to greater reason and knowledge.

Compared to the epistemological relativism and scepticism in Wang Ni's dialogue, this hierarchy of greater and smaller perspectives seems to fundamentally contradict the relativist and scepticist view. The problem is how the recognition of multiple perspectives that are each particular and true in and by themselves can coexist with the assertion of an infinitely bigger perspective that includes and unifies all perspectives. This is also the paradox of Nietzschean 'strong truth perspectivism' (Danto 1965: 80):

> If [strong] perspectivism is a perspective, then there are perspectives in which statements are untrue only in a perspective; if [strong] perspectivism is not a perspective, then it is untrue that every statement is true in some perspectives and untrue in others.

'Strong' perspectivism self-contradictorily either allows absolutism, which is what Wang Ni's relativism entails, or is absolutist itself, which is embodied by the great cosmic perspective. Apart from the interpretation that the *Zhuangzi* naturally contains inconsistent views and we should accept that, I argue that the text provides an answer to this perspectival paradox. First, it is implied in the optional construction of 'if you look at them from the viewpoint of their disparities [...] if you look at them from the viewpoint of their sharedness' that the perspectives of difference and commonality are parallel alternatives that one can choose to switch between. In this sense, it seems that neither the holistic nor divisive perspective is superior. Nevertheless, the sage who is talking about both the universality and difference of things shows that his perspective is something more than either perspective: he does not adopt either of them but recognizes them both. Allowing both big and small, individual and holistic perspectives to exist is already beyond exclusively seeing from any one perspective, which is what passage 2.5 further expounds as the 'axis' viewpoint:

> From the viewpoint of 'that' there is one kind of right and wrong, from the viewpoint of 'this' there is another kind of right of wrong. Do 'that' and 'this' really exist? or do they in fact not exist? Where neither 'that' nor 'this' finds its opposite is called the axis of the Way. Once the axis is found at the centre of the wheel it responds endlessly [to all situations], so 'right' is endless and 'wrong' is also endless.

The metaphor of the wheel's axis shows how there can be a pivotal point upon which all perspectives — including oppositional ones — turn. The circle's radius can be understood as the equal validity of each perspective, and a sector between any two radiuses can be understood as one perspective. But only an inclusion of all sectors leads to the complete area of the circle. Thus the all-encompassing holistic viewpoint of the axis is both every individual perspective and all individual perspectives put together, i.e. the axis viewpoint is both a perspective and a meta-perspective, a set and sub-member of itself. Returning to the paradox of 'strong' perspectivism, we see that absolutism contradicts perspectivism only when one is not *thoroughly* strong perspectivist and still thinks that absolutism and perspectivism are essentially different. In fact, in this Zhuangzian perspectivism which is both a perspective and all perspectivisms, absolutism is no longer a problem, because it would be yet another perspective that is subsumed under the meta-perspective of the axis, which both endorses absolutism and surpasses it. In practical terms, someone with axial understanding would not argue against an absolutist, but would affirm that absolutism is one way of interacting with the world, and see that there are many alternatives to absolutism which are no less effective or reasonable. At this point we realize that the *Zhuangzi*'s perspectivism far exceeds the relativist pluralist worldview which some critics believe it to hold, since its main thrust is not so much the particularity of each individual perspective as the 'additive sum of perspectives', which in the Nietzschean view constitutes knowledge as 'interpreting things from all perspectives at once' (Hales and Welshon 2000: 123). This may explain why in passage 17.2, bigger perspectives are preferred to smaller ones, since that means a greater scope of knowledge and rational modes; this may also explain why Wang Ni questions the knowledge that a knowing subject can obtain, since it is impossible for any individual to be capable of an omniperspectival interpretation and attain non-partial knowledge.

What, we may now ask, are the implications of the *Zhuangzi*'s perspectivism for conceptualizing new modes of rationality? In fact, the omniperspectival standpoint is pan-affirmation, which in logical philosophy leads to the problem of trivialism. More specifically, to be both part of a whole and the whole itself — which happens in the axial standpoint where perspective and meta-perspective coincide — reveals a thoroughly holistic affirmation which the critic Ziporyn calls 'omnicentric holism'. This can be visualized by the image of a grain of salt thoroughly melted in a cup of water, so that the salt is in every drop as well as the whole body of water.

> [Such a holism] holds that any point in the system can be made the centre to which all else is subordinated and which all else supports and explains. All points in the system [...] are integrated to such an extent that, by the time the system is fully comprehended, any point can be the end to which all the other are means, any point can be taken as the ultimate point, and this point will necessarily incorporate all the other aspects of theory and practice in the system (Ziporyn 2000: 24).

Putting this back to the wheel metaphor, this means a circle, the centre and circumference of which are everywhere, which is precisely the image of the cosmos that the Renaissance philosopher Nicholas de Cusa hypothesized in his *De docta ignorantia (On Learned Ignorance)*. In this omnicentric circle, every point can be the axis point, which means that every point can be the point from which both a particular perspective and all perspectives are possible. In this way, the wheel is thoroughly strong perspectivist and everything is affirmed from every viewpoint, so all modes of reason and knowledge, including irrationality and ignorance, are equally accepted.

The problem of trivialism emerges here, since in an omnicentric perspectivism, contradictions are no longer contradictory and 'la parole est toujours "légitime", c'est-à-dire qu'il y a toujours un certain point de vue sous lequel elle est recevable' ('Speech is always "legitimate", which is to say that there is always a certain viewpoint from which speech is allowable') (Jullien 1998: 129). In other words, when the encompassment of perspectives and their propositions are affirmed, the law of non-contradiction is broken and one has to allow sentences such as 'this sentence is not true', i.e. 'both A and ¬A are true, that is, [...] A is both true and false' (Priest 2006: 1). In classical logic, if this happens, then there is an explosion of logic: *ex contradictione quodlibet*, 'from a contradiction anything', in which case we have trivialism, which holds that all propositions are true. Trivialism seems at first downright absurd and uncritical, which explains why it has been repulsed by Aristotle and the vast majority of European philosophers until very recently, when, with the development of non-classical logic such as paraconsistency, trivialism entered into serious philosophical discussion as exemplified in the works of Priest (2008), Berto (2007), Azzouni (2006) and Kabay (2008). Nevertheless, certain important thinkers in the history of philosophy — for instance Zhuangzi, Heraclitus, Cusanus, Nietzsche in the strong perspectivist sense — have in fact expounded views that are essentially trivialist, although they have not explicitly labelled themselves as 'trivialists'. Focussing on the *Zhuangzi*, besides the paradoxes in 2.5 that point to trivialism, we also have assertions of a reality that 'consists of the greatest possible totality — a totality so inclusive that it includes everything, even its opposite' (Kabay 2008: 19). As in the following (*ZZ*, 17.5):

> Now you may say, should people make right their master and do away with wrong, or make order their master and do away with disorder? [...] This is like saying that you are going to make heaven your master and do away with earth, or make the moon your master and do away with the sun. Clearly it is unacceptable. If people persist in talking this way without stop, they must be either fools or deceivers!

The order of logic and principles, i.e. right/wrong, order/disorder, is compared to the order of things, i.e. heaven/earth, moon/sun, and the author argues that so-called opposites in logic are in fact necessary and complement each other just as the contrasting pairs of things in the material world do. To try to eliminate the 'negative' opposite is thus narrow-minded and foolish, and the maximal inclusion of all things and views — especially the contradictory ones — is advocated instead. As the *Zhuangzi* asserts in another instance (2.6): 'There is nothing that is not so, nothing that is unallowable'. This pan-affirmation is therefore essentially trivialist, since trivialism negates nothing, not even its own negation, and agrees with and accepts everything.

This trivialist worldview can be used to better understand the *Zhuangzi*'s views on rationality and knowledge. Firstly, if every view and perspective is affirmed, then every possible mode of thinking and viewpoint can be rational. This means that rationality would be the sum total of perspectives, including the human and non-human, the non-logical and unintentional. So rationality is not, as Western philosophers have typically insisted, the patent of human beings but an inherent quality of the cosmos itself. As Viveiros de Castro demonstrated in his study of Ameridian cosmology (1998: 476), it is 'the point of view [that] creates the subject'. And since 'the world is inhabited by different sorts of subjects or persons, human and non-human, which apprehend reality from distinct points of view' (Castro 1998:

469), we understand that a thing is a perspective, rather than a perspective being an exclusively human mode of perception and reasoning. In this sense, although there are infinite individual rationalities and standpoints, the entirety of reason is cosmological instead of human, impersonal instead of subjective. Secondly, the trivialist worldview annuls the distinction between the order of language and the order of things since it does not consider contradiction as a problem. Contradiction is a problem only in discourse but not in reality and facts, the latter being unable to '"speak"' of each other or of themselves' (Borenrieth cited in Berto 2007: 8). By allowing contradiction to exist in both logic and reality, trivialism asserts that language is a part of rather than counterpart to reality and that linguistic and logical principles are not necessarily different from the principles by which facts and things exist. This frees language and logic from the referential demand and they can both reflect and not reflect reality faithfully. In extension, reason is liberated from the demands for principiation and consistency. Thirdly, if the reader takes into account the *Zhuangzi*'s trivialist worldview, then the textual inconsistencies are automatically justified and there is no need to resolve anything, and no possibility for any objection. One may object that by showing a preference for the axial, i.e. all-encompassing viewpoint, instead of the particular and limited one, the *Zhuangzi* undermines itself because omnicentric holism and trivialism should affirm everything equally. But this attack misses its mark, because in trivialism, self-consistency is just as acceptable as self-contradiction. From the very start, 'the denial of trivialism cannot be rationally sustained, because the conclusion to any argument cannot be an alternative to trivialism' (Kabay 2008: 78). The trivialist can therefore make all statements freely without fearing whether they undermine each other. In this way, the rationality of the text itself is no longer in question, because the text expresses inconsistent views but its trivialism allows this, and it is in fact reasonable that a self-contradictory text should use trivialism to liquidate the problem of contradiction, since trivialism is consistent with everything. Thinking back now on the common perception that the *Zhuangzi* is anti-rationalist and opposes the reduction of living reality by logic and language, we understand that this view is partial and much simplifies the question at hand, since before any divisive conceptual framework may be established that posits language and the world as counterparts, the very notions of logic, language and reality in the *Zhuangzi* should be examined.

As regards trivialism's relevance to re-understanding knowledge in Zhuangzian terms, firstly, although the text does assert the difference between small and great knowledge — the former attained by exclusively linguistic means and the latter by the encompassment of all perspectives — the trivialist rationality that includes all ways of thinking and is non-exclusively human shows that this difference only exists among individual knowing subjects, not in knowledge itself. In other words, that which constitutes knowledge and that which can be known by any individual being are not to be confused. The former is the totality of the cosmos and sum of knowledge of all particular perspectives and beings, because every being *qua* perspective is itself part of what can be known and what constitutes the totality of knowledge, as well as knowing something. What can be known by any particular knowing agent is, however, partial and uncertain, as shown in Wang Ni's argument that individual beings cannot acquire omniperspectival and non-partial knowledge. Therefore perfect knowledge = total knowledge = all perspectives and beings and their relationships. Knowledge exceeds the subject-object framework and is, like rationality, cosmic, impersonal and subjectless, for it is everything that exists as well as everything that is known. Precisely because of these non-anthropocentric characteristics of knowledge, once knowledge becomes the object of pursuit of any human agent, it becomes elusive. This is why both assertions of knowledge and epistemological nihilism appear in the *Zhuangzi*, the former being a cosmic dimension and the latter a question about human endeavour. Secondly, despite the realization that it is impossible to gain perfect knowledge, the question of what knowledge humans can gain is no less urgent, and the *Zhuangzi* provides some clues to this question through the trivialist affirmation that ignorance is paradoxically a form of knowledge. This view is repeated throughout the text, and exemplified in the following dialogue between a sage called 'No-beginning' and a novice 'Great-clarity' (*ZZ*, 22.7):

> No-beginning said: 'Not knowing is profound, knowing is superficial; not knowing is internal, knowing is external.'
>
> Thereupon Great-clarity sighed and said: 'Not knowing is to know? Knowing is not to know? Who knows the knowing of non-knowing?'

Ignorance is seen as a greater and deeper kind of knowledge, almost as something that pertains originally to one's being, i.e. 'internal', instead of something that is acquired and added onto existence, i.e. external. The paradox of knowledge being ignorance is not absurd but has a deeper significance. Cusanus's theory of *docta ignorantia*, 'learned ignorance', gives an example of such a paradoxical understanding of knowledge. In Cusanus's view (1990: 9), human intellect cannot, 'by means of reasoning, combine contradictories in their Beginning, since we proceed by means of what nature makes evident to us'. But this is a fault in human reasoning rather than in contradictions, for the totality of beings necessarily enfolds all contradictions. Thus, the world is fundamentally 'inapprehensible' and this inapprehensibility is the basis of learned ignorance, meaning that 'the more [one] knows that he is unknowing, the more learned he will be' (Cusanus 1990: 6). This kind of ignorance is different from the Socratic knowledge of ignorance, because it is neither negative nor simply the recognition of one's epistemic limitations but also a positive quality that opens up to the infinite potentiality for knowledge. This positivity of ignorance is what the *Zhuangzi* dialogue above shows: that non-knowing is also a form of knowledge. Furthermore, the classical Chinese term for 'to know': *zhi* 知, also means 'to be conscious of', 'to be acquainted with', so that another possible translation of 22.7 would be 'Unconsciousness is profound, whereas to be conscious of what you know is superficial'. This corresponds to Wang Ni's view that each being is a perspective and in extension, a part of the totality of knowledge, because being is a more profound way of knowing than cognition. For example, a person does not need to be fully conscious of his body's every process and function to exist; in fact what one is unconscious of far exceeds what one is conscious of. In this sense, we can understand No-beginning's preference for non-knowing over knowing as an affirmation that simply existing itself is a more direct and spontaneous way of knowing than knowing by cognitively acquiring structures, principles and information. The nature of Zhuangzian epistemology is therefore ontological rather than cognitive. In the *Zhuangzi*, therefore, we discover that rationality is the sum of all ways of thinking, whereas knowledge is the totality of all perspectives and beings. Reason and knowledge are thus not only human and subjective but also cosmological and impersonal. These ideas are important for understanding how the *Zhuangzi*, although it does not present a systematic critique of reductive thinking, still has great relevance to constructing one, since it shows a maximally non-reductive thinking. This is also the case, as we will see, with Artaud and Michaux.

Artaud is typically seen as vehemently anti-intellectualist. Nevertheless, it is often unclear whether Artaud's anti-intellectualism primarily aims at annihilating reductive and institutionalized rationality and knowledge, or rather emphasizes that the destruction of normalized thinking is the condition for creating a more perfected and flexible form of reason. To clarify this issue we need to first read more attentively Artaud's attacks upon Western rationalism. In fact, Artaud objects to the 'anatomy' and inflexibility of formal logic rather than the use of thought to guide actions. For him, formal logic is fundamentally flawed because it is modelled upon Euclidean geometry and demands strict and clear definitions. Logic thus chops up, i.e. anatomizes the flux of mental activities and impoverishes the richness of idea clusters, as Artaud writes (2004: 159):

> J'ai toujours été frappé de cette obstination [...] à vouloir penser en dimensions et en espaces. [...] Mais je suis encore plus frappé de cette inlassable, de cette météorique illusion, qui nous souffle ces architectures déterminées, circonscrites, pensées, ces segments d'âme cristallisés, comme s'ils étaient une grande page plastique et en osmose avec tout le reste de la réalité.
>
> [I have always been struck by this persistence [...] in wishing to think in dimensions and in spaces. [...] But I am even more struck by this tireless, this meteoric illusion that infuses into us these fixed, circumscribed and studied constructions, these crystallized segments of the soul, as if they were a large malleable page and in osmosis with all the rest of reality.]

The demand for the clear-cut dimensions and structures of thought such as defined semantic fields is a human illusion that leads to intellectual osmosis. For Artaud, the experience of one's mind is precisely the opposite (I: 94):

> A chacun des stades de ma mécanique pensante, il y a des trous, des arrêts, [...] je ne veux pas dire une pensée en longueur, une pensée en durée de pensées, je veux dire UNE pensée, une seule, [...] mais je ne veux pas dire une pensée de Pascal, une pensée de philosophe.
>
> [At each of the stages of my thinking mechanism, there are holes and interruptions, [...] I do not mean a thought in linear temporal extension, a thought in duration of thoughts, I mean ONE thought, a single thought, [...] but I do not mean some kind of Pascalian thought, the philosopher's thought.]

Instead of a linear and continuous flow of thoughts, Artaud's mental experience is fragmented and holed; unlike the mathematical and systematized thought of the paradigmatic philosopher, Artaud's thought is one undifferentiated block that cannot be geometricized or sub-categorized: 'UNE pensée'. Remarkably, Artaud still uses the term 'mécanique' to describe the totality of his thought, implying that although thought processes are not clear-cut, well-structured or systematic, neither are they a complete chaos devoid of principles of function or organization. This already indicates that what Artaud finds objectionable is the institutionalization and normalization of rationality rather than rationality per se. This anti-institutional attitude is prominent in his iconoclastic exhortations:

> On peut brûler la bibliothèque d'Alexandrie... et il est bon que de trop grandes facilités disparaissent et que des formes tombent en oubli, et la culture sans espace ni temps et que détient notre capacité nerveuse reparaîtra avec une énergie accrue [...] des cataclysmes se produisent qui nous incitent à en revenir à la nature, c'est-à-dire à retrouver la vie (IV: 13).
>
> Pour faire mûrir la culture il faudrait fermer les écoles, brûler les musées, détruire les livres, briser les rotatives des imprimeries (VIII: 187).
>
> [Let the library of Alexandria be burnt...and it's a good thing that certain excessively powerful establishments disappear and some cultural forms fall into oblivion, so the culture without space or time which our neurological power preserves will reappear with increased energy [...] disasters happen and they urge us to return to nature, which means to rediscover life.]
>
> [To bring culture to maturity we should close down schools, burn museums, destroy books, and smash the rotary presses of printing houses.]

Artaud's pugnacious defiance of cultural institutions parallels the *Zhuangzi*'s demolishments of established culture and morality (*ZZ*, 10.2):

> Utterly abolish the sagely laws of the world, for only then will it be possible to discuss things with the people; [...] throw away compasses and L-squares, shackle craftsmen's fingers, for only then throughout the world will people be in possession of their skills; [...] reject benevolence and duty, for only then will the virtue of the world equal the primordial undifferentiation.

For both authors, the paradigms and monuments of culture such as moral principles or the library of Alexandria are more detrimental than beneficial to the cultivation of intellect and ethics. Once principles are upheld, frameworks for moral and immoral behaviour arise and appropriate people's thoughts and actions; once exemplary knowledge is established, learning and culture follow upon this form and obscure the possibilities for alternative forms latent in living reality. Thus what Artaud demolishes is the petrification of culture and using it in an authoritarian way, but Artaud has no anti-cultural stance — in fact he precisely affirms culture — in a deeper, non-power-orientated, and living sense: the destruction of schools and masterpieces are for the purpose of 'faire mûrir la culture' and 'retrouver la vie'. Artaudian anti-intellectualism is not a nihilism of culture and reason, for it is not destruction for destruction's sake. Destruction is the precondition for the regeneration of a more wholesome and profound culture: 'S'il y a une culture, elle est à vif et elle brûle les organismes. Car pas de culture sans foyer' (VIII: 160). ('If a culture exists, then it should be red-raw and burn the institutions. Because there is no culture without the furnace.') Because the meaning and value of thought and culture — which for Artaud are as unquantifiable, indefinite and free as the flux of nature and life — have been reduced and distorted by the accumulation of conventional ideas, social structures and codes, there is the need to restart everything on a *tabula rasa* so that culture and thought remain constantly alive and open to new possibilities.

If Artaud's anti-rationalism is an attack on rigid and power-dominated institutions of thought rather than an embracing of madness or absurdity by abandoning all reason and culture, the same goes for his supposed anti-epistemology. Although this anti-epistemological view about Artaud is well-established in existing criticism (e.g. Bonardel argues that Artaud is 'hostile à toute connaissance scientifique' (1987: 342), and Vidieu-Larrère (2001: 149) thinks the late Artaud 'rejette et renie tout ce qui peut être assimilé à un quelconque savoir'), Artaud's views on knowledge throughout his literary career are much more ambiguous than direct rejection, and owing to this ambiguity critics have often understood Artaud as more anti-epistemological than he actually is. More specifically, Artaud criticizes epistemology in very much the same way as he criticizes rationalism, that is, he attacks certain limited understandings and ideological uses of knowledge and its methods rather than the category of knowledge itself, which is precisely what eludes delineation and needs exploration and experience. As Artaud declares, knowing the truth is not about definitions and distinctions but about bodily experience:

> La vérité n'est pas une question de définition. Poser la question comme si on posait un problème d'école, en nous demandant quelle idée nous nous faisons de la vérité, quels sont nos moyens d'y atteindre, et quel est le discriminant, [...] c'est poser la question d'une manière fausse (V: 111).
>
> Pour moi qui dit Chair dit avant tout *appréhension* (2004: 147).
>
> Sur les routes où mon sang m'entraîne il ne se peut pas qu'un jour je ne découvre une vérité (I: 106).
>
> [Truth is not a question of definition. Posing the question just as one poses a scholastic problem, asking ourselves what idea we have of the truth, what our means to attain it are, and what the standard is for making distinctions, [...] is posing the question in the wrong way.]
>
> [For me, that which says Flesh means above all *apprehension*.]
>
> [On the paths where my blood leads me it is not possible that one day I will not discover some truth.]

Morfee has aptly commented that these statements show that 'truth' for Artaud is something 'felt' through the body, which is the source of an 'instinctual, pre-verbal knowledge' (2005: 43). Knowledge and understanding for Artaud are experiential and existential rather than propositional or linguistic. This accords with his view that culture and thought are a living flux rather than fixed in monuments and books. Rationality in the definite form of logical language cannot be an adequate means to deep knowledge, and the knowledge that results from such anatomical reason would also be impaired. 'Le savoir rationnel empêche la connaissance, celle-ci d'ailleurs ne se raisonne pas. Elle se possède ou non et son assimilation ne se peut démontrer' (VIII: 98). ('Rational knowledge obstructs understanding, which as a matter of fact does not submit to reasoning. Understanding either holds its own or does not, but its assimilation cannot be demonstrated.') Note that both 'savoir' and 'rationnel' are used in the sense of restricted and normalized thought, and 'connaissance' differs from 'savoir' here precisely because it is not reasoned and acquired through deduction and demonstration, but is assimilated into one's being in a way similar to the surreptitious growth of an organism. Referring back to the *Zhuangzi*'s view above (22.7) — that knowledge is profound when it is unconscious and is part of existence itself, whereas in comparison the knowledge added to life is superfluous — we can understand Artaud's claim about the indescribable absorption of knowledge and its being experienceable through the body as an affirmation of knowledge's ontological nature. This explains why Artaud sometimes expresses the view that there is no need to try to know anything, because the most spontaneous and fundamental knowledge is already in existence itself: 'Celui qui n'est pas ne sait pas' (1989: 32) ('He who is not knows not'); 'Il n'y a rien à savoir, il n'y a qu'à être, cela suffit' (XVIII: 103) ('There is nothing to know, there is only being, and that is enough'). Furthermore, if existence already automatically entails knowledge, as these quotations show, then knowledge is not an exclusively human attribute, but, just as in the *Zhuangzi*, an inherent quality of the cosmos. That knowledge should have a maximal field as its source is asserted by Artaud when he reflects upon how man as a limited being could aspire to cosmic horizons (VIII: 116):

> Avec Bergson j'ai l'impression de lire un Homme qui par ses moyens individuels, c'est-à-dire limités, tâtonne et essaie de retrouver les Eléments d'une connaissance qui figure de manière collective, c'est-à-dire illimitée, dans certains livres essentiels: Popol Vuh [a Guatemalan mytho-historical narrative], Sepher ha-Zohar [a Kabbalistic classic], Zend Avesta [Zoroastrian sacred texts], Véda, Livre des morts.
>
> [In regard to Bergson, I have the impression of reading a Man who, by his individual and in other words limited means, gropes and tries to recover the Elements of an understanding that exists collectively, which means limitlessly, in some fundamentally important books: Popol Vuh, Sepher ha-Zohar, Zend Avesta, the Vedas, the Book of the Dead.]

That knowledge should be 'collective' and 'illimitée' testifies to its cosmic dimensions, and Artaud's reference to ancient texts that are highly esoteric and metaphorical rather than explanatory and logical shows that this infinite knowledge to which man aspires cannot be within the scope of an exclusively logical rationality. Great cosmic knowledge needs a greater mode of rationality that includes non-logical methods of reasoning, intuitional insight, and pre-logical practices of science such as alchemy, which fascinated Artaud (see IV: 'Le théâtre alchimique'). Therefore, to say that Artaud has an attitude of anti-science or anti-epistemology is too simplistic. While it may be understandable for Artaud to be read in this way, using as he does the terms 'reason' and 'knowledge' to denote, on different occasions, either their institutionalized and limited forms, or their vibrant and expanded forms, what he is really attacking is the idea that the scope of science and knowledge be circumscribed by logic, propositions and the human mind, and not the existence of and necessity for science and knowledge per se.

Artaud's criticism of narrow definitions of reason and knowledge shows that his 'anti-rationalism' and 'anti-epistemology' are more nuanced and complex than usually understood. In addition to this, Artaud also gives specific examples of the greater and deeper understandings of rationality and knowledge that he appreciates. From his syncretist approach of deriving thought modes and knowledge from different cultures and times, and from his advocation for the maximal flexibility and scope of thought, we see that for him, there is a plurality of rational and epistemic forms, the Enlightenment model of which is only one possible form, and certainly not the optimal. To rediscover and reintegrate into life other thoughts that modern Western culture has obscured, Artaud notably emphasizes non-logical reasoning such as analogy and induction over causality: 'Le génie réside-t-il dans cette structure analogique des images qui fait que d'une manière soudaine et imprévue et par le rapprochement de deux termes éloignés la Vérité apparaît' (VIII: 18). ('Genius lies in this analogical structure of images that, suddenly and unexpectedly, by bringing together two estranged terms, makes Truth appear.') Analogical thinking is also reflected recurrently in Artaud's writings, e.g. when he sees the Tarahumara Indians dancing, he correlates their movements with natural phenomena and the cosmic environment (IX: 90–91):

> Les Indiens dansent des danses de fleurs, de libellules, d'oiseaux [...]
>
> Même si, en principe, ces danses imitent le mouvement de la nature extérieure: le vent, les arbres, une fourmilière, [...] elles acquièrent chez les Tarahumaras un sens hautement cosmogonique, et j'eus l'impression d'avoir devant moi et de contempler l'agitation de fourmis planétaires au compas d'une musique céleste.
>
> [The Indians dance the dance of flowers, dragonflies and birds [...]
>
> Even if, in principle, these dances imitate the movement of external nature: the wind, the trees, an ant-hill's swarming, [...] for the Tarahumara people they take on a highly cosmogonic significance, and I had the impression of contemplating before me the agitation of planetary ants governed by the rhythm of celestial music.]

The notions that the human body is a microcosm and that its movements correspond to non-human existences and their patterns of activities are not logically deduced but connected by analogies here. Artaud uses analogy to argue that the Tarahumaras are integrated in nature and unrestricted by anthropocentrism. This movement between different levels of thought and existence is a way to surmount the limitations of causality. In Artaud's words: 'On ne sort pas du cercle de la cause et de l'effet, mais on peut échapper aux mauvais effets d'un plan par les lois d'un autre plan' (VIII: 154). ('You cannot break away from the circle of cause and effect, but you can escape from the bad effect of one level through the principles of another level.') Causality always leads to the vicious circle of further causes and effects, and to break out of this infinite regress one should think in terms of relating different planes of thought to find methods and solutions that are undeducible on any one plane. So the principles and modes of one system of thought can be transposed and applied to another system to solve the latter's problems, regardless of their difference. Here Artaud asserts implicitly that there is no essential split between different thoughts and cultures and one can flexibly use and combine ideas from all sources, given the appropriate circumstances. This is a thoroughly syncretist and anachronistic view which shows that Artaud believes in the communicability rather than incommensurability between different forms of thought. This is why when he finds European intellectual traditions insufficient for articulating the semantic field of reason and knowledge that he envisages, he turns towards various non-occidental cultures — not to find an alternative to rationality as constructed in European metaphysics, but richer and deeper forms of thought. For instance, Artaud admires Chinese culture precisely because he sees a fundamentally rational dimension in it (VIII: 278): 'Il n'est pas de civilisation ni de culture plus *rationnelles* que la civilisation et la culture de la Chine.' ('There is no civilization or culture more *rational* than the civilization and culture of China.') It is surprising that Artaud should characterize China as extremely rational, especially when the dominant view in Europe at his time — supported by prominent sinologists (e.g. Granet, Maspero) and stemming from Eurocentric philosophical discourses about an unchanging Orient (e.g. Hegel's *Lectures on the Philosophy of History*) and the colonialist view that non-European cultures are primitive-minded instead of rationalist (e.g. Lévy-Bruhl) — was that Chinese thought is concrete, imaginative and pre-logical rather than abstract, scientific, and rational. Artaud's emphasis on Chinese *rationality* shows how far he is from Eurocentrism. More importantly, he does not search for the rational paradigms of Europe in Chinese thought and upon finding similarities confirms the Chinese as rational. Rather, he recognizes its non-Occidental thought modes as rational on their own terms, as the examples of Chinese reason which he gives show: the *I-Jing*, the canonical manual of divination that uses hexagrams instead of words to give instructions and interpretations (VIII: 134): '*I-King* traité d'énergétique, de divination, de cosmologie jusqu'à l'atome' ('The *I-Jing*, a treatise of energetics, divination and cosmology up to the smallest particle') and Chinese medicine, which visualizes the body as a holistic system of vital breath and is diametrically different from the Western organ-based and anatomical model (VIII: 194): 'Les trois cent quatre-vingt points de la médicine chinoise qui régissent toutes les fonctions humaines font de l'homme ce bloc d'unité.' ('The 380 points of Chinese medicine that govern all the human functions make a block of unity out of the human being.')

That distinctly non-logical and non-linguistic ways of thinking should be seen as rational and epistemological shows that Artaud's notions of reason and knowledge reverse the commonly-accepted Western perception that pre-logical thought is more primitive, that myth and magic are less developed forms of history and science, and that religious beliefs and practices are less principled and rational than philosophy. For Artaud, European cultures are neither more advanced nor more rational than other cultures, because the very belief that there exists a common standard to measure the advancement and rationality of cultures is fallacious. Artaud in fact thinks that Europe has abandoned a higher form of culture that certain tribal and non-western cultures have preserved:

> C'est là une haute idée de culture, à quoi l'Europe a renoncé (VIII: P188).
>
> Et toute vraie culture s'appuie sur les moyens barbares et primitifs du totémisme, dont je veux adorer la vie sauvage, c'est-à-dire entièrement spontanée (IV: 15).

> Comme la vie, comme la nature, la pensée va du dedans au dehors avant d'aller du dehors au dedans. [...] Je vais de l'abstrait au concret et non du concret vers l'abstrait (VIII: 192).
>
> Le contenu significatif et humain de toutes les fables et légendes me paraît moins enfantin que toute l'école scientifique, biologique et anthropologique moderne (VI: 398).
>
> [It is precisely the lofty idea of culture that Europe has abandoned.]
>
> [And all culture that is genuine depends upon barbarian and primitive ways of totemism, the savage life of which I wish to worship, for that means completely spontaneous life.]
>
> [Like life, like nature, thought goes from the inside to the outside before going from the outside to the inside. [...] I proceed from the abstract towards the concrete but not from the concrete towards the abstract.]
>
> [The symbolic and human subject-matter of all fables and legends seems to me to be less childish than all modern scholarship in science, biology and anthropology.]

If totemism, concrete thought and nature are richer, more philosophical and advanced forms of culture than modern science, abstraction, and social institutions, then Artaud is expressing the view that the 'raw' is more developed than the 'cooked', nature more cultivated than culture. This view has in fact become prominent in post-Lévi-Straussian anthropology, expounded in particular by Viveiros de Castro and Descola, who term it 'supernaturalism', meaning that nature is super-cultivated instead of cruder and more original than culture. Castro gives the example of Awareté cosmology (1998: 477), in which '*Culture is the Subject's nature*; it is the form in which every subject experiences its own nature affect'; whereas Descola argues that nature has never existed as 'savage' nature but as a community including both human and non-human (2005: 23): 'La nature n'est pas ici une instance transcendante ou un objet à socialiser, mais le sujet d'un rapport social; prolongeant le monde de la maisonnée, elle est véritablement domestique jusque dans ses réduits les plus inaccessibles.' ('Here, nature is not a transcendent authority or an object to be tailored for society, but the subject of a social relationship; by extending the world of the household, nature is truly domestic down to its most inaccessible nooks.') Anthropology is in fact always already an 'anthropology of nature', culture is a culture of nature, and for Artaud, rationality and knowledge are always mental activities and capacities beyond language, logic and cognition. This view reflects Artaud's desire for thought and being to progress towards the supernatural, i.e. super-cultural state (VI: 398): 'Je crois, moi, au Surnaturel.'

Returning to the conceptual relationship between Artaud and the *Zhuangzi*, we find that Artaud's supernatural and eclectic views of reason and knowledge can relate to Zhuangzian perspectivism and trivialism. Firstly, for the *Zhuangzi*, every thing is itself a perspective, which is at root a cosmological view that refuses the human/non-human divide. This is similar to Amerindian cosmology, which, as Castro argues (1998: 477), posits a common 'sociocosmic field' where 'whatever is activated or "agented" by the point of view will be a subject'. So the whole of nature and culture, i.e. supernature, are this 'sociocosmic field'. Supernaturalism happens when subjectivity pertains to each perspective rather than exclusively to humans. Artaud's views above therefore already indicate their underlying perspectivism, since he recognizes the non-exclusively human scope of culture and thought and the plurality of viewpoints. Exclusivity of thought forms is, furthermore, particularly depreciated (I: 189):

> Toutes les revues sont les esclaves d'une *manière de penser,* et, par le fait, elles méprisent *la pensée.* [...] Car il n'y a pas d'état de l'opinion, il y a des opinions diverses qui valent plus ou moins d'être formulées. Mais l'humanité est inguérissable, on n'empêchera jamais les hommes d'être certains de leurs pensées et méfiants de celle d'autrui. [...] Nous avons une opinion qui vaut la peine d'être exprimée.
>
> [All presses are slaves of a certain *mode of thinking,* and, because of this, they despise *thought.* [...] Because there is no state-of-the-art of thought, there are diverse views that are more or less worthwhile formulating. But humanity is hopeless; it will never be possible to stop people from being sure about their own thoughts but suspicious of others. [...] We have a view that is worth the effort of expression.]

Artaud criticizes the common tendency to value one's own opinions and depreciate others' views, which becomes the source of ideological conflicts and fear for words. But thought is neither singular nor fixed and all opinions have some meaning and value. Recalling the *Zhuangzi*'s (2.4) mockery of various disputers who attack each other, each advocating what he thinks is right, we see that Artaud has the same attitude towards the intolerance of different perspectives. Since the diversity of viewpoints and subjectivities has always already existed, why should it not be accepted? Moreover, any view is always worth expressing, Artaud believes, not for its truth-value or correctitude, but for its being an expression of a perspective that is one among the plethora of perspectives that constitute thought. This explains why Artaud writes in abandonment and expresses himself freely without worrying whether his statements are comprehensible or consistent — especially in his disconnected and rambling later writings — because their expressive value already justifies their existence regardless of their propositional value.

Secondly, from the cosmo-social character of nature and culture to the affirmation of non-logical and non-cognitive forms of reason and knowledge, Artaud shows a maximal inclusivity of all thought forms and an aspiration to a cosmic field of understanding that are the fundamental characteristics of omniperspectivism and trivialism. For example, we first find Artaud describing how he sees not only from certain viewpoints but also the totality of viewpoints (I: 318):

> Le cerveau veut dire trop de choses qu'il pense toutes en même temps, dix pensées au lieu d'une se précipitent vers la sortie, le cerveau voit d'un bloc la pensée dans toutes ses circonstances et il voit aussi toute la multiplicité des points de vue.
>
> [The brain wants to say too many things which it thinks about all at once; ten thoughts instead of one dash towards the outflow point; the brain sees a block of thought in all its situations as well as sees the full multiplicity of these viewpoints.]

The corpus of one's thought is not constituted by organized and linear language, not to mention logic, but by a block of diverse co-existing idea clusters. To grasp one's thought is to take it as a whole, so that the brain sees the multiplicity of viewpoints, which is also a meta-viewpoint that allows all possible viewpoints. But once this meta-viewpoint becomes possible, as the *Zhuangzi* shows (17.5), one sees non-differentiation and the necessity of opposites to exist. As Artaud professes (I: 322): 'J'ai perdu tout point de comparaison, point de sensation pour le bien et pour le mal, pour le bon et pour le mauvais, en matière et en qualité!!!' ('I have lost all benchmarks, all standards of sensibility for right and wrong, good and bad, in both substance and quality!') Not knowing how to make distinctions, Artaud naturally does not recognize contradictions: 'De toutes choses l'Un et de l'un toutes choses. | C'est des contraires que viennent la concorde et l'Harmonie' (VIII: 151). ('Of all things One and of one all things. | It is from opposites that concord and Harmony originate.') That contraries should ultimately produce harmony instead of conflict is exactly the *coincidentia oppositorum* that trivialism proposes. Furthermore, Artaud explicitly attacks the law of non-contradiction and refuses to see contradiction as a problem: 'Résoudre ou même annihiler tous les conflits produits par l'antagonisme' (IV: 80); 'Et la Loi est de revenir au repos, au-dessus du possible et de l'impossible. [...] Le principe de contradiction est dans la nature même de l'être' (VII: 267). ('Resolve or even annihilate all conflicts produced by antagonism'; 'And the Principle is to return to rest, beyond the possible and impossible. [...] The principle of contradiction is in the very nature of being.') We can now better understand Artaud's radical syncretism, for his pan-affirmative worldview leads to an ultimate transcendence of differences, as he declares (VIII: 194):

> Tous ces ésotérismes sont les mêmes, et veulent en esprit dire la même chose. Ils indiquent une même idée géométrique, numérale, organique, harmonieuse, occulte, qui réconcilie l'homme avec la nature et avec la vie.
>
> [All these esotericisms are the same, and in spirit mean the same thing. They point to the same geometrical, numeral, organic, harmonious and occult idea that reconciles man with nature and life.]

This trivialist aspect in Artaud is relevant to understanding his non-rational and inconsistent way of writing, because his thought is not constructed around a dualist framework and is, as Rogozinski says (2011: 21), a spiral constantly deviating from and returning to itself. Contradiction and paradox are thus necessary for Artaud's literary expression. Paradoxically, his unsystematic and self-contradictory style can be understood as *consistent* with his view that contradiction is not a problem.

Artaud's views on rationality and knowledge thus include the important dimensions of criticizing narrowly defined and power-orientated forms of thought, opening up the scope of knowledge to vast cosmic horizons, and syncretist and anachronistic approaches to different forms of thought. Neither reason nor knowledge is rejected but they are valued in an expanded sense that does not fit with logic and propositions. Through the *Zhuangzi*'s ideas, Artaud's intellectual eclecticism and paradoxical claims are better understood and shown to have perspectivist and trivialist tendencies, which are fundamental for supporting the flexible, non-dualist and non-anthropocentric notions of reason and knowledge that he advocates. The *Zhuangzi*'s and Artaud's critiques on reductive thinking are therefore very similar. From their aspiration to a maximally inclusive thought, we now turn to consider Michaux's understanding of rationality and knowledge and how it may relate to Artaud and the *Zhuangzi*.

Repeatedly, Michaux criticizes logical reductionism. But he also does much more than simply criticize. On various occasions, Michaux delineates alternative and greater forms of reason and knowledge. To begin with, the picture Michaux presents of the rational and absurd is very ambiguous and the conventional meanings of these two terms are often reversed. A good example is *Au pays de la magie*, where all kinds of magical and inexplicable phenomena proliferate, to the extent that magic is naturally accepted, whereas the demand for logic becomes insignificant or even absurd. For example, when the 'I' persona sees a lizard crammed with hordes of people and asks how that is possible, the wise men of the magical land do not deign to answer him (1977: 72):

> Par quelle magie et dans quel but invraisemblable des gens se fourraient-ils ainsi à l'étroit dans ce tout petit corps de lézard, voilà quel était le sujet de mon étonnement et ne lui parut pas mériter une question, ni une réponse.
>
> [By what magic and for what incomprehensible purpose did these people squeeze themselves so tightly into this tiny lizard body — this cause of my astonishment did not, however, seem to him to deserve either question or answer.]

Michaux's 'I' persona, instructed by European rationalist thinking, constantly struggles to understand what he sees and hears in the magical land precisely because he exercises his reason. In contrast, the Magi, the wise men there, do not ask questions based upon logic or common-sense, and 'haïssent nos pensées en pétarade. Ils aiment demeurer centrés sur un objet de méditation' (1977: 83) ('they hate our razzle-dazzle thoughts. They love to stay concentrated on one object of meditation'). As Broome comments (in Michaux 1977: 141): 'The contrast between European thought and magic thought is developed here: the former pursued in short, sharp bursts and scattering mental energy wastefully in all sorts of directions; the latter concentrated, enjoying continuity and unity, and centred at the very core of the phenomenal world.' Apart from this anti-rationalist dimension, however, there is also an extremely rationalist dimension to the magical land, especially in the way its inhabitants organize life. For instance, childless adults enter a 'marché de parents' where children can choose to be adopted by them (1977: 80): 'Mais mieux vaut un père adoptif qui vous convient, qu'une famille entière naturelle qui ne vous convient pas, tel est leur principe.' ('But better have an adoptive father whom you like than an entire biological family that you do not get along with; this is their principle'.) Also, when someone dies, instead of spontaneously grieving, the family hires a professional mourner to cast a charm invoking sorrow for a fixed number of days (1977: 61). These practises are so rationally calculated that they seem absurd, but they show how the magical land is a mixture of both logic and magic. As Michaux's 'I' persona observes, the inhabitants 'mêlaient aussi involontairement la merveille à la science' (1977: 72) ('also involuntarily mix the miraculous with science'), which means that they are oblivious of the distinction between reason and non-reason.

This shows that although Michaux does mock the rigidity and unimaginativeness of rationalism, he neither sets up a dichotomy between logic and magic, nor poses science and miracle as mutually exclusive.

In fact, it would be more accurate to say that Michaux does not simply criticize Western rationalism, for his main thrust is to criticize the prioritisation of logical reasoning that forcibly systematizes thought processes. As he states (2000: 178):

> Pour étayer des pensées, il faut en supprimer. Abstraire. Le raisonnement est par définition une pauvreté, puisqu'on n'arrive à une conclusion qu'en faisant abstraction, en supprimant les gêneurs. De plus pendant que tu raisonnes, ta propre pensée originale s'est modifiée, donc tu mens.
>
> [In order to support your thoughts, you have to obliterate them. Abstraction. Reasoning is by definition an impoverishment, since a conclusion cannot be reached without abstraction, obliterating the inconvenient thoughts. In addition, while you reason, your own original thought changes, therefore you lie.]

Rational language and abstraction result in the impoverishment and distortion of ideas. The formal clarity that is achieved therefrom is not a virtue but a vice. Michaux prefers the artistic and literary expressions that reflect the rich muddle of thought (1929: 169):

> Il y a dans ma nature une forte propension à l'ivresse. Je suis un homme en *mane* et tout m'est bon. Ainsi, quand je lis, les premières pages ne m'intéressent pas. Elles sont trop claires. Mais après plusieurs heures, cela devient flou, alors j'en retire une grande satisfaction.
>
> [In my disposition there is a strong tendency towards drunkenness. I am a man in *manic trance* and everything is all right for me. Thus, when I read, the first pages do not interest me. They are too clear. But after several hours, things become indistinct, then I derive great contentment from it.]

The first pages of a book — usually introductory expositions and outlines of structure and central topic — do not interest Michaux precisely because they are too clearly written and self-justifying, and thus are overwrought and uninteresting. Michaux prefers a more turbid flow of expression that appeals to his sensibility of 'ivresse' and 'mane', i.e. that liminal state between self-awareness and unconsciousness, where mental processes are not clearly segmented or structured, and therefore not reduced or suppressed.

The idea that rationality — especially logic and its control over one's thoughts and acts — should not be prioritized is further explicated when Michaux writes in *Misérable miracle* that reason carried too far and carried out too thoroughly could become a form of madness and folly (1972: 165, my italics):

> De tous les animaux l'homme apparemment est celui qui tient sous contrôle le plus grand ensemble de barrages et de passages libres, de 'oui' et de 'non', de permis et d'interdits.
>
> Les chaînes de réflexes, pas si réflexes que ça, arrangent bien des choses, mais n'arrangent pas tout. *Qu'est-ce qu'il y a de plus fatigant dans la vie et qui conduit le plus sûrement à la folie? C'est de rester éveillé. C'est de rester à son tableau de bord.*
>
> Tout ce qui dure est intenable au surveillant. Il lui faut prendre congé. Il lui faut son repos, sinon c'est *la maladie du contrôleur, c'est-à-dire la folie.*

[Of all animals man is obviously the one who has under his control the biggest set of barriers and open passages, of 'yes' and of 'no', of permissions and prohibitions.

Links of reflexes (not so reflexive as all that) sort things out well, but do not sort out everything. *What is the most tiresome thing in life and which results most certainly to madness? To stay vigilant. To preside over one's dashboard.*

All that lasts is untenable to the watchman. He needs to take time off work. He needs his rest period, if not there would be *the disease of controllers, which is madness.*]

The conventional meanings of 'folie' and 'contrôle' are completely reversed here: the controlling, rationalizing agent who presides by his 'dashboard' of administration gets sick and goes mad, the reason being precisely this awareness of what one should and should not do. Like the *Zhuangzi*'s view (2.9) that exclusively using argumentation to classify the world of beings actually defeats any rational classification, Michaux argues that exclusively using principles to govern and calculate one's experiences is irrational and detrimental. After all, is the desire for rational control itself rational? Michaux believes that rationality is fundamentally a defence mechanism and nothing more than what can be called 'a case of cosmological special pleading' (Hall in Callicott and Ames 1989: 110). As Michaux writes (1966a: 276): 'Pas seulement les rêves mais une infinité de pensées sont "pour en sortir", et même des systèmes de philosophie furent surtout exorcisants qui se croyaient tout autre chose.' ('Not only dreams but also innumerable thoughts are for the purpose of "getting out", and even philosophical systems were, above all, exorcisors, while believing themselves to be something totally different.') So even the paradigm of rational thought: philosophy, functions like shamanic exorcisms and dreams: it boils down to escaping everything that humans fear. Thus Michaux bunches together rational and abstract thought, dreams and fantasies, muddled words, magic and science, showing an attitude that embraces all forms of thought without distinct categorization.

This non-exclusivity in Michauldian thought corresponds to the pan-encompassing trivialism of the *Zhuangzi* and can be further explored through the latter's lens. Firstly, in regard to logical contradictions, Michaux permits them and uses them abundantly. He gives examples of the Magi's knowledge, which is about fantastically paradoxical phenomena and creatures in the magical land (1977: 83): 'les primordiaux crépusculaires'; 'le chaos nourri par l'échelle'; 'le scorpion-limite et le scorpion complet'. These present logical and epistemological impossibilities: what is a primordial twilight? a time before the first daybreak in time? How can chaos, namely, formlessness be nourished by a ladder, an instrument of inflexible and definite form constructed in different grades? Knowledge of such inconceivable things is possible in the magical land because contradictions are no longer seen as conflictory, which is also Michaux's view. Secondly, as the *Zhuangzi* does in 2.5, Michaux also flips around contradictions, as in the pithy 'Même si c'est vrai, c'est faux' (1954: 66). This is a restatement of the liar paradox, the classical example in trivialism against the law of non-contradiction, which leads to the conclusion: 'If it is true, then it is false, and vice versa' (Castro and Walford 2011: 144). Michaux points out that there are situations where non-contradiction cannot be the standard for truth. Also, he may be referring to the effect of words, as Castro believes (2011:

145), for words' effectiveness 'has nothing to do with the truth. Even the truth — especially the truth, it is tempting to say — is capable of prodigious effects of falsity and falsehood'. This shows that Michaux does not think language should always be judged by its truth-value. Thirdly, Michaux expresses the view found in the *Zhuangzi* 17.5 discussed above: that opposites complement and transform into each other, and that one should fully accept these alternating opposites rather than eliminate one negative pole. For instance, in *L'Infini turbulent* Michaux's thoughts constantly oscillate between diametric poles (1964:15):

> De même dans une autre série le 'non' (le 'contre') est suivi d'une cessation de 'non' (d'une cessation d'opposition), puis du 'non' réapparu, puis de la cessation de l'opposition, puis encore de 'non', puis de cessation du 'non' et du refus, etc.
>
> [Likewise, in another series the 'no' (the 'against') is followed by a discontinuation of 'no' (by a discontinuation of opposition), then by the reappearing 'no', then by the discontinuation of opposition, then again by 'no', then by the discontinuation of 'no' and of refusal, etc.]

Michaux's thoughts are bounced back and forth between negation and the negation of negation, showing a mind in a fluctuating and unpredictable state. Neither 'le non' nor its cessation has the final say and there is a suspension of judgment. But this flux of contradictions does not bring anxiety or chaos to Michaux, who on the contrary feels a profound poetic peace:

> Au-delà de l'antipathie, du non, du refus
> AU-DELÀ DE LA PRÉFÉRENCE
> [...]
> j'entendais le poème admirable, le poème grandiose
> le poème interminable
> [...]
> sans rimes, sans musique, sans mots
> qui sans cesse scande l'Univers (1964: 82).
>
> [Beyond antipathy, beyond no, beyond refusal
> BEYOND PREFERENCE
> [...]
> I heard the marvellous poem, the grand poem
> the never-ending poem
> [...]
> without rhyme, without music, without words
> incessantly it cadences the Universe.]

> Qu'est-ce que l'extase? C'est dans l'âme une unité exceptionnelle au point de paraître miraculeuse, où, sans la plus petite, la plus infime exception, tout va dans le même sens (*Ibid.* 211).
>
> [What is ecstasy? It is a unity in the soul so exceptional that it seems miraculous, where, without the smallest or the minutest exception, everything means the same.]

Beyond all contradiction, Michaux finds an ecstasy of *in*-difference, an ataraxic feeling of unity. This experience of undifferentiation resulting from the transformation of contradictions into each other can be understood as seeing from an axial perspective, which, as the *Zhuangzi* shows, allows all views to co-exist despite their differences. By adopting this omniperspectivism one transcends all contradictions and treats things equanimously, i.e. without preference. Thus all thoughts, feelings and perceptions in the mind string together a poem of the Universe, one without word or sound, that is, unmediated. Its unity arises from the great understanding of the centre of the wheel from which all is perceived; its peace is like the restfulness of the axis that is itself immobile yet keeps the wheel turning.

Besides this trivialist attitude underlying Michaux's works, there is also a perspectivist attitude akin to the *Zhuangzi*'s. Michaux also appreciates the view that each viewpoint has its own particularity and should be recognized on its own terms, and that each thing, even every part of a thing, is a perspective. For example (2000: 103–04):

> La jambe est intelligente. Toute chose l'est. Mais elle ne réfléchit pas comme un homme. Elle réfléchit comme une jambe. La jambe est sensible. Elle n'a pas d'émotions d'homme. Elle a des émotions de jambe.
>
> [The leg is intelligent. All things are. But the leg does not think like a man. It thinks like a leg. The leg is sensitive. It does not have man's emotions. It has the leg's emotions.]

The leg — one body part — is taken as a viewpoint per se, as a locus of thought and feeling independent from the brain or the whole body. This idea can be stretched by analogy to other situations, e.g. despite the fact a person belongs to a community, the logic of the collectivity does not apply to his personal logic; or, despite the fact that the ability to reason stems from the whole fabric of the mind, the way the mind works does not necessarily apply to the way reasoning works. Neither should the whole totalize the part nor the part monopolize the whole. Thus, if things are infinitely multiple and/or infinitely divisible, there will be an infinity of different perspectives and ways of thinking. Even if things are not infinite in quantity or divisibility, they are still extremely numerous and there would still be a vastly rich field of perspectives.

In the *Zhuangzi*, this multiplicity of viewpoints and thought modes does not mean an infinitely fragmented vision of the world, because the trivialist worldview allows both difference and sameness, multiplicity and oneness. If Michaux is examined in this aspect, we find that his emphasis on the part, i.e. an individual perspective, does not exclude the possibility of seeing the world as a whole i.e. an omniperspective. His admiration for the non-exclusivity of Hindu religions shows this (1967b: 62): 'La religion hindoue comprend monothéisme, polythéisme, panthéisme, animisme et cultes du demon.' ('The Hindu religion includes monotheism, polytheism, pantheism, animism and cults of the demon.') That monotheism can co-exist with polytheism shows that for Indians, oneness is not totalization but inclusion. This contrasts starkly with the totalizing monism in much of modern Western thought: monotheism, monogamy, unidirectional, i.e. irreversible linear time. To Michaux, a monism that homogenizes all perspectives is intolerant and fallacious (1981b: 27): 'En te méfiant du multiple, n'oublie pas de te méfier de son contraire, de son trop facile contraire: l'un. C'est toujours de l'assouvissement, l'unité.' (While distrusting the multiple, don't forget to distrust its opposite, its all-too-easy opposite: the one. Unity, it is always about assuagement.') Michaux is no more interested in making the world one than many; it is always already both. Neither the simplistic multiplicity of incommensurable differences, nor the authoritarian monism that applies universally is commendable. Instead, Michaux aspires to see all perspectives simultaneously and recognize the particularity of each perspective. This is why he writes both 'Les poutres tremblent et c'est vous. Le ciel est noir et c'est vous. Le verre casse et c'est vous' (1978b: 42) ('The timbers tremble and it's you. The sky is black and it's you. The glass breaks and it's you'); and 'tout s'atomise, et "se distrait" et se met "en discordance"' (1966b: 148) ('everything is atomized, "distends" and falls into "disharmony"'). By being simultaneously holist and atomist, Michaudian perspectivism ties in with his trivialist affirmation of opposites and envisions an *in*-dividual — in the sense of both personal microcosm and macrocosmic undividedness — field of reason and knowledge. Thus Michaux's interest in the problem of reason is on articulating an alternative, more inclusive reason and knowledge rather than censuring the paradigms of Western rational thought. Furthermore, Michaux's concern is not predominantly about self-knowledge but the breakdown of barriers of human subjectivity so one can open up to cosmic horizons, as implied in (1977: 37): 'On me parlait d'horizon retiré, de Mages qui savaient vous enlever l'horizon et rien que l'horizon, laissant visible tout le reste.' ('Someone told me about the withdrawn horizon, about Magi who knew how to remove the horizon — and only that — from you, so that all the rest would be made visible.') The metaphor in the *Zhuangzi* of expanding one's understanding by seeing beyond the well-frog's vision can well illustrate Michaux's idea of losing one's individual horizon.

Michaux also offers some examples that illustrate more specifically what his expanded reason and knowledge mean. For instance, the notion of an intelligent unconsciousness as a more perfected and spontaneous way of thinking and knowing is very much present in his works. This stems from Michaux's surprising argument that thought does not need self-awareness, so that unconscious thought and knowledge minimize and ultimately annul the thinking agent. This idea relates to the Zhuangzian notion of spontaneous non-knowing as profound knowledge, and shows that for Michaux and the *Zhuangzi*'s authors, thought is experiential and sensorial rather than purely linguistic and cognitive. As Michaux declares (1966b: 11):

> Comme l'estomac ne se digère pas lui-même, comme il importe qu'il ne se digère pas, l'esprit est ainsi fait qu'il ne puisse se saisir lui-même, saisir directement, constamment son mécanisme et son action, ayant autre chose à saisir.
>
> [...]
>
> Cet abîme d'inconscience journalière soudainement découvert, confondant et tel que je n'allais plus pouvoir jamais l'oublier, m'avertissait de la rechercher ailleurs, elle aussi omniprésente, au point que l'on pourrait presque dire que le penser est inconscient. Il l'est sans doute à 99%. Un centième de conscient doit suffire.

[Just like the stomach that does not digest itself, just as it is important that the stomach precisely does not digest itself, the mind is made in such a way that it

> cannot grasp itself, cannot directly and continuously grasp its own mechanism and action, for it has other things to grasp.
>
> [...]
>
> This suddenly-revealed abyss of everyday unconsciousness, so disconcerting that I would never be able to forget it, cautioned me to seek for it elsewhere. It was also omnipresent, to the extent that you could almost say that thinking is unconscious. It is definitely 99% unconscious. One-hundredth of a percent of consciousness should be enough.]

Michaux's discovery that the mind cannot grasp itself, that thought is not controlled but happens unawares makes him question the rationalist structures of subjectivity and objectivity. The flux of thoughts exists as a mental phenomenon, a fact out there, in the sense that we can say 'something happens in my mind' but not that 'I brought it about', nor that 'this (language, for example) constructs my mind'. Without the thinking agent and the known object, thoughts are like random energy waves that flit about in the mind (1978b: 218): 'Mes pensées? Mais les pensées ne sont justement peut-être que contrariétés du "moi", pertes d'équilibre (phase 2), ou recouvrements d'équilibre (phase 3) du mouvement du "pensant."' ('My thoughts? But thoughts are perhaps simply that — antinomies of the 'I', losses of balance (stage 2), or repossessions of balance (stage 3) of the "thinking" movement.') 'Mais la phase 1 (l'équilibre) reste inconnue, inconsciente' — 'Le moi' is simply a site of thinking energies in and out of balance, yet the first state of stability, phase 1 — where thoughts and 'le moi' originate — is unknown. The self and the intellect cannot be pinned down to language or any other definite cause; they are nothing more than a site where the traffic of thoughts and feelings freely circulate, so any form of reason and knowledge will be open, malleable, fundamentally unintentional and uncontrolled, incessantly in flux (1969: 96): 'Le véritable et profond flux pensant se fait sans doute sans pensée consciente, comme sans image.' ('The genuine and deep thinking flux happens undoubtedly without conscious thought, just as it happens imagelessly.') If non-knowing in the *Zhuangzi* 22.7 is deeper than knowing because it is unconscious and a priori without deliberate cognitive acquisition, then Michauldian unconscious thought can be a kind of intelligence more profound than constructed or acquired thought patterns. The indefiniteness and spontaneity of unconscious thinking give it infinite potentiality for expansion and change of form and content: 'Comprendre c'est d'abord se couler dessous, être au plus profond niveau, être informe, pour prendre ensuite nouvelle forme' (Michaux 1969: 96). ('To understand is, firstly, to flow beneath, to be at the deepest level, to be formless in order to take on new forms afterwards.') Clearly, although this intelligent unconsciousness cannot be called 'rationality' or 'knowledge' in any conventional sense — which involves intentionality, differentiation, certainty, the knowing agent and epistemological object — it redefines reason and knowledge by including intuition, sentience and all mental and physical resources that create thought.

Besides this unconscious intellect as alternative and expanded reason and knowledge, Michaux also presents the notion of sophisticated simplicity. It is well-known that Michaux particularly favours the figures of the child and imbecile, but my argument concerns firstly, that Michaux does not appreciate the child and imbecile for any original innocence or return to simple nature, but because they represent an understanding higher than the intellectual systems and common-sense of adults and normally rational people; secondly, how this sophisticated simplicity relates to the *Zhuangzi*'s and Artaud's views about the notion of cultivated nature. More specifically, Michaux expresses Da Vinci's idea that 'simplicity is the ultimate sophistication' when he writes about innocence and ignorance (1929: 48): 'Parfois je lis attentivement tel et tel grand écrivain classique. Ils ont l'air puceau, on devine que même pour leurs contemporains c'étaient des puceaux.' ('Sometimes I read closely one or another of the great classical writers. They seem to have a childlike innocence. I suppose that even for their contemporaries they were childlike.') The thoughts of great writers strike Michaux as the reflection of a childlike and inexperienced mind that perceives the world in wonderment and probes at reality rather than accept it. The child is a metaphysical being that asks the big questions of life (Michaux 1963: 52): '"Pourquoi y a-t-il constamment des choses? Pourquoi suis-je moi et non pas lui? Pourquoi est-ce Dieu qui est Dieu?" Âge d'or des questions et c'est de réponses que l'homme meurt.' ('"Why do things go on existing constantly? Why am I myself and not him? Why it is God who is God?" The golden age of questions and it is from answers that man dies.') Adults' attempts to answer or bypass these questions are in fact a regression in understanding ; Michaux's wish is to remain in childlike wonderment (1929: 169): 'J'ai toujours les yeux grands ouverts comme les nourrissons et ne les tourne que quand ça bouge, comme les nourrissons.' ('I always have my eyes wide open like babies and I only move my eyes when something moves, as babies do.') This image of the infant with wide-open eyes and in stupefaction at the new and marvellous world connects beautifully with the Zhuangzian image of the daimonic sage (22.3): 'You will have an innocent eye like a newborn calf and not try to find out the reason why!' Newborn calves, like infants, have a stunned look and stare transfixedly rather than flit their eyes around. Wonderment at the world has therefore, both in Michaux and the *Zhuangzi*, a greater grasp of reality and being than analysing why and how these phenomena came about.

Besides this childlike metaphysical tendency that is richer than adult understanding, Michaux also emphasizes that 'imbecility' should not be taken in the mentally retarded sense, as he defends the imbecile (1929: 78):

> J'ai remarqué que ces théories renversées par de successifs savants l'étaient justement par cet endroit où l'imbécile de 15 ans avait mis le doigt.
>
> Les derniers de la classe, [...] beaucoup d'entre eux étaient ainsi faits qu'ils eussent compris la vie par le plus simple, par le plus bas, et le plus sûr.
>
> [I noticed that those theories which were demolished by successive scholars were precisely the issues which the 15-year-old simpleton had put his finger on.
>
> The pupils at the bottom of the class, [...] many of them were made thus so they would understand life in the simplest, the humblest, and surest way.]

In an anti-intellectualist vein, Michaux thinks that the complicated theories expounded by scholars boil down to the discoveries and reflections that an imbecile could make. This shows that these theories are neither truly sophisticated nor need specialist knowledge, and that the 'imbecile' does have good understanding. Moreover, the 'imbecile' has the wisdom of simplicity that intellectuals often lack, namely, understanding life in the most down-to-earth and concrete sense. Michaux's 'imbecile' is therefore not pathologically and mentally impaired but someone who contents in a simple lifestyle, has a no-fuss attitude, and disregards institutional and overwrought thought systems. This understanding of imbecility as simplicity and non-principledness is clear in Michaux's warning that 'il ne faut pas être imbécile trop tôt. | Vers 30 ans, les études faites, c'est permis, on peut redevenir simple, et faire ainsi des découvertes.' (1929: 77) ('You should not become stupid too early./ Towards the age of thirty, having finished your studies, then it's permissible, and you can re-become simpleminded, and thus make your discoveries.') Appreciating this 'imbecility' does not advocate the abandonment of knowledge and learning, but an unlearning after learning, i.e. purging the ideological thought patterns and structures that seep into all dimensions of life (1981b: 9): 'Toute une vie ne suffit pas pour désapprendre, ce que naïf, soumis, tu t'es laissé mettre dans la tête — innocent! — sans songer aux consequences.' ('An entire life is not enough to unlearn what you — oh naïve one, not thinking about the consequences! — have unwittingly and submissively allowed to be instilled into your head.') The simplicity achieved through this unlearning process is the result of intensive cultivation, the emphasis being on the great wisdom of the 'imbecile' rather than stupidity, as in Saint Paul's words which Michaux quotes (1981b: 79), albeit in a non-theological sense: '*Stultus fiat ut sit sapiens*' ('May one become stupid so that he may become wise').

Michaux's advocation of becoming simple and innocent now shows itself not to mean regression to a primordial state of intellectual purity, but a progression towards a super-rational and super-cultivated state. As seen already, super-nature exists in both Artaud and the *Zhuangzi*, where the dichotomy of the 'raw' and 'cooked' and the naïve nostalgia for an original nature are refused. Likewise, the notions of simplicity and sophistication, understanding and stupidity are reversed in Michaux and shown to be interpenetrable. Simplicity stems from cultivation, ignorance is nourished by knowledge, innocence and imbecility are not born but acquired qualities. Schipper's comment (1982: 61) on the supreme paradox of the Zhuangzian sage goes for Michaux as well: 'La véritable spontanéité, le "tel quel", doit être acquis par l'entraînement et la culture de soi.' As in the *Zhuangzi*'s example (3.2): an ingenious cook Ding can butcher oxen so skilfully that the ox dies without feeling pain, but Ding says that he does not calculate every technical step but lets his hands guide the knife spontaneously. Ding reaches this super-technical state of natural action after spending nineteen years learning and practising the art of butchery. His spontaneity is learnt rather than pre-existing as a basic instinct on a blank slate of knowledge. From Ding's example we better understand that Michauldian simplicity and Artaud's primitivist tendency are precisely not Romantic idealizations of a 'natural' state untouched by culture, and that 'returning' to simplicity and concrete life is in fact a complex and progressive evolution.

It is remarkable that although Michaux criticizes the predominance of logic and modern science as the only rational and epistemic methods, he does not, as the Eurocentric exoticist does, advocate irrationality and non-Western shamanic practises and spirituality as an alternative. Instead, he breaks down these dichotomies that define rigidly reason and knowledge and takes a non-exclusive approach to all thought modes. This non-exclusivity of Michaux's thought reflects the same trivialism and holist perspectivism that is present in both the *Zhuangzi* and Artaud, delineating un-selfconscious, cosmic, simple but super-cultivated forms of understanding.

Conclusion

Part of the feeling of wonder that comes from reading through the morass of paradoxes in Artaud, Michaux and the *Zhuangzi* is the realization that they show all modes of thought — including contradictory ones such as the logical and non-logical, the cognitive and intuitive, the human and cosmic — can contribute to reason and knowledge. Expanded semantic fields of reason and knowledge are brought into view, as well as the notion that the rational and epistemic are qualities inherent in the cosmos rather than exclusively human. In this sense, although these texts show anti-intellectualist tendencies, they reflect profound and complex thought and are knowledge-poietic, albeit in a non-determinate and non-systematic way. They contribute prominent views to rethink reason and knowledge: perspectivism and trivialism, which offer the vision of a world of infinite possibilities, imaginations, contradictions, and flexibilities. This requires the reader to rethink how they should receive these texts. As the *Zhuangzi* says about itself (2.12): 'I'm going to try speaking some abandoned words and could you hear them also in abandonment?' Speech and thought that express non-conventional reason and knowledge should be received non-conventionally. So the reader would do well to challenge her own preconceptions about reason and knowledge when reading these texts, for the ideas and literary expression of these texts also have the methodological implication of demanding an expanded understanding of reason and knowledge on the reader's and critic's part. Without the recognition that the conventional critical expectations of consistency of thought must be abandoned when reading Artaud, Michaux and the *Zhuangzi*, it would be difficult to do justice to their paradoxical, fragmented and sometimes nonsensical writings that confront any interpretative systematization. By deriving a critical method from these texts' linguistic methods and philosophical views, the self-theorization of the texts also takes place, since they inherently provide the means to read themselves.

Besides perspectivism and trivialism, these texts also help to advance the idea of cultivated simplicity, which shows that the tendency towards pre-logical and un-selfconscious thought and knowledge in these texts is not a regression to origins but a progression towards a higher, more complex yet simultaneously holistic and spontaneous thought and experience. As Bachelard has observed (1936: 1–4), what is outside rationalism is not necessarily irrationality, but could be 'surrationality', which is a 'conscious, critical, rational project [...] produced by intellectual reforms, its goal being the liberation of rationality from the encrusted habits of convention'. Surrationality can be principled, rational and even scientific, as well as anarchist, non-logical, and mythic. The ideas of non-knowing, supernature and simplicity in Artaud, Michaux and the *Zhuangzi* are similar to surrationalist reforms of thought, so the labels of 'anti-rationalist' or 'irrationality' are misleading and should be avoided.

The conceptual interaction between the three texts also shows that not only is the *Zhuangzi* relevant to and necessary for rethinking the French writers, but also that such an inter-reading of ideas creates site-specific dialogues. The first site of dialogue occurs when the syncretism and fragmented format of the *Zhuangzi* become crucial for rethinking authorship and literary production in Artaud and Michaux, in the sense that single consistent authorship is a fiction in their case and their way of composition is neither argumentative nor book-orientated. The second site is where the *Zhuangzi* shows that the use of logically rational language both deflects into nonsense and reflects upon the surrational, and vice versa, that the use of illogical or disorientating language can show insight into rational thinking. This explains how Artaud and Michaux when writing rationally can analyse their mental chaos, and when writing illogically and dionysiacally can make a surrational critique of normalized thinking. The third site is formed when the *Zhuangzi*'s omniperspectivism and trivialism are read into Artaud and Michaux's works and liberate them from problems of self-contradiction and paradox by affirming all expressions and perspectives and indicating a non-rationalist and consequently non-reductive approach to the texts' interpretation. Lastly, the Zhuangzian preference for spontaneous and unconscious knowing over institutionalized and deliberately acquired learning creates a space where we may understand Artaud's vehement anti-intellectualism and Michaux's advocation of ignorance as expressing the urgent need of a deeper and more flexible epistemology rather than intellectual nihilism. Thus, the *Zhuangzi* has made possible the argument that Artaud is neither mad nor unreservedly anti-Enlightenment, and that Michaux is neither Romanticist nor simplistically primivitist.

At this point there arises a serious question which Davidson argues (2004: 184) to be one that any discussion of what is beyond conventional rationality and knowledge poses: if this non-rational excess is explained too well, there is the danger of rationalizing, that is, re-appropriating by means of reasoning, this excess back into the scope of rationalism; but if this excess is left insufficiently examined or labelled conveniently with vague terms such as 'mystic', there is the danger of seeing it as an ideal Other dichotomous to reason, which misses the point that reason and knowledge are always more or less inherently non-rational. In other words, how can non-rationality be truly articulated without destroying itself as a concept? The reading this chapter offers does risk making these literary texts too rational, but this is, I believe, still preferable to leaving their critical challenge to normalized reason under-explored. After all, something is always lost and gained in any interpretation, but this fact should not hinder the effort to interpret and understand. Just as Artaud said, we should not be afraid of speaking because we cannot speak the truth. Moreover, this reading does not reduce these texts' transgressive power, nor makes them uniform and clean perspectivists and trivialists (if they indeed exist, since uniformity is fundamentally what they resist). Simply the recognition that such thought dimensions can be found in these texts and are fundamental to their worldview suffices to bring out the distinct transformative power they have on thought.

Notes to Chapter 2

1. Fintz (1999) and Trotet (1992) are good examples of this approach.
2. Halpern (1998) and Milner (2000) have commented on Michaux's anti-intellectualist attitude and preference for ignorance, and his experimentation with drugs, as an endoscopic means to explore his own body; Parish (2007: 72) sees Michaux's drug writings as an epistemological experiment to reveal his own psyche.
3. Graham (1985), and Carr and Ivanhoe (2010) believe that the *Zhuangzi* is anti-rationalist but uses sound reasoning to refuse the exclusive use of rationality as the sole principle for action and means to knowledge. Hansen (1983b), however, does not even think that rationality and logic are concepts that apply to the *Zhuangzi*, not to mention anti-rationality. Another approach is the argument of mysticism, made by Roth (1999) and Kohn (1992), who understand rationality and knowledge to be subsumed in the undifferentiated flux of mystical intuition induced by meditation and body cultivation, so that they are ultimately an experience of cosmic energy rather than intellectual states per se. As regards epistemology in the *Zhuangzi*, Hansen (1983a) and Yearley (1983) argue for a radical scepticism, whereas Soles thinks that the *Zhuangzi* is epistemologically nihilist (1998: 160), since it 'calls into question the legitimacy of the category of *knowledge* itself'.
4. My approach ties in with a more recent critical tendency of emphasizing how language and reason are crucial for the *Zhuangzi,* e.g. Levi (2010), who argues that the text reflects upon the debates among the most sophisticated logical disputers and rhetoricians at the time; or Coutinho (2004), who highlights the relationship between linguistic strategies and conceptual modes alternative to logic and clarity.
5. See Graham (1978), and Lenk and Paul (1993: 123).
6. For more contradictions see Robinet (1996: 110).
7. See Hamdan (2002) and Chamayou (2001).
8. The view that this passage is a parody of monism is held by Graham (2001) and Trauzettel (1999).
9. Artaud may be intending a double entendre here, since 'cave' is also the slang for 'idiot'.
10. 'Mamtram' may be Artaud's pun on 'mantra'.
11. 'Tastée' is like 'mamtram', a non-existent word in French, but with connotations of 'tâter' (to feel) and the tongue ('taste-vin').
12. See Morfee (2005), Graham (1985), and Broome in Michaux (1977), who hold the anti-rationalist thesis.

CHAPTER 3

Cosmology: Spirals of Time and Space

Nothing is simpler nor more ubiquitous, yet simultaneously more elusive than time and space. From Aristotle through Kepler to Kant and Heidegger, it seems that no major thinker in intellectual history has not dwelt upon the puzzle of defining time and space. The texts of Artaud, Michaux and the *Zhuangzi* join this sphere of intellectual discourse too. Fundamental cosmological questions such as the nature of time, the size of cosmic space, and human beings' experience of the cosmos recur throughout their texts, albeit often in highly idiosyncratic and enigmatic expressions. Naturally we may wonder if their cosmological interest and ambiguous views on the topic relate to their anarchic, holist, and non-dualist notions of rationality and knowledge. For instance, does an anarchist and perspectival rationality point to protean and non-logical conceptions of time and space? Can a non-dualist thought that overlaps with emotions and sentience extend to experiential and organic time and space? If reason and knowledge are cosmic, does that mean that cosmological time and space can think and feel?

This chapter investigates these questions, with a view to gaining a better understanding of the overall question of what time and space mean to Artaud, Michaux and the *Zhuangzi*. This overall concern is important because although these texts have been recognized to engage with time and space, the topic has seldom been dealt with directly. Most discussions on space in Artaud focus on bodily and theatrical space. For example, Grossman's *Artaud/Joyce* (1996) reads Artaud's writings as textual space as well as a reference to a cosmic body that dilates its dimensions infinitely to include the world; Weingarten and Cohn's study (1963) on Artaudian theatre points out the emotive dimension of space but does not explore what space is. Likewise, Michauldian space is often subsumed under the theme of corporeality and psychic experiences (such as dreams, drug hallucinations, mystic contemplation),[1] and only a few critics such as Bréchon (1987) and Badoux (1963) have noted Michaux's tendency to negate time in his repeated descriptions of intemporality and eternity. On the *Zhuangzi*'s side, similar to the situation in Artaud and Michaux criticism, its cosmological views are often seen as an instrument or by-product of its philosophical (here meaning 'non-scientific') concerns, especially epistemology, mysticism and ethics.[2] Although most critics of these texts have recognized their highly original treatment of time and space, there is hardly any detailed examination of what infinite space, time-space unity or temporal transcendence means: i.e. is space infinite in divisibility, size or number (given the possibility of multiple spaces and worlds)? Are time and space substantial entities per se or ungraspable relationships between things? Is temporal transcendence a negation of time *tout court* or simply transcending the temporal limitations of humans? These are the particular aspects of time and space pertinent to these texts' complex cosmology, and which will be better articulated in the following discussion.

To start talking about cosmological time and space in Artaud, Michaux and the *Zhuangzi*, however, also means that they have some connection and relevance to more general debates about cosmology. Although these texts are firmly established in literature, and to a certain extent in philosophical thought as well, they have almost never been considered to be engaging with or contributing to the history and philosophy of scientific thought. But this is a misleading view. A good example of studying literary and artistic figures with their contemporary context of scientific thought is Parkinson's study (2008) on the Surrealists' interaction with modern science, especially the revolutions of non-Euclidean geometry, modern mathematics and relativity. It shows that avant-garde writers and artists, even those with anti-technological and anti-science tendencies, are often au fait with the intellectual developments in science and reflect upon them in creative activities. Artaud and Michaux are no exceptions here, for we shall see that they can be related to mathematical theories on infinite sets and psycho-pathological studies of spatial experience. Nor is the *Zhuangzi* only philosophical and not scientific, for it was one of the earliest Chinese texts to attempt a conceptualization of the universe in temporal and spatial terms. Moreover, the cross-over between philosophical and scientific thought that these texts embody questions the very distinction between philosophy and science, which is largely a modern post-Enlightenment view that should not be taken for granted (up to the Enlightenment, most philosophers were also scientists or mathematicians). Thus cosmology in the context of Artaud, Michaux, and the *Zhuangzi* should be understood in both metaphysical and scientific senses, and above all in the sense of blurring their boundaries.

Cosmogonic time and infinite regress

> That which is substantial but resides nowhere is called 'yu'; that which has continuity but no beginning or end is called 'zhou'. (*ZZ*, 23.11)

The quotation above gives the *Zhuangzi*'s definitions for space, *yu* (宇), and time, *zhou* (宙), which are highly abstract and have great significance because their compound form *yuzhou* means 'cosmos' in Chinese. And in fact, the earliest known use of the compound form *yuzhou* is found in the *Zhuangzi*, which shows the text understands time and space primarily in the cosmological sense. Intriguingly, the definition of time (*zhou*) given in the quotation already paradoxically negates the temporal concepts 'beginning' and 'end', so it seems apt to start discussing cosmology by thinking about time in cosmogony, or originary time. Cosmogonic time is presented in a particularly ambiguous way in both the *Zhuangzi* and

Michaux. For the *Zhuangzi,* if time neither begins nor ends then it seems logical to conclude that cosmogony never happened, and that the universe has always already existed. Nevertheless, the *Zhuangzi*'s refusal of temporal origins is much more ambivalent than a straightforward anti-cosmogony, as this discussion of the beginning of time shows (*ZZ,* 2.8):

> There is a beginning, there is a 'not yet having begun to be a beginning', there is a 'not yet having begun to be "not yet having begun to be a beginning"'. There is something, there is nothing, there is 'not yet having begun to be nothing', there is 'not yet having begun to be "not yet having begun to be nothing"'. Suddenly there is nothing, but it remains unknown whether this 'there being nothing' really exists or not. Now I have already said something, but I do not yet know whether what I have said really said something or in fact nothing.

This extremely sophisticated passage presents a radical scepticism about origins and in extension, existence itself. This scepticism is argued by showing how uncertain any 'beginning' is. First, the term 'not yet', *wei* (未) is used to denote the state prior to anything, even prior to 'there being nothing', for that is a state that can be conceptualized as 'nothing', and is already one step further from neither-something-nor-nothing. 'Not yet' is also highly ambiguous since it neither confirms nor negates a beginning: something that has 'not yet' happened may after all happen, just as well as it may never happen. But at the stage of 'not yet', any beginning or cosmogony remains unknown. Second, the author here finds that if 'not yet' can characterize the state before any beginning, then this 'not yet' state can infinitely extend backwards into a sequence of beginnings before beginnings. To use a numerical representation, if the beginning can be numbered 0, then the state before the beginning is -1, and because -1 cannot be a beginning one cannot stop at -1 but needs to go further to -2, i.e. the state before the state-before-the-beginning, and so on *ad infinitum.* But then another problem arises: would not -1 be one step forward from -2? namely, the state-before-the-beginning can be considered a beginning when compared to the state preceding it? Therefore paradoxically, time both never begins and constantly re-begins. Thus the author realizes that origins are unspeakable. Third, if original time is uncertain and beyond understanding, how and whether any state or anything came to existence are also uncertain, and not even the state of nothing can be affirmed. The text then concludes that we do not know whether there is anything or not. Thus according to the *Zhuangzi,* Leibniz's question 'why is there something rather than nothing' already assumes too much. Cosmogony, just like any beginning point in time, is inexplicable.

The *Zhuangzi* thus hovers between the beginning and non-beginning, being and non-being, cosmogony and anti-cosmogony. As Ye (1997: 254) describes, this is a 'meta-metaphysical' view that endeavours to transcend the duality of existence and non-existence. There seems to be the desire to reach the primordiality of primordiality, the 'root of the root' (*ZZ,* 22.2), when time was void and any distinction or conceptualization of 'something' and 'nothing' impossible. But the author also clearly refuses the naivety of any such nostalgia, for he realizes that trying to locate origins is as impossible as trying to find the ultimate point in an infinite sequence.

In another passage, however, cosmogony is affirmed but as an unfortunate event, showing again the preference for pre-cosmogonic time (*ZZ*, 7.7):

> The south sea emperor was Fast, the north sea emperor was Sudden, the emperor of the centre was Hundun [渾沌, meaning 'undifferentiation', 'confusion', 'dark waters'] [...] Hundun treated Fast and Sudden very generously. So [they] discussed how to repay Hundun's kindness: 'All men have seven openings to see, hear, eat and breathe. Hundun alone does not have any. Let us try boring them.' Every day they bored one opening, and on the seventh day Hundun died.

This passage hints at a creation story, ending with the death of the dark confusion and acquisition of distinct abilities to experience the world in different aspects. Remarkably, the cosmos — or order — begins with death rather than birth. Hundun existed as a self-sufficient and impermeable ball, a happy 'Humpty-Dumpty' of non-distinguished pure experience, until he obtained organs of sensory differentiation that forced him into the consciousness of things and their conditions in time and space. The story therefore precisely does not express a nostalgia for a golden age immediately after the beginning of time and the world, because cosmogony is *itself* the 'fall', but a wish for the pre-originary state where time and space remain unspeakable and existence unconceptualizable. This wish cannot be understood as nostalgia, since this pre-primordiality is a void that offers no 'home' to return to (*nostos*). Thus, in these passages 2.8 and 7.7, the *Zhuangzi* presents originary time as an impossible question, and nevertheless shows elliptically a desire for the 'time' before time, although it cannot be conceptualized as 'time'.

Originary time in Michaux is discussed in no less ambiguous terms than in the *Zhuangzi*. In the aspects of cosmogonic uncertainty and scepticism, Michaux's *Fables des origines* are exemplary. The *Fables* offer fictional anecdotes about the Creation and origins of civilization. But remarkably, instead of giving one version of cosmogony Michaux gives three: in Tale one, God was infuriated when nobody responded to his summons, so he turned everything into stones, hence creating the world, albeit as a desert rather than a garden; in Tale two, God was bored so he created the world and mankind to amuse himself; in Tale three, God created the world after passing a vote. With these different origins contradicting each other, 'cette question de l'origine [...] ne va cesser de se défaire et de se déliter; au point qu'il n'y aura plus d'origine du tout', ('this question of origin [...] will unceasingly undo itself and disintegrate, to the point where there will no longer be any origin at all'), as Noël remarks (in Michaux 2000: 52). We can think that there are multiple originary times that coincide with multiple cosmogonies, but that leads to the problem of how one world could have been created multiple times; or we may think that time never originated from anything but always already exists, but then it makes no sense to talk about any beginning point such as cosmogony. We may even think that maybe Michaux does not care about making sense here; he would rather that cosmogony be nonsense, for the effect of confusion is also one that contradicts cosmogony, the advent of order. But it would be more interesting to see if Michaux's story can be pursued further, beyond sheer incomprehensibility. If we refer to the metaphor of the infinite sequence in the *Zhuangzi*, non-originary eternal time is just like a sequence extending two ways: ...-2, -1, 0, 1, 2.... Every point in the sequence is equal in position to every other point, therefore any 'beginning point' is impossible, although there are infinitely preceding points to each particular point. In this sense, Michauldian originary time is, like the Zhuangzian, fundamentally paradoxical and unconceptualizable, but not nonsensical.

Besides the unthinkability of originary time in the *Fables*, we also find a revolt against the Creation. This objection can be understood as the desire for pre-primordiality, which the *Zhuangzi* story expresses. More specifically, as the *Fables* continue, we read that immediately after cosmogony, the world deteriorates in the proliferation of suffering and cruelty. For example, a father, upon realizing that he is eating his child who accidentally fell into the cooking pot, feels no sorrow but finishes eating with relish and then kills his neighbour's children for more meat; on another occasion, a man is chastised for being honest about his sexual desire, and thereupon everyone in the community becomes hypocritical and scheming. The message that these stories seem to convey is that existence itself is bad, an incurable disease as in Novalis's view of life as sickness. Cosmogony is portrayed as the root of all trouble, the worst thing that ever happened. The question that then emerges, as Michaux himself suggests in Tale three — is why God created the world at all, to which an answer is also implied (Michaux 2000: 114):

> 'Ne serait-il pas bon de créer des choses?', se demande Dieu.
> [...]
> Et les paroles disent: 'oui!', une seule dit 'non'.
> Les dieux passent outre, et le monde est créé.
> Mais le Dieu 'non' se venge sur l'homme — parce qu'il est la créature la plus intelligente.
> Cela, tu le vois tous les jours.
>
> ['Wouldn't it be nice to create things?' God asked himself.
> [...]
> And the voices said: 'Yes!', whereas only one said 'No'.
> The gods disregarded the 'No', and the world was created.
> But the God 'No' took its revenge upon humanity — for it is the most intelligent creature of all.
> And you see this kind of thing happening all the time.]

Here, because all gods except one approved, God created the world. The god who disapproved is, however, '[le] plus intelligent', which means that not creating the world is in fact the wiser choice. The concluding sentence then darkly refers to the grave consequences of the stupid decision of Creation, foreshadowing the following stories of human folly and suffering. Michaux seems to expand Nietzsche's advocation of Silenus's wisdom that 'the best thing for a human being is never to be born' to the entire cosmos, and suggests that the state where nothing whatsoever ever begins to exist is preferable above all. Michaux is thus distinctly anti-Leibnizian here, since he diametrically opposes the view that the world we have is 'the best of all possible worlds', the Creation being not a random choice but an absolute necessity, the best thing that God could have done. At this point, the story of Hundun becomes particularly relevant, because as in the *Zhuangzi*, cosmogony according to Michaux is also caused by stupidity, and is the 'fall' itself, leading to no edenic time to be nostalgic about. Nevertheless, by suggesting that it would have been better if nothing ever began, Michaux simultaneously expresses a desire similar to the *Zhuangzi*'s: the predilection for the pre-natal state, 'le commencement des commencements', in Michaux's own words (2000: 115). Although this wish is not nostalgia, it is an expression for return that is more profound than the nostalgia for origins, for it goes beyond all origins to retrieve a meta-original state in which cosmogony would be nullified, and to return to a 'time' (though it is not any time but there is no other term to use) when time had never begun. Primordiality can be understood in two ways, as Mircea Eliade proposes: one is the state at or immediately after the cosmogonic moment, the other denotes the undifferentiated primordial totality even prior to cosmogony. The second understanding corresponds with the pre-originary state in both the *Zhuangzi* and Michaux. And although this state is not an origin since it does not necessarily give rise to anything, nor is situated in any conceivable time and space, it is nevertheless a state that is more original than all origins because it is prior to all beginnings. But then that is impossible because time is born only at the beginning, so 'before-the-beginning' is temporally unthinkable, in fact unthinkable from *any* aspect. Ultimately, both Michaux and the *Zhuangzi* contradict themselves: a pre-existential time cannot be preferable simply because it cannot *be*. And even if it existed, there would be nothing to which it can be preferred, for the basis for any kind of evaluation is absent. Consequently, any discourse about originary time says both something and nothing, as the *Zhuangzi* (2.8) points out. Thus, the Rousseauian Romanticist nostalgia that Bowie (1973) and Smadja (2010) attribute to Michaux simplifies the problem. Michaux neither believes in Eden nor knows where to locate originary time. It is an ungraspability about which Michaux can only speak in a language that collapses into contradiction and silence (1954: 169): 'Si l'origine, le sujet, le nœud en était dans le Passé, [...] alors qu'il était dans l'Avenir, [...] l'effrayant, l'innommable.' ('If its origin, subject, or crux was in the Past, [...] whereas it was in the Future, [...] the dreadful, the unnameable.')

Thus the concept of 'beginning' is fundamentally challenged by both the *Zhuangzi*'s authors and Michaux, who orientate themselves towards an infinite stretch of time with infinite undifferentiated temporal points that cannot be demarcations of 'beginning' or 'end'. Now we may turn to compare the *Zhuangzi* and Artaud to examine another important question in thinking about time: the negation of time. Just after discussing time as infinite continuity in the *Zhuangzi*, the very idea of negating time seems self-undermining. But as the discussion about rationality has shown, we cannot expect an overall consistency in Artaud, Michaux and the *Zhuangzi*, and as readers we do not need to artificially iron out their contradictions. Moreover, it will become clear later that Artaud and the *Zhuangzi* do not negate unconditionally the very existence and concept of time, but only certain specific temporal modes.

To start with, instead of one absolute universal time, the *Zhuangzi* presents a plurality of temporal modes each with its own scale and appropriate for particular existences. As the text reads (1.1):

> Small time does not come up to great time. The morning mushroom does

> not know the time of evening until dawn, the summer cicada does not know spring and autumn. [...] South of Chu state there is a tree called Mingling, for which five hundred years is one spring and another five hundred years is one autumn.

The text clearly states that there are different kinds of time, for time is experienced on different scales and for more or less limited durations by different creatures. The view of time as infinite and undifferentiated continuity therefore does not apply to all time modes, but only to cosmic time, termed *zhou* (宙, as already mentioned). *Zhou* is time on the largest scale, namely, immeasurable and infinite time (*ZZ*, 22.5): 'If you add to it, it will not increase; if you deduct from it, it will not decrease'. *Zhou* is also a highly technical term. It denotes an abstract and quantitative time, which differs from the lived, qualitative time that particular existences such as humans experience. It is impossible, in fact, for any individual being to fully experience or know about cosmic time, because any limited thing when measured against infinity is (almost) zero. In the *Zhuangzi*'s words (22.5): 'Although things may live long or die prematurely, how much difference does that make? [...] Human life within heaven and earth is like the passing of a white colt glimpsed through a crevice: one instant and it's over'. The striking metaphor about the transience of human time emphasizes that infinite cosmic time reduces all limited temporal modes and the differences between them to nothing. When it comes to time, the *Zhuangzi*, like Spinoza, tends to see everything *sub specie aeternitatis*. Thus, the longeval Mingling tree is not much superior to the morning mushroom in temporal duration, and humans neither need to pursue longevity nor lament short life. The realization of the contrast between time itself and lived time is not particular to the *Zhuangzi* but a shared view among early Chinese thinkers. But contrary to focusing on lived human time as other thinkers such as Confucius do, the *Zhuangzi* considers human time too insignificant and is primarily concerned about vast cosmic time. The text exhorts people to reach towards the experience of temporal infinity and transcend the limitations of human time: 'Forget the years and forget duty, be set into motion in the limitless' (2.12), or 'be without past and present, then you will enter into the realm of neither-death-nor-life' (6.4). These exhortations present a negation of the limited temporal mode experienced by individual beings, since to forget the passing of years and demarcations of past and present is to refuse to experience temporal limitations and be affected by them. Nevertheless, this forgetting does not negate time itself, but treats any limited temporal mode *as if* it did not exist, so that even a limited individual being can approach cosmic time.

What the *Zhuangzi* negates is limited time and the limited perception that follows it. Although there is no individual being that can coincide with limitless cosmic time, it is infinitely better to recognize one's own insignificant duration than to exaggerate its importance and see nothing beyond one's own horizons. The idea is that the realization of one's own limited time already transcends this limitation. It is no wonder, therefore, that the *Zhuangzi* depreciates history, which is not only a limited mode of time but also its deliberate construction and preservation. This depreciation shows above all in the text's references to historical characters and periods, which are extremely imprecise or simply historically wrong. The fictional dialogues between Confucius and Laozi, Gongsun Long and Prince Mou provide good examples. As Schipper observes (in Huang and Zuercher 1995: 114), Daoist texts categorically ignored 'ordinary history and geography'. But in the *Zhuangzi* we find not only a disregard for but also a conscious attack on history. As soon as historical time appears, there is decline (*ZZ,* 8.3): 'Since the three dynasties [i.e. the first three historical periods that founded dynastic lineage], how troubled and disorderly the world has been! [...] Everyone has been bartering his nature for some other thing'. History is utterly undesirable because it results from the establishment of rulers and administrated society. In other words, history is the institutionalization and hierarchization of time. Moreover, as is well noted, history in ancient China meant primarily written records, which are a conservation of human memory. This becomes another point of attack because the *Zhuangzi* advocates a memory-less existence on the here-and-now: books recording the words of ancient sages are 'only useless dregs' and are not 'truly valuable' (*ZZ,* 13.9); to become wise one must 'sit and forget' (*ZZ,* 5.9). To paraphrase Graham (1985: 187), the Zhuangzian sage is a mirror because mirrors do not store previous images and always clearly respond to current situations. A memory-less person has no prejudices nor uses antiquity to judge the present. Therefore, as the expansion of individual memory into collective memory, history is a dysfunctional mirror that preserves old reflections and has increasingly less clarity and free space for the new and living.

In sum, the *Zhuangzi* negates time in the limited and historical sense through the perspective of cosmic time. This is remarkable given the text's historical context, since the paradigmatic early Chinese view on time — according to not a few sinologists (Needham 1969, Wu 1995) — emphasized concrete, lived, historically knowable and recorded time. The *Zhuangzi*'s predilection for abstract, non-historical, unknowable and immeasurable time is, in contrast, rather non-Chinese and more similar to the Indian view on the time of 'kalpa'. Thapar expounds that 'kalpa' is an overwhelming enormity of time that 'deliberately transgresses' historical time: 'If every hundred years [a] mountain is brushed with a silk scarf held, [...] then the time taken for the mountain to be eroded is a *kalpa*' (2005: 21–22). This way of negating human time through cosmic time is precisely the same in the *Zhuangzi*, and shows the tendency of a mythic thinker to abolish any temporal mode that limits one's gaze upon eternity.

The negation of limited temporal modes is also a prominent theme in Artaud's works. Firstly, like the *Zhuangzi*, Artaud has an anti-historical attitude and is far more concerned about the non-anthropocentric conception of time. This is evidenced by Artaud's rewriting of history as mythic and cosmic time in *Héliogabale*. Artaud *re*-presents the short-lived reign of the notorious emperor as an evolution of cosmic forces from conflict through interpenetration to resolution. For instance, the two queen mothers Julia Moesa and Julia Domna resemble cosmological bodies and are described as forces of female energy: 'Mais Julia Domna ressemblait à une pierre de lune, et Julia Moesa à du soufre écrasé au soleil' (Artaud 2004: 407). ('But Julia Domna resembled a moonstone, and Julia Moesa resembled sun-crushed sulphur.') The disorder that Heliogabalus brings to Roman society is seen as the clash between chaos and order, myth and history: e.g. Heliogabalus introduces esoteric religious practices that originate from the worship of primordial cosmic gods (Artaud 2004: 409):

> Le temple d'Elagabalus [...] est depuis plusieurs siècles le centre de tentatives spasmodiques où se mesure la gourmandise d'un dieu, [...] peut-être s'appelle-t-il le Désir dans la vieille cosmogonie phénicienne; — et ce désir, comme Elagabalus lui-même, n'est pas simple, puisqu'il résulte du mélange lent et multiplié des principes qui rayonnaient au fond du Souffle du Chaos.
>
> [The temple of Elagabalus [...] was, for several centuries, the centre of spasmic endeavours by which a god's gluttony was meted out, [...] maybe this god is called Desire in ancient Phoenician cosmogony; and this desire, like Elagabalus himself, is not simple, for it comes from the gradual blending of proliferating principles that radiated from the depths of the Breath of Chaos.]

Besides, Heliogabalus upholds a matriarchal society that distinctly subverts the long-established patriarchy in Roman society and thus seeks to reverse the course of history (Artaud 2004: 408):

> La filiation se fait par les mères: c'est la mère qui sert de père, qui a les attributs sociaux du père; et qui, au point de vue de la génération elle-même, est considérée comme le primo géniteur.
>
> [Family lineage was traced through mothers: it was the mother who acted in the role of father, who had the social significance of the father, and who, from the viewpoint of reproduction itself, was considered the progenitor.]

These references to cosmic principles, Chaos and female dominance are clearly anachronistic in Heliogabalus's historical context, which is third-century Rome and Syria. But ahistoricism is precisely Artaud's intention, as he goes on to describe a non-human time when there were 'luttes de dieu à dieu, et de force à force,' and the 'respiration des faculties cosmiques' which, in the 'avance historique', gradually lost contact with men and became detached from life (2004: 428–29). Similar to the *Zhuangzi*, Artaud also sees history as a diminutive time compared to time on the cosmic and mythic scale; and the 'avance historique' is ironic because it in fact entails the decline of primordial forces. Moreover, seen from the *Zhuangzi*'s perspective that history goes hand in hand with institutionalization and hierarchization, Artaud's advocation of anarchy in *Héliogabale* can be understood as the wish to abolish history together with its ordered society. As Jacobs argues (1977: 125), although history 'plays the moral counterpart to anarchy, reduces the multiplicity and differentiation of the origin', this didactic use of history is ironized because the true resolution of disorder and conflict turns out to be anarchy itself:

> Toute la vie d'Héliogabale, c'est de l'anarchie en acte, car Elagabalus, le dieu unitaire, qui rassemble l'homme et la femme, les pôles hostiles, le UN et le DEUX, c'est la fin des contradictions' (Artaud 2004: 451)
>
> [The entire life of Heliogabalus is about anarchy in action, for Elagabalus, the undivided god, who resembled both man and woman, the two antagonist poles, the One and the DUAL, is the end of contradictions.]

Anarchy not only subverts history but also heals life's schism from cosmic time and energies, returning life to the resolution of harmony instead of contradiction. Thus, all the supposed infamies of Heliogabalus: coprophagia, pansexual promiscuity, extravagance, and antinomianism are interpreted by Artaud as cosmic conflicts that eventually lead to a harmonious *an*-archy: a non-beginning of time and history, a non-hierarchized unity. Although anarchy is indeed 'the disorder that arises when separate principles are at war with one another' (Boldt-Irons 1996: 866–67), it is also the oneness that returns when principles are no longer separated. Anarchy as resolution is depicted literally in Heliogabalus's violent death: he as the incarnation of Chaos ends up with his body liquidated, mingled with his mother's remains and washed into the river Tiber, thus returning to the pre-natal state of existing in a watery womb of undifferentation.

Artaud's eccentric rewriting of Heliogabalus's history is both a negation of history and a recovery of cosmological time. Artaud's non-anthropocentric way of thinking about time corresponds to the *Zhuangzi*'s challenge to human subjectivity in its advocation of forgetting limited time in order to approach the infinite. But does Artaud, like the *Zhuangzi*'s authors, also favour memory-less existence? Logically speaking, if men's collective memory of time is given short shrift by Artaud, then individual memory of time would be even more insignificant. This proves to be true when we examine Artaud's statements about personally-experienced time (XVII: 9, 22, 32):

> Je ne suis pas celui qui se manifeste avec le temps.
> [...]
> J'abomine mon histoire et je ne peux pas partir ni la quitter. Je la vis, non depuis 49 ans seulement, mais depuis toujours.
> [...]
> Le présent a sa loi qui est d'être sans souvenirs et sans futur, sans passé.
>
> [I am not one whose existence is expressed by time. [...]
> I abhor my own past and I can neither go away nor abandon it. I live it, not only for 49 years so far, but for all time. [...]
> The present has its own principle, which is to be without memories, without past or future.]

Artaud does not see the 49 years of his life as a limited experience of time but as an always already existing eternity. The refusal to be conditioned by time and memories, and wish to always live the moment, without future projection or past influence, show the same attitude as that of the *Zhuangzi*'s mirror-like sage: namely, refusing historical determination; for memory is the means for determining who and what we are, i.e. maintaining one continuous identity tracing back to an origin. And as is well-noted by critics, Artaud is preoccupied with destroying the identity construct and is an anti-originary thinker because he detests derivation. For him, time in both personal and cosmological senses cannot constitute a string of demarcating events. To use the *Zhuangzi*'s metaphor of time as an infinite sequence with infinite equal temporal points to explain this, time is both 'depuis toujours' and the moment *in statu nascendi*. As Artaud asserts: 'L'éternité est toujours 0, étant partout la même sans bouger' (XVII: 52) ('Eternity is always 0, being everywhere the same without moving'), as well as 'le commencement est le point d'intensité maximum après lequel tout recommence' (XVIII: 96) ('the beginning is the maximal point of intensity after which everything re-begins'). Translated into an infinite sequence, Artaud's view on time would look like this: ...0, 0, 0, 0, 0, ... — a truly undifferentiated time where temporal order no longer matters because there is only one self-identical order throughout.

Among the important affinities between Artaud, Michaux and the *Zhuangzi* on the question of time, the most prominent is their common preoccupation with cosmological, abstract, and immeasurable time. This shows that we need to rethink the dominant critical tendency of seeing these texts as primarily interested in time that is concretely experienced through the body or subjectivity. Moreover, the importance of time as a defining characteristic of these texts is highlighted — especially when Artaud and Michaux are read interactively with the *Zhuangzi* — because the paradoxical views about temporal origins and the negation of history and memory provide the bedrock for these texts' views about self-contradiction, undoing identity, and non-anthropocentrism. Lastly, these texts' tendency to see all temporal modes *sub specie aeternitatis* supports the interpretative approach of not confining them to their historical contexts. If history and any finite timespan are considered unimportant, then some 2000 years separating the *Zhuangzi* and Artaud and Michaux do not present any insurmountable gap. The dimension of time both in and of these texts can extend towards an indefinite openness.

The space of infinity, thought and experience

The question of space is indispensable for painting a fuller picture of cosmology in the three texts. Here, space can be examined from two aspects: the concept of infinity and animate space. Beginning with infinity, the different ways in which the *Zhuangzi* and Artaud understand infinity in space connect with their concern for infinity in thinking about time. In the *Zhuangzi*'s case, we find recurrently the assertion of an infinite cosmos. The first quotation above, about cosmic space *yu* (宇) as 'substantial but residing nowhere', affirms that space is a concrete but unlocatable reality. In other words, space physically exists but cannot be grasped or determined sensorially as a stone or tree can be. The characteristics of space are further clarified in another passage about the limits to the 'four directions': namely, the cardinal directions, an idiomatic Chinese expression to denote space in general. 'Vast and expansive, the four directions are inexhaustible, having no demarcations or boundaries' (*ZZ*, 17.6). Space extends omnidirectionally, continuously and infinitely, like an unlimited amount of fluid of homogeneous concentration spreading out. This understanding — excepting its substantialist view of space as a concrete existence rather than a void — is remarkably close to the modern idea of homogeneous, continuous and shapeless space throughout the universe. In ancient China's context, this sharply differs from the dominant view of space as square, exclusively humanly-demarcated and known territory; and in the West, this is a view that strictly emerged after Newton. It is no wonder, therefore, that the *Zhuangzi*'s thought is considered to be well ahead of its time and to represent the 'infinite cosmos' view. Nevertheless, the *Zhuangzi*'s intriguing expressions concerning infinity refuse to be resolved by such an overall conclusion and demand closer examination. In particular, there is the problem of the size of infinite space, since the *Zhuangzi*'s authors clearly realized that 'infinitely big' does not seem applicable because infinity questions the very notion of size. For in what sense is size infinite? If space can be infinitely big, then can it be infinitely small too? We find discussions of big and small infinitesimals that attempt to clarify in what sense space is infinite (*ZZ*, 17.4):

> 'The ultimately fine has no shape, the ultimately big cannot be encompassed. Is that indeed so?' [...]
>
> 'The fine is smallness in the extreme, the gigantic is bigness in abundance, therefore it is easy to distinguish them. [...] For fineness and bigness depend upon that which has shape; but the shapeless cannot be divided by numbers, and that which cannot be encompassed cannot be exhausted by numbers. [...] That which has nothing to do with fineness and bigness cannot be discussed with words, or attained and examined through intuition or mental visualization.'

This dialogue shows that infinite space can be understood as both infinitely big and infinitely small, macrocosmic and microcosmic. But there is a limit to which the shape, or size of anything is discernible. In other words, that which has size i.e. 'fineness' and 'bigness' is finite. Both infinitely big and small spaces are shapeless, and therefore cannot be fully known. This is why the author asserts that both big and small infinitesimals are immeasurable and have 'nothing to do' with size, implying that there is no end to both spatial expansion and diminution. A problem now appears: although with finite space, the difference in size is distinguishable, how can one talk about the difference between infinitely big and small space when size is inapplicable? In the absence of measurability and size, how can one even describe infinite space as 'big' or 'small'? But then clearly there seems to be a difference, and an infinitely great one, for it can be understood as the infinite enlarging of the difference between a room and a grain of sand. So the question is: are there bigger and smaller infinities, although their 'bigness' and 'smallness' cannot be understood in the conventional sense of quantity for finite spaces? Or, in mathematical terms: are there infinite supersets that have infinite subsets?

The *Zhuangzi* seems to already provide an answer to these questions, for we find in another instance the assertion that 'Outside the limitless there is once again limitlessness' (1.1). This shows clearly a bigger infinite space enfolding a smaller infinite space, which, counter-intuitive as it seems, confirms infinite supersets containing infinite subsets. In fact, this problem can be clarified if we refer to set theory. To start with a few mathematical terms: 'integers' are the natural numbers plus their negative counterparts: ...-2, -1, 0, 1, 2,...; 'cardinality' is the number of members of a set S; and a 'power set' is the set of all subsets of S. The infinite set paradox was brought to attention by Galileo, who discovered that 'each of the natural numbers (the upper of the two series below, G1) can be paired off in a one-to-one fashion with its square (as [...] in G2)' (Dainton 2010: 277):

G1	1	2	3	4	5	...	91	92	...	n
G2	1	4	9	16	25	...	8281	8464	...	n^2

G1 and G2 are equinumerous and infinite, i.e. G1 and G2 are of the same size. But puzzlingly, there are also infinitely many numbers in G1 that cannot be found in

G2 — e.g. 2, 3, 5, 6 — which seems to mean the two sets are not of the same size. This paradox was solved by Cantor, who proved that G1 and G2 have the same cardinality — namely, the elements of G1 and G2 can be put into one-to-one correspondence (i.e. bijection), *and* that G2 is a proper subset of the other. Cantor also proved that if two infinite sets are not bijective, then one set is bigger than the other. Cantor's theorems profoundly rethink the understanding of infinity because they mean that infinite sets do not, as common intuition leads us to believe, all have the same cardinality; and even when they do, one infinite set can be a proper subset of another infinite set. Thus the question in the *Zhuangzi* of whether infinite spaces of different sizes exist can be answered affirmatively. Also, from Cantor's theorem we can also deduct, that a) 'for any infinite cardinality, there is a larger infinite cardinality. [...] It follows that there is no set of all sets, or no set of everything' (Suber 1998: 1–59); and b) vice versa, for every infinite set there is an infinite number of infinite subsets that have an ever smaller cardinality. If we use the first idea to understand the *Zhuangzi*'s statement that outside infinity is again infinity, then the paradox becomes perfectly allowable. Infinite space is always enfolded by a greater infinite space, but being enfolded does not mean 'finite' or 'discontinuous'. Cosmic space is therefore not visualized as a container of totality but a continuous never-ending expansion of different infinite spaces. With the second deduction about infinitely smaller subsets, we better understand the *Zhuangzi*'s view that spatial diminution is endless and that ever smaller space is 'immeasurable': not only in being too small to measure but also in being infinite.

It now seems that infinite space in the *Zhuangzi* can be understood through the fundamental mathematical theorems about infinite sets. This is not to say, however, that the text offers a proto-form of certain ideas that was later developed in modern science, since no such continuity of thought exists, nor should ancient ideas be judged according to any supposed progressiveness from the modern standpoint. What is manifest is that the *Zhuangzi*'s approach to conceptualizing infinity resonates with modern mathematical theories on infinite sets, and that the latter provides a perspective through which the former is better understood. In fact, critics have already observed that mathematical notions and numbers hold great significance in the *Zhuangzi*'s esoteric sections, although no substantial study yet exists on the topic.[3] The discussion here therefore points out that a mathematical rather than philosophical or mystical reading of infinite space can equally bring out important aspects of interest. For the *Zhuangzi*, infinite space is both maximal and minimal and enfolding each other in continuity. As Levi said (2010: 7), Zhuangzian cosmic space is like the Klein bottle: an unbroken, boundary-less and non-orientable surface. But in addition, it is open instead of self-enclosed. These characteristics of space can, in fact, also be found in Artaud.

Infinity is one of the key words in Artaud's philosophical vocabulary, and is at the centre of his conception of space. Infinity is seen as a dimensionless but spatial entity that is immeasurable, 'd'insondable immanence' (XI: 103). More specifically:

> L'infini c'est quelqu'un dont la dimension même est sans mesure (XIVi: 29).

> L'infini n'est pas une idée mais un être que je manifeste par l'existence des systèmes étoilés.

Je peux être une planète de feu roulante pour l'éternité (XIX: 95).
Placer l'infini entre le 0 et le 1
c'est admettre a priori un nombre, une mesure arbitrairement calculée et chiffrée de l'étendue de la totalité.
Alors que l'infini ne peut se trouver que hors du nombre et de la masse de quelque monde, état ou être, dimensionnel ou non dimensionnel que se soit (XXV: 130).

[The infinite is someone whose very dimension is immeasurable.
The infinite is not an idea but a being which I express by the existence of sidereal systems.
I can be a planet of fire rotating for eternity.
To put the infinite between 0 and 1
is to permit beforehand a number, a measure that is arbitrarily calculated and quantified by the entire expanse of totality.
Whereas the infinite can only exist outside numbers and outside the mass quantity of whatever kind of world, state of being or existence, dimensional or non-dimensional.]

In the first citation, Artaud affirms, like the *Zhuangzi*'s authors, that infinity is an entity of 'measureless' dimension, meaning possibly both that infinite space is extremely big, and cannot be mathematically calculated. The second quotation clearly shows a cosmological understanding of this infinite entity, since it is a concrete existence of space manifested by astral systems. In the third quotation, Artaud goes further to assert that infinity is beyond number, mass and dimension. Intriguingly, however, Artaud first hypothesizes that there is a mathematical infinity between 0 and 1, and then negates it — not because such an infinity cannot exist but because it makes infinity numerically representable. How are we to understand this? It could be that Artaud is making a reference to modern mathematics, since from the mathematical viewpoint, between 0 and 1 there is an infinite number of fractional numbers and irrational numbers (real numbers that cannot be written as a simple fraction, e.g. Π). One may first visualize 0, 1 and everything between them as one finite line segment with the two ends 0 and 1, and the infinite set of real numbers |R| as an infinite line. Then, according to Cantor's theorem about infinite sets, the number of points on any segment equals the number of points on an infinite line. Therefore the cardinality of the infinite set of numbers between 0 and 1 equals the cardinality of |R|, which is a non-denumerable infinite set. By Cantor's definition, the cardinality of the infinite set of natural numbers |N| is assigned the number $\aleph_0$ (aleph-null). An infinite set is countable when its elements can be counted one at a time and be put into one-to-one correspondence with |N|'s elements, although the counting will never finish. |R| is non-denumerable because it cannot be mapped bijectively with |N| and has a bigger cardinality than $\aleph_0$, which is, as demonstrated by Cantor, $\aleph_1 = 2^{\aleph_0}$. This has two implications that are relevant to understanding Artaud: first, that infinity can be represented and calculated by using the aleph numbers; and second, that when translated into spatial terms, an infinite 'n-dimensional space has the same number of points as one-dimensional space, or any finite interval of one-dimensional space (a line segment)'.[4] In this sense, a line — what is not considered space in the physical sense — is, in terms of infinity, equal to hyperspace.

Whether Artaud read about Cantor is uncertain, although given his interest in the philosophical and religious significance of numbers (notably shown in his *Nouvelles révélations de l'être (New revelations of being)*), it is likely that he did. In any case, his statements about infinity and space certainly can relate to Cantor's ideas, and if it is by coincidence, this affinity in thought shows even better that Artaud is of his time. His views connect to Cantor because, firstly, he rejects the mathematical method of representing and calculating infinity, which may be a reaction to this development of set theory that somehow 'tamed' infinity by making it more conceptualizable; secondly, Artaud's paradoxical statements about space show affinities to the counter-intuitive theorems about hyperspace and one-dimensional space. For example: 'C'est le volume qui est le plat/et non le plat' (VII: 177); 'L'espace, la nécessité de se déplacer d'un point à un autre point plus éloigné pour être' (XX: 153), ('Space, the need to move from one point to another farther point in order to be'), which visualizes space as one line rather than three-dimensional. Thus, Artaud on the one hand insists on maintaining the unknowability of infinite space (XVIII: 114): 'comprendre c'est polluer l'infini', and on the other hand sees infinite space in a highly abstract way akin to that of modern science by identifying infinite-dimensional space with one- or even zero-dimensional space (XVII: 108): 'L'insondable espace sur point X où tout recommence et se rejoint.' ('The unfathomable space at point X where all things re-begin and meet each other.') This explains why infinity for Artaud is a concept that both affirms and negates space, as critical views already show: Mèredieu (1992: 36) sees Artaudian infinity as 'un retournement de tous les espaces (internes et externes)' ('an overthrowing of all spaces (both interior and exterior)); and Bonardel thinks that with infinity, Artaud constructs an 'espace a-spatial' (1987: 311). But in addition to these views, however, Artaud's paradoxical and obscure views on space can be the product of his exploration of clear mathematical thought instead of some indeterminable or chaotic mysticism.

If Artaud's notion of infinite space is compared with the *Zhuangzi*'s, some essential similarities emerge. Artaudian space, being the mutual enfolding of the most complex infinite-dimensional space and the most minimalist zero-dimensional point, shares with Zhuangzian space the characteristics of being both maximal and minimal, yet infinitely continuous throughout different sizes and dimensions. Also, Artaud's infinity resists full comprehension, especially 'mental visualization', to use the *Zhuangzi*'s words (17.4). As Leibniz remarks about infinity (cited in José 1964: 109), although 'we cannot *imagine* [i.e. mentally picture] anything to be actually infinite, [...] we are quite capable of having an *idea*' of it, even if this idea does not embrace infinity *in toto*. This explains well why although Artaud and the *Zhuangzi* offer many abstract ideas about infinite space, we cannot arrive at an image of its totality. The picture of a cosmic limit that paradoxically can and cannot be surpassed — as in the puzzle of ancient thinkers such as Lucretius about throwing a spear over the limit — is therefore a fundamentally self-undermining way of approaching infinity. This is why resorting to the non-visual approach of mathematics when reading Artaud and the *Zhuangzi* proves to be more constructive. That both texts can be related to Cantor's theorems about infinite sets is very telling. It shows that despite the great cultural and historical differences, these thinkers approach the question of infinite space in more or less the same way: namely, using highly abstract thought instead of visual metaphors; thinking outside common-sense knowledge and logic about size; and mixing philosophical, mathematical, and imaginative modes of thought. This conceptual interrelationship between Artaud, the *Zhuangzi*, and modern mathematics shows that different contexts and linguistic media do not restrict thought to distinct spheres. Just as Artaud himself declares, mental space is just like physical space; its dimensions are (inter)changeable and do not constitute absolute boundaries (XVII: 105): 'Je transporte tout l'Extrême-Orient de la terre dans l'extrême-orient du coeur, ici, près de moi, à Rodez.' ('I transfer the entire Far-East on earth to the far-east of the heart, here, near myself, in Rodez.') Precisely because Artaudian space is infinite not in the dimensional or quantitative sense but in the qualitative, the empirical sizes of different spaces no longer matter and all spaces can be interlaced.

Michaux's thought on space also connects with the concept of infinity but roots it in concrete and panpsychic experience instead of abstraction. This brings up the second issue about space: animate space. To start with, Michaux's descriptions of spatial infinity outline an overwhelmingly powerful physio-psychic experience (1961: 25–26):

> Sentiment de l'infini, *de la présence de l'infini,* de la proximité, de l'immédiateté, de la pénétration de l'infini, de l'infini traversant sans fin le fini. Un infini en marche.
>
> [The sensation of the infinite, of the presence of the infinite, of its closeness, immediacy, and penetration, of the infinite that goes through the finite incessantly. An infinity in motion.]

Infinity is sentential, a presence that can be felt, a spatial intimacy produced by its penetrating movement. This is why infinity is primarily a concrete, spatial sensation for Michaux:

> Mon calme violé mille fois par les langues de l'infini oscillant, sinusoïdalement envahi par la foule des lignes liquides, immense aux mille plis, *j'étais et je n'étais pas,* j'étais pris, j'étais perdu, j'étais dans la plus grande ubiquité. Les mille et mille bruissements étaient mes mille déchiquetages (1972: 24).
>
> Je me mets en travers peut-être des courants de l'Infini (1954: 173).
>
> [My tranquillity was ruptured thousands of times by the tongues of infinity swinging back and forth, it was invaded in curvatures by the swarm of fluid lines, enormous by a thousand-fold, I was and I was not, I was captured, I was lost, I was in the biggest ubiquity. These thousands and thousands of murmurs were my thousand fragmentations.]
>
> [Maybe I am putting myself against the currents of infinity.]

Like sea waves, infinity is incessant spatial displacement as well as an organic materiality that totally immerses one's body and feelings. In fact, this invasion of infinity into the space of one's physio-psychic existence and their subsequent intermingling is so complete that infinity shows itself as not only Michaux's spatial experience but more importantly, an emotivity inherent in space itself. Emotive qualities are attributed by Michaux not to the human subject who experiences space, but to this space of infinity itself (1964: 21): 'L'infini peut être abordé selon trois modes, selon le mode pur, selon le mode diabolique, selon le mode démentiel. Le bienheureux infini, le pervers et satanique infini, l'horrible et traumatisant infini.' ('The infinite may be approached through three modes: through the pure mode, the diabolical mode, and the insane mode. The fortunate infinite, the perverse and satanic infinite, the horrible and traumatizing infinite.') Space that is injected with infinity can be in turn mad, traumatic, or undilutedly ecstatic. These feelings are not reflections of the psyche of the human experiencer, but characteristics pertaining to the entire immersive space, surroundings and the individual alike. As Michaux notes, the experience of infinitization reveals this immersive space as emotive but non-human (1966b: 148):

> L'infinisation, la perpétuation, l'atomisation, l'indéfinie parcellisation, aggravée par les mouvements antagonistes et contradictoires qui rendent tout absurde, ne permettent plus que l'ambivalence, les réitérations, la rétivité, le refus et un inhumain détachement.
>
> [The infinitization, perpetuation, atomization, and indefinite division, aggravated by the oppositional and contradictory movements that made everything absurd, do not allow anything beyond ambiguity, repetitions, rebelliousness, refusal and an inhuman detachment.]

Through infinity, one realizes that space is fragmented, agitated, absurd, negative and detached. In other words, space is animate: a formless hotchpotch of both psychic and physical dimensions that generates sensations, thoughts, emotions itself. Space is, Michaux repeatedly says, the subject of its own experience:

> L'amour, c'est une occupation de l'espace (1963: 23).
>
> Une ligne rencontre une ligne. [...] Une ligne pour le plaisir d'être une ligne [...] Points. Poudre de points. Une ligne rêve. On n'avait jusque-là jamais laissé rêver une ligne. [...] Une ligne attend. Une ligne espère. Une ligne repense un visage (1954: 115–16).
>
> [Love is a possession of space.]
>
> [A line meets another line. [...] A line for the pleasure of being a line. [...] Points. Powder of points. A line dreams. So far people have never allowed a line to dream. [...] A line anticipates. A line hopes. A line re-thinks a face.]

Such a space that can dream and think is a poetic space of riddles. But it is also a space that asserts itself as a thinking, sentient existence. This is not an agent understood in the same way as the human subject who acts from intention and choice, but an impersonal panpsychic agent that thinks and acts without any motive or telos. In this way, Michauldian space is not an entity distinct and independent from everything it contains, but is enmeshed with and constituted by everything. This can be well illustrated by Minkowski's theory of 'dark space', i.e. a space that dissolves the self and the consciousness of distinct spatial positions and bodies.

> I no longer have the black night, complete obscurity, *before* me; instead, [...] it penetrates my whole being, it *touches* me in a much more intimate way than the clarity of visual space. [...] Dark night [...] is taken in its positive value — in its materiality (Minkowski 1970: 405).

> One could almost say that while the ego is permeable by darkness it is not permeable by light. The ego does not affirm itself in relation to darkness but becomes confused with it, becomes one with it.
>
> Contrary to light space, it will have no 'beside' or distance, no surface or extension, [...] but there will nonetheless be something spatial about it; it will have depth — not the depth which is added to length and height but a single and unique dimension which immediately asserts itself as depth. [...] [This space] will be mine without being subjective in the current sense of the word (*Ibid.* 429–30).

Darkness is therefore a spatial experience opening up to non-differentiation without annihilating but absorbing individual consciousness. The importance of night space is, of course, an 'expérience spirituelle' for Michaux, as Bruchez has pointed out (2007: 134). But this spirituality does not primarily pertain to Michaux but to the whole spatial situation. This is clearly shown in Michaux's descriptions of himself fusing with space (1966b: 116, 118, 122):

> Un ciel noir s'étendait partout avec beaucoup d'étoiles. Je m'y abîmai. Ce fut extraordinaire. Instantanément dépouillé de tout comme d'un pardessus, j'entrais en espace. J'y étais projeté, j'y étais précipité, j'y coulais. Par lui happé violemment, sans résistance.
>
> [...]
>
> Je recevais le ciel et le ciel me recevait.
>
> Simultanément, j'étais dans une expansion extraordinaire. L'espace m'espacifiait...
>
> [...]
>
> J'étais dans une extase d'espace.
>
> [A black sky spread everywhere with many stars. I plunged into it. It was extraordinary. Immediately stripped of everything like peeling off a shell, I entered into space. I was projected into it, I was hastened towards it, I sank into it. Was engulfed by it, without resisting.
>
> [...]
>
> I received the sky and the sky received me.
>
> Simultaneously, I was in extraordinary expansion. Space was spatializing me...
>
> [...]
>
> I was in an ecstasy of space.]

Ultimately, the self, everything in space in fact, *is* space. Michauldian spirituality is not only a state of self-cultivation but an inherent quality of cosmic space that emerges only when the individual being no longer clings onto its individuality. Michaux holds the view of animism that characterizes much ancient and tribal cosmological thought, which has modern advocates such as William James. If consciousness is diffused in space and everything, then there is no need of subjectivity for consciousness to exist. In James's words (1976: 4, 5): 'There is only one primal stuff or material in the world [...] "pure experience"'; and 'consciousness [...] is entirely impersonal — "self" and its activities belong to the content'. Michaux's views on space thus reveal a cosmology of panpsychism.

Thinking back now on the *Zhuangzi*, does it contain animist views about space that can be related to Michaux? Indeed, Zhuangzian space, besides being infinite and unimaginable, is also an organic and substantial existence. This is because space is rooted in cosmic breath: *qi*, the primal matter-energy. 'Throughout the world is the one cosmic breath' (*ZZ*, 22.1), and all shapes, spaces and things originate from this vital breath (*ZZ*, 18.2): 'In the intermingling of the indeterminate and undifferentiated, something changed and there was cosmic breath, cosmic breath then changed and there was shape, shape changed and there was life.' The cosmogonic image here shows an indeterminate and inexplicable moment of coming-into-existence, well suiting the *Zhuangzi*'s ambiguity on cosmogonic time, but is very clear that cosmic breath is the source of life. Cosmic breath therefore constitutes the world and pervades all things and space, being the 'equalizing [...] fundamental unity of the cosmos' (Michael 2005: 14). Furthermore, 'cosmic breath is that which is empty and allows for things' (*ZZ*, 4.2). Thus understood, space is cosmic breath — this animate and pan-cosmic force — as well as all things, since cosmic breath also constitutes everything. This hylozoist cosmology now shows itself to correspond to Michaux's panpsychic space, for 'panpsychism is [...] the view that matter is intrinsically active (hylozoism)' (Lamberth 1999: 187). For both Michaux and the *Zhuangzi*, things and space share one being, so the thoughts and feelings that arise belong to this collective existence. Space is not an inanimate framework in which things are positioned and interact, but an experiential material existence that is co-sentient with — ultimately, *is* — all things.

The idea that space thinks and feels, although dismissed in modern science as a spiritualist doctrine, has had serious advocates in intellectual history, most prominently Parmenides. As Garelli points out in his study on Artaud (1982: 110), Parmenides's saying 'τὸ γὰρ αὐτὸ νοειν έστίν τε καί εἶναι' should be translated as 'Car la même chose sont pensée et être' ('Because thought and being are the same thing'). This statement affirms that everything that exists thinks. Nevertheless, it was understood by Enlightenment philosophers such as Berkeley to assert that a (human) being is necessarily a thinking being. Garelli then argues that Artaud returns to the original Parmenidean view and sees the universe as a field of 'co-appartenance qui fonde dans la même Unité, Lieu et Parole, Temps et Espace, Penser et Monde' (1982: 127). Artaud writes in *L'Ombilic des limbes* that 'l'espace rendait son plein coton mental où nulle pensée encore n'était nette et ne restituait sa décharge d'objets' (2004: 106) ('space produces its abundant mental tissue where no thought has yet been unclear or not released its discharge of things'), upon which Garelli comments that (1982: 104): 'Ce qu'affirme Artaud, ici, est très précisément que l'espace pense.' ('What Artaud is asserting is precisely that space thinks.') But Artaud not only attributes thought and sentience to space, he also recognizes the physio-psychic identity shared between space and the individual mind and body. For instance:

> L'homme n'est pas seulement *répandu* dans son corps, il est répandu dans le dehors des choses (XI: 103).
>
> Suis-je donc le ciel ou la mer ou les vagues des immensités que j'entends mugir dans mon cœur (XIVi: 28)?
>
> Il n'y a pour moi jamais rien d'inanimé.
> L'animation est le sol de la terre afin de permettre le sursaut qui produit du merveilleux, [...] La terre et les pierres sont des états de conscience (XIX: 214).

> [Man is not only pervasive within his body, he is also pervasive on the outside of things.
>
> So am I the sky or the sea or the waves of vastnesses which I hear roaring in my heart?
>
> For me there is never anything inanimate.
>
> Animation is the soil of the earth in order to allow the startling jolt that the marvellous creates, [...] the earth and stones are states of consciousness.]

These statements express the view that the spaces of body and environment, mind and nature coincide, and that Artaud is just like Michaux and the *Zhuangzi*'s authors, a thorough animist. This animist aspect, so far little-remarked, is an important dimension of Artaud's thought. It not only shows Artaud's organicist approach to space and cosmology but also fits with his epistemology. As already discussed, for Artaud, reason and knowledge are impersonal cosmic attributes that do not exclusively depend on the human mind to exist. This view is naturally complemented by an understanding of space as living and conscious.

Through these inter-readings of all three texts, an understanding of infinity as an inherent, abstract but experienceable quality of space instead of limitlessly big size emerges. Space also becomes an animate, pan-conscious materiality that both envelops and exists *as* everything. The texts also approach these questions about space by combining different fields of thought, notably mathematics and metaphysical symbolism in Artaud and the *Zhuangzi*'s case, psychological discourse and empiricism in Michaux's. Imagination and conceptual rigor, literary creation and scientific hypothesis are not mutually exclusive, nor necessarily bad bedfellows. Moreover, these texts' views on space add something to their existing critical reception. It shows how very unsolipsistic and non-anthropocentric their understandings of space and the cosmic totality are. Although self-cultivation and the body are crucial in spatial experience, there is no narcissistic projection of subjectivity that expands until the entire cosmos is its mirror. Moreover, Artaud and the *Zhuangzi*'s connections with mathematics bring to attention the extent to which these writers engaged with their contemporaneous scientific concepts and developments — something that has been underestimated. Through the comparative dialogue of these texts, their shared concerns and approaches become clearer, and a conceptual wormhole is created between them: the distance between them suddenly becomes proximity. Artaud, Michaux and the *Zhuangzi*'s views together, by complementing each other, say something about the conceptual context of the thought on time and space and the texts themselves — something that is not evident if each is considered on its own. That these texts can echo and interact with each other, as well as relate to the same notions such as Cantorian infinity and Jamesian empiricism, shows that cosmological thought — and thought in general — is neither always nor entirely restricted by the historical contexts and cultural spaces that produce specific ideas and approaches to science and metaphysics. This demonstration that more ancient ideas can be similar to more modern ones, or vice versa, is not using the modern worldview (especially the scientific) to judge the ancient, nor nostalgically looking towards ancient wisdom to solve contemporary problems, nor an anachronistic mistake. Thought is not only local, it transcends its locality simply by spreading to different minds. The totality of thought — which for these thinkers takes cosmic dimensions — is where temporal, geographical and linguistic boundaries can be surpassed. The case of these three texts shows that the intellectual history of cosmology is an interactive field rather than a chronological string. This fluidity of thought boundaries is particularly relevant to cosmology, since it is the branch of thought that presents the greatest challenge to linear time and commonly accepted spatial demarcations. This concords with Artaud's view that physical spatial differences are not absolute, and sometimes can be obliterated (XIVii: 193): 'Je n'ai jamais fait de différence entre ce qui était près et ce qui était loin.' Comparative thought itself is a conceptual Klein bottle.

Cosmological time and space in context

Contrast only becomes sharper when a text that has undergone a process of deterritorialization returns to its original context. If Artaud, Michaux and the *Zhuangzi*'s views on time and space are put back into their contemporary contexts of cosmological thought, the question of how they relate and contribute to the history of time and space philosophies can be further clarified. Generally speaking, their ideas show both a high level of interaction with and great difference from their contemporaneous intellectual trends. Starting with the *Zhuangzi*, it contrasts with the dominant tendency of ancient Chinese thinkers to emphasize linear, recorded history and demarcated, civilized space. In particular, Zhuangzian time is quite atypical of Chinese views of time and more similar to the Indian conception of immeasurably long, anti-historical time. This shows that pre-Buddhist Chinese thought is not necessarily radically different from Indo-European thought, despite the lack of Indo-European influence. Furthermore, the *Zhuangzi* subverts the prevalent correlative cosmology. Sinologists such as Henderson (1984) and Schwartz (1985) have shown that Chinese cosmology emphasized 'the systemized correspondences between processes and classes of things in the natural realm and the human realm' (Chang 2009: 222), for instance, the changes in stars and cosmic breath indicating historical change and spatial positions. This is the widely accepted correlative cosmology in early Chinese thought. But the *Zhuangzi* overthrows this paradigmatic correlative method because it 'rejected the accepted criteria for classifying things, [and] removed any basis for the drawing of analogies' (Henderson 1984: 95–96) — namely, the basis of shared qualities. For example, when the text 'compares a high ministry of state to a rat's rotting carcass' (Henderson 1984: 96), it is parodying analogy and refusing to use it in the way that reinforces conventional meaning. Instead of analogy, Zhuangzian cosmology, based on abstraction and non-visualization, is a remarkable alternative to correlative cosmology. Moreover, the *Zhuangzi*'s ambiguous treatment of the question of cosmogonic time surpasses its contemporaries in sophistication and boldness in cosmological speculation. Although the idea of Creation by a divine agent is absent in ancient China, the vast majority of textual evidence confirms that the universe was born at some point, and time then evolved from this beginning point in various ways. Only the *Zhuangzi* goes so far as to question whether cosmogony happened at all, whether things exist at all outside the conception of things, and whether time should be thought in terms of beginning and end. Although for most people at the time — thinkers, rulers, and common people — the importance of time and space lay in their functions and symbolisms in human life and society, e.g. in establishing morality, rituals and power legitimacy, for the *Zhuangzi* it is precisely the super-human aspects of time and space that are appreciated: their unknowability, infinity, indifference to limited individual existences.

In Artaud and Michaux's case, the recognition that they are important thinkers of time and space makes the lack of philosophical exploration of cosmic time and especially space in the nineteenth and twentieth centuries a bit less glaring. As intellectual history shows, the gap between the humanities and the sciences notably increased from the Enlightenment onwards, and by Artaud and Michaux's time, cosmology was mainly the concern of theoretical physics. Although there were important philosophers of time such as Bergson, McTaggart, and Heidegger — who, apart from McTaggart, mostly addressed time through experience and phenomenology — very few thinkers outside the scientific field addressed the nature and substance of space. These are issues which Artaud and Michaux, however, directly reflect upon, albeit through literary writing instead of scientific experiments, showing that scientific cosmology does not make philosophical reflections on cosmology obsolete. Furthermore, Artaud's and Michaux's cosmological views are remarkable because they present a different approach to time and space in contrast with some established paradigms — for instance, the Kantian view, which sees time and space as *a priori* conditions, as frameworks for thought and being, rather than as intrinsic properties of anything themselves. Apart from the time and space ingrained in humans beings' 'modes of behaving' (Melnick 1989: 25), time and space in themselves — if they exist at all — cannot be known. Kant thus does not assert any substantial reality in time and space: as part of our empirical sensibility, they seem to be real but could be only part of phenomenal appearances; as part of non-phenomenal reality, their existence is impossible because the noumenal has no place for that which affects our senses.[5] In contrast, Artaud's and Michaux's cosmologies do not introduce a split between the phenomenal and noumenal, nor draw any clear line between what is accessible to human subjectivity and what is beyond. Human existence is bathed in a pan-conscious fluid of space, and is part of the whole extent of cosmic time. Time and space are substantially real, and this reality is given out there in the universe, not justified through human definitions of what is real. In regard to a few other paradigms of time philosophy that metaphorize time into different shapes, most famously, the Nietzschean eternal return and the Bergsonian 'irreversible' time of the *durée,* we see that Artaud and Michaux reflect primarily on cosmic and abstract time rather than the lived time of becoming, and avoid the dichotomy in seeing time either as cyclical or linear. If tracing back to primordial time is impossible (according to Michaux), then we cannot say time is a linear extension, as in the fundamental linear continuity that underlies Bergsonian temporality; if time is without past or future, being an infinite series of 'toujours 0' (Artaud XVII: 52), then any return becomes meaningless, either in terms of Nietzschean recurrence, or the regular restarting at the instant of birth à la Mircea

Eliade. Besides, if there is a concept of the past in cyclical time, eternal return would be a linear repetition of cycles following upon each other, each time numerically different. Thus the past would be accumulating infinitely, and the eternal return becomes yet again a *linear* time model. Artaud and Michaux offer ways to think out of this impasse precisely because they do not try to define the shape of time. Time may be like infinity, much more conceptualizable than visualizable. The very approach of trying to put time into a convenient geometric shape could be self-undermining. The non-visual approach made possible by Artaud and Michaux shows that a deep understanding of time is possible without a clear image of it.

Conclusion

Highly diverse as Artaud, Michaux and the *Zhuangzi*'s articulations of time and space are, when put into dialogue, they connect to each other in some important aspects, with the *Zhuangzi*'s ideas further bringing out the cosmological dimension in the two Francophone writers' thought. Through their views, we may envisage a cosmos of unitary reality 'whose being does not exist "behind" or "in" everything spatial and temporal but *as* everything spatial and temporal' (Neumann 1989: 243). Once again this confirms that although these texts are not scientific texts aimed at proving a systematic cosmological theory, cosmology is an indispensable part of them that demands the reader's attention. The *Zhuangzi* — despite not teleologically constructed for a specific purpose — can be considered a cosmological text as well as a mytho-poetic one; and Artaud and Michaux prove to be thinkers who, in a time when the gap between philosophy and science increasingly widened and when cosmology and space in particular were becoming inquiries exclusive to physics, sought to bridge this gap and return to a more holistic state of thought.

It is also understood from these texts' paradoxes about and conceptual probing into the questions of time and space that their attitudes of spatio-temporal undifferentation and logical trivialism overlap. In other words, cosmology is interlocked with epistemology and is equally important. This inter-relationship also shows how the encounter between these texts creates site-specific ideas that are particular points and intersections, which then provide more possibilities for further dialogue. One idea sheds light on another not because it already explains the other by itself, but because these two ideas are juxtaposed into a conceptual collage. Thus, for instance, panpsychic space says something about the cosmic knowledge that is constituted through all beings and perspectives, and vice versa. Or, time and space themselves are conceptual sites where comparison can be enacted, for comparison itself is an approach that juggles with and transcends the limits of chronology and geography. Especially when the texts in question hold cosmological views that overthrow the normal assumptions about time and space and advocate the indifferentiation of time sequence and spatial demarcation, comparative and interactive dialogue is even better supported, for the disparity of particular historical and geographical contexts of these texts is no longer an obstacle to putting them into the same intercultural and conceptual space. It may be said that in the space of literature and thought, everything could occupy the same space simultaneously.

Notes to Chapter 3

1. See Zanghi (2002), who discusses Michaux's correlation of inner and outer, bodily and cosmic spaces; and Verger (2004), who treats dream space, with some exploration of time, and sketches Michaux's landscape of imagination. Trotet (1992) also studies the notion of 'le vide' by relating Michaux to Daoist, Zen and Hindu ideas, indicating a space of free spiritual movement.
2. For these views see Michael's *The pristine Dao* (2005), which points out that the *Zhuangzi* considers time and space as mythic states transcending the known world, without beginning or end. But Michael's emphasis is on the religious significance of this mythic cosmology. Zhang (2002) and Li (1988) both recognize that the *Zhuangzi* is important in the development of cosmological thought in China and that it uses a highly abstract terminology for time and space that contrasts with the concrete thinking of its time. They also argue for the 'infinite cosmos' view and for time-space being one unity — both prominent ideas in the *Zhuangzi* to which I will refer — but which end up as an expression of the *dao*, an inexplicable thing itself.
3. Only Ye (1997) briefly mentions the symbolism of numbers in the *Zhuangzi*.
4. See Weisstein's explanation on this website: <http://mathworld.wolfram.com/Aleph-1.html> [accessed 7 February 2015]
5. See Goosen (2008: 26) for a discussion about Kantian space and time.

CHAPTER 4

Cosmology: Nature beyond Form

From Artaud's advocation of a pest-like theatre 'où se retrouvent à vif toutes les puissances de la nature' (2004: 518), from Michaux's horror and fascination when confronted with the 'fleuve' of nature, which is also 'son propre fleuve de sang' (1963: 45), and from the *Zhuangzi*'s affirmation of the ultimate as a state in which 'neither heaven [or 'nature'] nor man is victor over the other' (*ZZ*, 6.1), nature is shown to be fundamental in the three texts' worldviews, but existing as a question that needs probing rather than a concrete thing or defined notion that can be taken for granted. In fact, it is only natural that nature should be an important concern of these thinkers, for it relates to their cosmological interest and is indispensable in the overall structure of cosmological thought. Parallel with the question of cosmic structure, namely, time and space, nature is also a crucial issue underlying cosmological understanding. Whitehead has remarked that 'the meaning of nature' principally involves 'the character of time and the character of space' (1920: 54), which shows that nature is not only a concrete entity as commonly understood but extends the questions of time and space into the issue of cosmic principiation. This is already reflected through these texts' views on time and space shown in the previous chapter, for instance in the panpsychic space that reveals a pervading cosmic life force. The non-subjective and experiential quality of time and space also reflects an impersonal way of cosmic functioning which is nevertheless fully integrated in the experience of each particular being. Temporal and spatial indeterminateness and impersonality therefore point towards natural principles such as transformation and fate. A tension however exists. Is not fate about determination rather than amorphousness? Should not an endlessly metamorphosizing nature be open to multiple possibilities, thus defeating fatality? Living impulses, rivers of blood and bodily circulation, cosmic agon and balance — these are what Artaud, Michaux and the *Zhuangzi* seem to tell us about nature. But what kind of nature is this? Or rather, what multiplicities of natures do these images and metaphors depict? How do natural principles — if any — function in the entirety of time-space that these texts outline? These are the questions that this chapter will explore and clarify.

But before enquiring into the theme of nature in these texts, certain existing views on the topic should be addressed, not least because they have already embedded Artaud, Michaux and the *Zhuangzi* in certain primitivist, romanticist, or spiritualist forms. Although Artaud's relationship to nature has never been studied in-depth, he tends to be considered as either anti-naturalist or primitivist, or both. According to the former thesis, supported by Barber (1993) and Deleuze and Guattari (1980), Artaud sees nature as an authoritarian predetermination that dictates existence and confines it to fixed forms, such as progeny through sexual reproduction, or naturally assigned functions of the body.[1] According to the primitivist view, however, Artaud has a mythic and surreptitiously Romanticist notion of nature that takes nature as the original and pre-linguistic state. For instance, Demaitre (1972) believes that Artaud's writings about Mexico show an essentialist nature; and for Sontag (1976), writing for Artaud is a 'denaturalization' of the more original state of speech. Thus the anti-naturalist view sees Artaudian nature as too totalizing and rigid, whereas the primitivist view sees it as too spontaneous and unconstructed in an 'original' authenticity. But is the best way of reading Artaud's attitude towards nature simply a confirmation of clichés of natural determinism or innocence? Rebelling against or primitivizing nature is neither transgressive nor interesting, for one must have a pretty inflexible understanding of what nature encompasses. There are many instances where Artaud provides us with clues showing — especially through his theorizations of 'la Cruauté' — that he endeavours to transform the very idea of nature. Likewise, neither has Michauldian nature escaped aesthetic stereotyping: nature as Romanticist, an Orientally-influenced harmony, or a pure poetic act of the sign. Boon reads Michaux's drug writings as a continuation of nineteenth-century Romanticist 'nature mysticism' (2002: 251); Trotet thinks Michaux understands nature's relationship with man as harmony and equilibrium, which are in turn views coming from Oriental spirituality, especially Daoism.[2] But the view that Oriental philosophies are non-dualist towards nature and man should be questioned, since dualism is not, as Descola observes (2005), the patent of European thought. Finally, Parish (2007) and Laügt (2008) have regarded Michaux's appreciation of the poetic sign as the primitivist predilection for the prototype ideogram of nature before its evolution into a more advanced stage of language, namely, culture. But Michaux is too self-conflictory about nature to subscribe to these attitudes. As we will see, sometimes he divinizes nature, sometimes he abhors it to the extent that its very presence means screaming pain and self-disgust. For Michaux it is too difficult to speak about nature, but it is equally difficult not to speak about it.

This dilemma about conceptualizing and linguistically expressing nature can also be found in the *Zhuangzi,* albeit contemplated with less self-conscious suffering. Maybe it is to the text's benefit that a precise term for 'nature' did not exist at the time of its writing, and the very notion was more a field of idea clusters than pinned to a few key terms. This means that certain terminological limits of discussing nature *as* nature are removed. But this relative linguistic freedom has also triggered interpretations that try to define Zhuangzian nature through other related terms such as *dao* and *ziran* (自然), translated as 'spontaneity'.[3] This terminological approach, which has its roots in nineteenth-century philology, neglects other important approaches, for it puts too much emphasis on specific words and their etymologies. And because the idea of spontaneity has typically been related to the *Zhuangzi*, primitivist ideas have once again found their way into Zhuangzian nature, for it is too easy to think about spontaneity as a perfect 'animal-like unity' (Moellegaard 2007: 124) to which human beings should return, an effortless existence or organicist harmony between nature and man.[4] This chapter contests the view that nature is a state of animality to which man can *regress*, and suggests more recognition of the tension between natural law and human contrivance in the *Zhuangzi*. Spontaneity does not come easily; in fact, being spontaneous and free is sometimes the hardest thing to do. There is more to say on Zhuangzian nature from the perspective of determinism than from that of freedom, as Graham and Billeter have already touched upon.[5]

In response to problems in the three texts' reception, this chapter intends to show that although the discourse of alienation and Romanticism about nature was entrenched in European thought, Artaud and Michaux should not be understood simply as a reaction to or perpetuation of it. And in the *Zhuangzi*'s case, not any view concerning nature in ancient China necessarily reflects an unalienated and holistic state that contrasts sharply with nature in post-Enlightenment Europe, for the opposition between man and nature also existed in China, and by the *Zhuangzi*'s time there was already the awareness of destruction of the natural environment and artifice. The dualism between nature and culture is not an exclusively Western problem, and these thinkers, especially Artaud and Michaux, try to avoid entering the discourse of alienation — itself a Romantic product — by, instead, taking it on and then attacking it.

'Nature' and nature

There are few terms like 'nature' in philosophical discourse that mean so many things. What sense of the word, however, would it carry when considered in the context of Artaud, Michaux and the Zhuangzi? No doubt, 'nature' immediately brings to the contemporary mind images of beautiful wildernesses untouched by human presence, the planetary environment, and the idea of primordial authenticity. These are by now the most commonly-accepted understandings of nature, namely, the Romanticist, ecological and essentialist views. But these views are neither universal nor timeless, since each of them carries the intellectual baggage of specific contexts. Romantic philosophies of nature, taking on Kant's transcendental sublime, have the 'basic tendency [...] to identify nature with spirit' (Hadot 2006: 273), making nature an ultimate mirror of the ego. This view aesthetically alienated man from nature because it introduced the dialectic of individual subjectivity and the external world. As the paradigmatic medium for discovering the authentic self, nature was increasingly established in opposition to society, namely, as a primitive state untouched by civilization and the original truth. The ecological understanding of nature then perpetuates the Romantic nature-culture dichotomy in the scientific and pragmatic sense. Against the background of post-Enlightenment alienation of nature as an epistemological object and resource to be controlled by reason and dominated by man (Adorno and Horkheimer 1995), the term 'ecology' was coined in 1866 by the German scientist Ernst Haeckel. Ecology then formulates the modern understanding of nature as environment. Finally, the essentialist view of nature sees nature as the determinant of true identity and the set of properties that one category of beings must have. This view is strongly represented in the history of European thought, from Aristotle, Renaissance humanism that emphasized a distinctive human nature to nineteenth-century biological essentialism that discriminated between race and gender on the basis that nature predetermined people's character and behaviour. These views, besides being historical products of Europe and therefore contingent, also assume the existence of one nature but multiple cultures, which is very questionable. This is what Descola (2005) calls the 'naturalist ontology', which sees the world as continuous in physicality but discontinuous in interiority. But naturalism is not endorsed by many non-European cultures that believe instead in other ontologies such as totemism, analogism and animism.[6] Thus not only does nature have many meanings in history and different cultures, but also that there are multiple natures just as there are multiple cultures.

Artaud, Michaux and the *Zhuangzi*, however, do not understand nature in any self-evident way. A distance from the ideas conventionally associated with nature is necessary, so we can envisage drawing closer to the phase when the term 'nature' did not have formulated meanings, or even when the term itself did not yet exist. As in Heraclitus's aphorism: *Phusis kruptesthai philei* (which may be rendered as 'what causes things to appear tends to make them disappear'), *phusis,* which is unsatisfactorily translated as nature, is something nebulous and 'demands to be hidden'. It could mean 'the constitution or proper nature of each thing', and/ or 'a thing's process of realisation, genesis, appearance' (Hadot 2006: 7–8). This shows that rather than a monadic and defined concept, nature is a semantic field articulated by diverse but related concepts and terms. Therefore, rather than try to match these texts' views with certain existing definitions of nature, it is more worthwhile to investigate the idea clusters in the three texts that can formulate a broad notion of nature.

Philosophers have long debated about how broad a notion can be before it becomes no longer a concept of anything specific. This has to be borne in mind when sketching out a semantic field for nature. More specifically, this 'sketch' proceeds from different questions: what are the concepts in the texts that relate to or can help formulate a field of understanding for nature? What will this conceptual field be like? In other words, if 'nature' can mean so many different things why should we call it 'nature' but not 'cosmic principle', 'growth' or 'being'? Do these texts suggest that 'nature' denotes a specific understanding with clear conceptual boundaries or that it ultimately means anything? To address these questions, certain ideas — based on but not limited to their classical Chinese expressions — in the *Zhuangzi* can be used to articulate an understanding of nature rather than identify something that resonates with modern meanings of nature. This approach is more historically and linguistically sensitive because the very existence of a Chinese term for 'nature' as well as a unified notion of nature at the *Zhuangzi*'s time were absent. Instead of showing that the *Zhuangzi* thus defines nature, I argue that nature can be understood in certain ways that the *Zhuangzi* shows. This Zhuangzian nature — relatively unmoulded by the modern ideologies about nature — can then be used to read Artaud and Michaux, thus allowing an idea of nature that is less burdened by European metaphysical problems to emerge. Therefore, although the word 'nature' is non-existent in the *Zhuangzi*, nor appears in high frequency in Artaud and Michaux, this does not mean that these texts do not engage extensively with thinking about nature. Moreover, even when they say 'nature', they can be using the word in different senses. 'Nature' is neither a single concept with strict definition, nor an umbrella term that can be used for everything.

In sum, there is too much baggage on the idea of nature and its place in Artaud, Michaux and the *Zhuangzi,* too much for the reader not to throw some away (ideally, as much as possible) before attempting to see these texts anew. On the other hand, the resistance to categorizing discourses about nature in these texts also implies the huge extent to which the notion of nature can be kneaded and perverted (in its etymological sense). Reading through the following analyses, the reader may discover that one of the biggest contributions of these texts to thinking nature is about how nature can be denaturalized — although this denaturalized nature remains, surprisingly, *still* nature. We may paraphrase Blanchot's aphorism (1969: 192) on humanity's (in)destructibility that 'l'homme est l'indestructible et que pourtant il peut être détruit' by saying that for these thinkers, nature can be denaturalized and yet it remains none the less natural. Indeed, the exasperating elasticity and strength of concepts such as the human or nature lie precisely in the split-second when they become other than themselves, only to find that this 'other' is self-identical.

Fate: Nature as principle

Antinomian as both Artaud and the *Zhuangzi* are, they often express a firm belief in principles of nature, or fatality. Fate here, however, is hardly seen as an enslaving bondage that restricts change and development, nor an authentic state that must be maintained immobile without acculturation, but is similar to an inherently given fact. Starting with the *Zhuangzi,* the concept of 'heaven', *tian* (天) is helpful in thinking about nature because it introduces the idea of a pervasive cosmic order, which is nature as order. Heaven has various meanings such as the material firmament, cosmic space, the numinous power 'responsible for everything which is independent of man's will' (Graham 2001: 15). It is therefore both an empirical existence and an abstract principle by which things operate, and does not necessarily define nature but shows how things are and function. The *Zhuangzi* expounds that heaven's main characteristics are its inevitability and predeterminative nature. Heaven is a law that 'rotates' (*yun,* 運) according to the cosmic 'cycles and numbers' (*ZZ*, 27.4), regardless of human desires: 'Death and life are destined; that they have the constancy of morning and evening is of heaven' (*ZZ*, 6.2). These facts that 'cannot help but be' (Wu 1982: 69) are the expression of heaven, the power that is 'daimonic and cannot not be done' (*ZZ*, 11.6). In other words, heaven is not only a force of principiation, it is the supreme power that always already exists and makes things exist as such. This means that if heaven illustrates the idea of nature, nature can be understood as a fatalist order. Therefore, heaven and nature do not need to be thoroughly understood, but must be accepted.

> Provide things and adjust them to your body, bury unforeseen troubles to nourish your mind, revere what is within you so that you can extend it to others. If you do this and yet many evils visit you, then it is all heaven's doing, not man's doing (*ZZ*, 23.8).

Although humans can take better or worse actions, there are situations that are fated by heaven and cannot be helped. Every being has a course of life given by heaven that cannot be refused. In the classical Chinese context, the force of fate itself is heaven (*tian*), whereas the heavenly-assigned lot of life is termed *ming* (命), meaning both biological life and the fortune of life that is mandated. In other words, *ming* is both the actual state of living itself, and the non-anthropocentric force that makes and directs the life of all creatures. A tension — or in good circumstances, a balance — therefore exists between the actual life and the heavenly-directed life, which seems to echo the passive fatalist view of fate as a forcible oppression that annihilates personal freedom. This is, however, far from what the *Zhuangzi* propounds. Fated life and actual life are not a dichotomous pair of obligation versus submission, but a dynamic and constant mutual interaction. Although '*ming* cannot be changed' just as 'time cannot be stopped', the wise person will 'follow and fulfil *ming*' (*ZZ*, 14.7, 14.3). Although *ming* is predetermined by heaven, it cannot be accomplished by resignation or idleness but requires appropriate and reflective action. In fact, 'the hardest thing to do is precisely to fulfil [one's own] *ming*' (*ZZ*, 4.3).

The fact that *ming* is fated by heaven but needs to be realized through action shows that fate is a potentiality of life rather than a given. As Puett describes (in Lupke 2005: 49), fate as heaven's mandate is a flexible, relational and self-changing process: 'we are mandated by heaven to do X, and if we do so, then the order desired by both heaven and man will be obtained'. Fate also depends on the person who carries *ming* and is partly shaped by his actions. So fate is self-changing and constantly being transformed, this being part of heaven's mandate too. Consequently, one cannot predict or calculate the movement of life and heaven as a procedure of mechanical causality. In the *Zhuangzi*'s words (19.10): 'I do not know why I should be so but I am so, that is *ming*'. Fate and heaven are not fully knowable to individual beings and 'happen without our understanding' (Poo in Lupke 2005: 110), without reason even. The *Zhuangzi* does not offer any explanation of how fate comes about, as do the Indian notions of *saṃsāra* (cycles of cause and effect) through *karma* (action), or the logical determinism in Europe stemming from sets of mechanical and mathematical rules. Instead, the *Zhuangzi* emphasizes that fate is beyond causality and human wisdom is attained by accepting and acting it out, not by understanding how it came about. In an anecdote about a sage suffering from extreme poverty and illness, the sage thus explains his plight to a friend (*ZZ*, 6.10):

> I am thinking about what brought me to such extremities, and cannot find an answer. How could my father and mother have wanted me to be poor? The firmament impartially covers everything, the earth impartially carries everything, why would they discriminate to make me poor? [...] Nonetheless I have come to these extremities — it is then *ming*.

The sage's conclusion that it is *ming* and he cannot blame anyone or anything for his misfortune illustrates the Zhuangzian view that the movement of heaven and fate neither needs nor can be justified by human reason and values. By ignoring factors such as personal choice and social circumstances, the sage attributes his problem to the cosmic rather than human sphere; by not seeking answers through causality, the sage avoids the infinite regress of further causes and effects. His attitude is not passive resignation but a fearless recognition of the inevitable and unknowable. Zhuangzian fatalism thus reflects a non-logical, numinous and transhuman power, which can be understood as nature.

This natural power, however, does not embody the presence of a theistic agent such as a god, but an impersonal and unintentional cosmic principle that is beyond morality. The sage above characterizes the firmament and earth as 'impartial' to everything, which is another way of saying that heaven is impersonal and amoral. As the *Zhuangzi*'s address to heaven further demonstrates (6.8): 'My teacher, O my teacher! You grind to dust the myriad things but it is not cruelty; your bounty extends to a myriad generations but it is not benevolence.' Heaven can destroy and create all things, just as nature can ravage and nourish them, but these acts have no moral intention behind them. They are as natural and self-evident as the changes of weather: sometimes there is sunshine, sometimes there are storms. Heaven, or nature, far surpasses all moral values that humans can conceive of, and if there is a 'goodness of the cosmos', '[it] is not necessarily a moral goodness' (Kohn 2009: 118). Although natural principle à la Zhuangzi has a numinous and daimonic dimension, it is precisely not a moral agent with personal concerns about the world. The *Zhuangzi*'s notions of heaven and *ming* outline a fatalism that is determinist but non-coercive and non-logical, transhuman but non-theological and amoral, and this fatalism can be understood as natural order: something that works upon all beings and gives rise to action but far exceeds human control. That the term for heaven, *tian*, should also mean the sky shows that natural order encompasses the vast realms beyond humanity and is a cosmological movement. Nature does not evolve around the needs of society but the forces that move stars. This confirms again the cosmic rather than social nature of the *Zhuangzi*'s thought.

Zhuangzi's conception of nature as fate ties into ways of seeing how Artaud's thought engages with nature. Beginning with the viewpoint on Artaud's notion of 'Cruauté', which is comparable to the notion of heaven, 'Cruauté' can be said to denote a super-human and amoral force that determines existence but is non-logical. Although 'Cruauté' is one of Artaud's most famous and discussed ideas, it is frequently misunderstood because critics tend to relate it to violence in theatrical representation and have not remarked upon on how crucial the understanding of 'Cruauté' as a determinative force of nature is. In both *Le Théâtre et son double* and his self-reflexive commentaries on this treatise, Artaud takes great care to state explicitly and precisely what 'Cruauté' means for him. First of all, it is not to be taken 'dans le sens materiel et rapace', since it is not about circumstances of 'la cruauté vice [...] qui s'exprim[e] par des gestes sanglants' (Artaud 2004: 566, 574) ('the evil cruelty [...] that is expressed by bloody actions'). This vulgarized and brute violence that is usually associated with cruelty is only 'un tout petit côté de la question' (Artaud 2004: 566) ('a tip of the iceberg'), a superficial understanding of human suffering. Artaud wants instead to speak 'philosophically' about 'Cruauté', which is 'un sentiment détaché et pur' in the sense of the 'appétit de vie, de rigueur cosmique et de nécessité implacable' (2004: 567). 'Cruauté' is therefore synonymous with what Artaud calls 'la Fatalité', or 'le déterminisme philosophique' (2004: 524, 566), and is the superior force by which Artaud realizes that 'nous ne sommes pas libres' (IV: 95). If these views are compared with Artaud's remarks on nature (VII: 287–88): 'La Force de la *Nature* est la Loi, et cette Loi est la *Nature des choses* qui de toute façon fait la Loi, qu'on l'accepte ou qu'on le nie', ('The Strength of *Nature* is the Law, and this Law is the *Nature of things* which upholds the Law by all means, regardless of whether you accept it or deny it'), we find the same ideas about inexorability and superior principle. In other words, 'Cruauté' stems from a fatalist and cosmic understanding of nature on Artaud's part, just as with the Zhuangzian view of heaven.

The importance of nature now emerges as the backdrop of Artaud's philosophy of 'Cruauté' and in extension, of his entire theory about the theatre. 'La nature ne laisse rien au hasard', Artaud declares (VIII: 41), so nature is precisely the basis of this fatal necessity. If Artaud's 'théâtre de la Cruauté' is 'le plus organique de tous les théâtres' (Grossman 2004: 93), it is because such a theatre '[fait] entrer [...] la nature entière dans le théâtre' (Artaud 2004: 556). The 'théâtre de la Cruauté' therefore means the theatre of nature, not a naturalist theatre that depicts the reality of daily life and society, but a theatre that makes us aware of cosmic principles, especially the principle that there is no absolutely free agent, not even the force of 'Cruauté' itself. 'Il y a dans la cruauté qu'on exerce une sorte de déterminisme supérieur auquel le bourreau suppliciateur est soumis lui-même' (Artaud 2004: 566). ('In cruelty a kind of higher determinism is carried out, to which the torturer hangman is subjugated himself.') Through experiencing the theatre as an aesthetic expression of natural order, human beings could, Artaud believes, reach the 'lucid' understanding that 'Cruauté' is beyond human control and knowability: 'Le ciel peut encore nous tomber sur la tête. Et le théâtre est fait pour nous apprendre d'abord cela' (IV: 95). ('The firmament could still collapse on us. And theatre is created to tell us this before everything else'.)

Besides being inexorable and transhuman, Artaudian 'Cruauté' also has the characteristics of amorality and numinosity as seen in the *Zhuangzi*'s heaven. Firstly, Artaud explicitly sees 'Cruauté' as 'amoralité' (V: 48), emphasizing that human conceptions of morality do not apply to it. This amorality takes on the Nietzschean notion of the superhuman, which is 'beyond good and evil'. For example, the forces of 'Cruauté' 'allaient droit leur chemin hors de nos petites distinctions humaines où tout se partage entre le mal et le bien' (Artaud 2004: 641) ('go straight on along their course, beyond our petty human distinctions where everything is divided between good and evil'). The cosmic order that 'Cruauté' embodies is characterized by 'cette amoralité fabuleuse qui appartient à la foudre qui frappe, comme aux bouillonnements d'un mascaret déchaîné' (V: 48–49) ('this wondrous amorality characteristic of lightning when it strikes, like the effeverscent bubbling of unleashed tides'). The metaphors used here are telling: lightning that strikes blindly on anything, and the tumultuous tidal current, the flowing of which is unstoppable. Both are images of natural events that happen unaffected by human desires and regardless of rational justification. They are the evidence that 'la nature parle plus haut que les hommes' (Artaud 2004: 641), and reflect the same amorality of natural destruction and nourishment seen in the *Zhuangzi* (6.8). As Artaud further expounds, to act amorally is also to act impartially, for 'Cruauté' does not prioritize acts that fit with the human understanding of goodness: 'La mort est cruauté, la résurrection est cruauté, la transfiguration est cruauté' (2004: 568), 'tout ce qui agit est une cruauté' (IV: 102). Without this impartial amorality, nothing would ever come to pass and the universe would not be this fascinating turbidity of bubbling energies that, like the pest which Artaud admires for its intense powers of transformation, breaks out into artistic activity.

Nevertheless, although Artaud considers 'Cruauté' as necessity, it does not denote a mechanical necessity such as causal determinism. Artaud in fact emphasizes the non-logical and unpredictable aspects of 'Cruauté' (2004: 574–75):

> Et quelque aveugle rigueur qu'apportent avec elles toutes ces contingences, la vie ne peut manquer de s'exercer [...] mais cette rigueur, et cette vie qui passe outre et s'exerce dans la torture et le piétinement de tout [...] c'est cela qui est la cruauté.
>
> J'ai donc dit 'cruauté', comme j'aurais dit 'vie' ou comme j'aurais dit 'nécessité', parce que je veux indiquer surtout que pour moi le théâtre est acte et émanation perpétuelle, qu'il n'y a en lui rien de figé.
>
> [Whatever blind relentlessness that all these contingencies may bring about, life could never stop from being effectuated [...] but this relentlessness, this life that goes on regardless and is effectuated by torturing and trampling on everything [...] this is what cruelty is.
>
> Therefore I said 'cruelty' just as I would have said 'life' or 'necessity', because I wish to point out above all that for me, theatre is action and perpetual emanation, and that there is nothing fixed in theatre.]

Artaud juxtaposes the paradoxical meanings of 'aveugle' and 'rigueur', 'nécessité' and 'rien de figé', showing that the determinism he is articulating is not a logical system that is fully knowable or fixed from the start. That life and action must happen is determined, but how and why they actually happen are radically uncertain, for life happens through an 'impulsion irraisonnée' (IV: 161). Thus, fate is also flexible because it is effectuated through different impulses, circumstances and relationships of life. How fate can fulfil itself despite its unpredictability and malleability seems to be, however, a mystery. As Artaud states, the action of 'Cruauté' invokes 'une impression d'inhumanité, de divin, de révélation miraculeuse' (IV: 90). This mystic and inexplicable dimension of Artaud's fatalism echoes the numinosity and daimonic nature of Zhuangzian heaven. But this mysticality does not reflect a theological understanding of fatalism, for Artaud attributes the higher order that 'Cruauté' embodies to 'forces primordiales' and natural principles (VII: 292, 341), and repeats that a truly 'cruel' act is 'désintéressé', 'détaché et pur' (IV: 136). As we have seen in the *Zhuangzi*, fate as nature is impersonal and unintentional. We can likewise understand Artaud's fatalism as a self-controlling non-agential power that pervades the world. 'Cruauté' thus outlines a fatalism that stems from nature but does not function by causality or logic, nor through divine agents.

It is significant that Artaud advocates fatalism in his philosophy of 'Cruauté', because since modern times, fatalism has been brushed away by philosophers as a ridiculous and superstitious belief that does not merit serious consideration. But fatalism in fact does not necessarily 'deny causal efficiency to human actions or [...] to any sort of events', as the philosopher Steven Cahn asserts (1967: 23), for it is fundamentally the thesis that 'the only actions which a man can perform are the actions which he does, in fact, perform' (Cahn 1967: 8). The natural determinism in Artaud and the *Zhuangzi* supports this thesis, although it does not undergo logical justification as Cahn's argument for fatalism does. The non-logicality of Artaud's fatalism is not surprising, since it fits well with his views on reason and his challenge to the law of the non-contradiction (as shown in chapter one). That Artaud should oppose the ideas of free will and agency and see nature as a numinous but non-theistic force is very telling. In one sense, Artaud is radically out of his time, for his intellectual context extends from the Surrealists, who advocated radical freedom in both art and life as exemplified by *amour fou,* to Sartre who emphasized human agency and choice in the absence of divine authority. In another sense, however, Artaud is very much of his time and goes even further than his contemporaries. By denying individual freedom and subjectivity in actions, Artaud truly leaves Romanticism behind — something that always haunted avant-garde art and thought; by advocating a determinism without rational justification or God, Artaud takes on Nietzsche's anti-Enlightenment legacy and his view of a superhuman but Godless nature; finally, by maintaining the presence of numinosity in life and nature, Artaud differentiates between the numinous and the god figure, and continues the hierophanic worldview exemplified by Spinoza. Hierophany is, as expounded by Eliade, the view that everything from the stars down to a simple stone is a manifestation, or appearance (*phanein*) of some divine (*ieros*) force or sacrality. Against the background of fatalism as a strand of thought with serious advocates like Aristotle and Diodorus Cronos, and which is revived into debate in the twentieth century by logical determinists such as Richard Taylor (1962) and Steven Cahn, Artaud's philosophy of 'Cruauté' shows its importance because it makes the case for fatalism on the basis of a spontaneous but auto-regulating and amoral natural principle, not on causal determinism or theology.

Seen from the key characteristics that relate to nature in the *Zhuangzi*, namely: being inevitable, superhuman, amoral and acausal, Artaudian 'Cruauté' and life reflect a philosophy of nature. Artaudian nature can be seen as both a principle and constant principiation, a determinism that, often inexplicably, directs and undergoes change. This idea about nature's movement leads to another important concern related to nature in the *Zhuangzi* and which connects to Michaux: metamorphosis through a dionysiac *diasparagmos*, the tearing apart of forms by life force.

Nature as *phusis* and life force

A common theme that runs through the *Zhuangzi* and Michaux's works is that of the source and growth of life, which shape an understanding of nature as primary source and metamorphosis. To better understand this we may start by considering the denotation of the ancient Greek term *phusis,* since it is less burdened by many modern connotations of 'nature' and better illustrates the *Zhuangzi*'s notions of a dynamic and primary life force. From existing studies, *phusis* is shown to denote an inborn quality that is crucial in determining how something exists. This includes dispositions towards a certain way of growth (*phuo*), which is simultaneously a process of acculturation. In more detail, as already mentioned, Heraclitus used *phusis* to indicate something ungraspable and fundamental to the constitution and process of realization of all things. Thus *phusis* relates to both aspects of predetermination and constant change, which are respectively fate and the direction of life. The word *phusis* itself provides support for this view. On one hand, it is 'usually accompanied by a genitive: it is the birth *of* or the aspect *of* something [...and] is always referred to a general or particular reality' (Hadot 2006: 18). On the other hand, *phusis* comes from *phuo* and involves the act of growth, thus overlapping, as Vergnières observes (1995: 6), with terms such as '"impulsion naturelle" (*ὀργή*), "manière d'être" (*ρυθμός*), ou "tournure du caractère" (*τρόπος*)'. Here, *phusis* reveals the same paradox we find in the *Zhuangzi*'s and Artaud's fatalism: that there is an innate principle given at the start of any existence that directs the latter's entire course of life yet to come, and that this innateness is a potentiality and malleable by different ways of cultivation. Aristotle summarizes this two-sidedness of *phusis* as its fundamentally being 'the essence of things which have a source of movement in themselves' (*Physics*, II.2). *Phusis* is 'indissociable' from *nomos*, or law (Descola 2005: 101), but it remains itself by constantly changing — just as there is a cosmic principle (according to the *Zhuangzi*, Artaud and Michaux) that makes things happen as they do happen, but which also depends on the constant happening itself to exist as such a principle. This idea of maintaining sameness through difference is crucial to understanding how the issues of fate and the flux of life complement rather than contradict each other in the three texts.

It is necessary to note that speaking in Artaud, Michaux and the *Zhuangzi*'s context, the denotations of *phusis* that work for them are mainly limited to the above three: innate principiation, primary source and dynamic potentiality. The Aristotelian view of *phusis* as the determination of an unchangeable identity and ultimate *telos* does not have echoes in the three texts. As already demonstrated, Artaud and the *Zhuangzi* have an acausal view of nature. When reading the *Zhuangzi* and Michaux together, however, nature is also non-utilitarian and non-teleological, flowing like a purposeless stream.

That heaven and fate should be self-changing in the *Zhuangzi* already implies the aspect of dynamic vitality in them. Heaven is often referred to in terms of the source of life, represented by metaphorical images involving nutrition and a pool of primary energy. Heaven is a 'pond' that 'gives' impartially (*ZZ*, 1.1, 32.10), so that everything 'receives food from heaven' and is nourished by 'the heavenly broth' (天鬻, *ZZ*, 5.5). This 'food' is both actual and metaphorical, it points to heaven's all-encompassing gift of existence itself and all the resources and circumstances that enable things to continue existing. And this source of existence is inexhaustible, like an infinite ocean, 'if you add to it, it does not increase; if you subtract from it, it does not diminish' (*ZZ*, 22.5). Heaven is thus like *phusis*, the primary source of life that always already exists and provides the force of growth, which is also the innate disposition of all things, characterized thus: 'There is nothing it does not send off, nothing it does not welcome, nothing it does not destroy, nothing it does not complete' (*ZZ*, 6.4). Nevertheless, unlike the ungraspability and abstractness of *phusis*, the *Zhuangzi* makes this disposition of life as concrete as it is abstract, for it is manifested by the matter-energy called *qi* 氣. *Qi* is 'the single breath that breathes through heaven and earth' (*ZZ*, 22.1), being the energy fluid that pervades and constitutes not only the sky, but the entire cosmos. Furthermore, this cosmic breath is thoroughly material because it is the organic tissue of all existences:

> Mingled in the amorphous and ungraspable, something changed and there was *qi*, then *qi* changed and there was shape, then shape changed and there was life (*ZZ*, 18.2).
> The life of man is the gathering of *qi*. When *qi* gathers there is life, when it disperses there is death. [...] Therefore the myriad things are one. [...] The foul and rotten transform back to the spiritual and wondrous, the spiritual and wondrous transform back to the foul and rotten. Therefore it is said: 'running through the world there is the one *qi*' (*ZZ*, 22.1).

From these descriptions of *qi*, all forms of existence — from human beings to animals, trees, stones, air and stars — can be understood as simply different shapes, degrees and stages of congealment of this breath-energy that is *qi*. Consistent with the *Zhuangzi*'s pan-animism of space as seen in chapter two, the universe depicted here is a hylozoistic mass, and every single existence shares itself physically with everything else. Heaven's breath-energy is our breath-energy, is fundamentally us — and in this fusion of everything, no differentiation exists between the animate and inanimate. If nature is understood as heaven, then heaven's *qi* reveals, in addition to the view of nature as principle, the view of nature as vitality, the primary substance of being.

But heaven and *qi* are not only the providers of cosmic life; another crucial dimension is that they work through transformation. As passage 22.1 above shows, things are constantly changing because of *qi*. Like *phusis*, *qi* is a flux that depends on change to exist, and directs the way all other things exist: their specific forms (including maintaining and losing these forms), their dispositions towards developing in certain directions, and their place in the larger cycles and patterns of cosmic mutation. The *Zhuangzi* uses *hua* 化: a term with various connotations of change, evolution, acculturation to denote this metamorphic function and process of *qi*. The process of *qi*-produced metamorphosis is illustrated by this story (*ZZ*, 6.5):

> Suddenly Master Lai fell ill, and, panting, he was going to die. His wife and children stood around him and wept. Master Li [Lai's friend] went to ask how he was, and said to his family: 'Shoo! Stand back! Do not disturb the process of transformation (*hua*)!'
>
> Then Li leaned on Lai's door and spoke: 'How wonderful is the process that fashions things! What now will it turn you into? Whither will it make you go? Will it make you into a rat's liver, or an insect's leg?'
>
> Master Lai said: '[...] That which made me live well is also that by which I die well.'

Instead of bewailing the suffering and imminent death of Lai, as his family do, Li talks ecstatically about the marvellous metamorphosis that Lai is undergoing and wonders about the infinite possibilities for his human form to become something else. Lai's body is 'only part of the continuous natural transformations of energy' (Kohn and Sakade 1989: 196–97). Death becomes impersonal, so grief is unnecessary. The uncertainty about the direction of change augments the awe at this numinous process, and Lai's affirmation of living and dying as equally positive ultimately renders death obsolete. In this flux of *qi*, what is usually distinguished as destruction and birth, formlessness and form are all one. The commentator Guo Xiang identifies this vital flux with heaven and the 'process of nature' (cited in Munro 1985: 49). If nature is thus understood to be embodied by *qi*, then the Heraclitean view that 'everything flows' (panta rhei) would be the reflection of this aspect of Zhuangzian nature.

We now see that Zhuangzian *qi* is similar in some important aspects to Bergson's *élan vital*, which is the impetus of life and creative force that seizes upon matter and gives it 'la plus grande somme possible d'indétermination et de liberté' (Bergson 2007: 252). Both the *élan* and *qi* are pan-animist, indivisible as a flux, and bring about the constant metamorphosis of forms of life. More importantly, they implicitly equate life with nature. One notable difference between Bergson and the *Zhuangzi*, however, is that the *élan vital* acts upon 'inert' matter and through this agonistic relationship, forms of life are created (Bergson 2007: 225), whereas the *qi* is both energy and matter, thus asserting a thoroughly animist world. Also, despite Bergson's emphasis on the indetermination of life force, he does not renounce the idea that evolution is progression in the long run. As Trotignon remarks (in Bloch 2000: 406), in Bergson's last work *Les Deux sources de la morale et de la religion*, mankind is seen as the culmination of evolution through the *élan vital*: '*L'homme seul* a brisé la chaîne, a traversé les mailles du filet.' ('*Only humanity* has ruptured the [evolutionary] chain, and slipped through the filtering mesh.') Thus there seems to be some lingering teleology and transcendence in Bergson's vitalist evolution. This is an important question in the philosophy of nature because, as mentioned above, nature has been understood as flux by Heraclitus but as teleology by Aristotle and Hippocrates, and the tug between the processual and essentialist, immanent and transcendent views of nature has continued throughout European thought. For the *Zhuangzi*, metamorphosis through the *qi* arguably involves evolution but the emphasis is on nature's continuity rather than its teleology. In the above story, Master Li's hypothesis that Lai could turn into a rat's liver or insect's leg overthrows the idea of progressive change, and the following passage explicitly denies any *telos* in evolution (*ZZ*, 18.7):

> The seeds have germs. When they get to water they become the water-plantain, when they get to the border between water and land they become the 'frog's coat', when they breed on dry land it becomes the plantain. When the plantain gets to rich soil it becomes the 'crow's foot'. [...] [Then] green plants produce leopards, and leopards produce horses, and horses produce mankind. Mankind then goes back into the germs.

This list of fantastic metamorphoses that shows a distinctly surreal (to use the term anachronistically) spirit is not meant as a documentary record of the precise changes of life forms but a poetic reflection on how, through infinite transformations, all existences share an interconnectedness that unites them in continuity rather than separates them. There is a sense of evolution in this continuity, not from the simple to the complex, but in terms of returning cycles. Vital flux and nature are thus non-progressive and non-teleological. Nature is purposeless and life is about itself, not about pursuing a goal of happiness, as Aristotle propounds. Jullien's view does say something about the Zhuangzian deferment of the pursuit of happiness, for Zhuangzian nature is nutrition rather than evolution (2007: 27): 'Nutrition is not progress toward something; it is renewal. The transformation that it brings about has no other purpose than to reactivate something.'

How will these Zhuangzian ideas of a non-teleological nature as the source, growth and transformation of life enter into conversation with Michaux? We may start by considering the recurrent topic of transubstantiation throughout Michaux's writings, which shows that the continuity of existence through metamorphosis constitutes one of his crucial concerns. In a passage entitled 'Nature', a man contemplates a river, only to find it a river of his own blood with his body floating as 'une île délicate' in it (Michaux 1963: 45). Is the man suddenly transformed into a river, or was he originally a river hallucinating that he was a man? But before this overwhelming flow of change, the distinction between a man and a river becomes unimportant. It is the experience that counts. Just as Michaux has one of his characters exclaim ecstatically (1948: 307): 'Métamorphose! Métamorphose, qui engloutit et refait des metamorphoses.' ('Metamorphosis! Metamorphosis, that engulfs and reshapes all metamorphoses.') Nature is seen as a river embodying the Great metamorphosis that enfolds all possible metamorphoses and perpetuates its own flow: 'Les choses immédiates sont la nature. La transsubstantiation est la nature. Les miracles sont la nature. [...] La joie parfaite' (Michaux 1978b: 113). Like the sages in the *Zhuangzi* who express joyous wonderment at all the changes caused by the *qi*, Michaux feels perfect joy both in the things existing here-and-now and in their natural propensity to melt into something else. A passage about the biological evolution of a fictional persona, equally fantastic to the *Zhuangzi*'s list of germs evolving to ground-beetles and then to mankind, reads thus (Michaux 1978b: 126):

> Pon naquit d'un œuf, puis il naquit d'une morue et en naissant la fit éclater, puis il naquit d'un soulier; par bipartition, le soulier plus petit à gauche, et lui à droite, puis il naquit d'une feuille de rhubarbe, en même temps qu'un renard; le renard et lui se regardèrent un instant puis filèrent chacun de leur côté. Ensuite il naquit d'un cafard, d'un œil de langouste, d'une carafe.
>
> [Pon was born from an egg, then he was born from a cod-fish and upon birth made it explode, then he was born from a shoe; by bisection, the smaller shoe on the left, and he on the right, then he was born from a rhubarb leaf, and simultaneously with a fox; the fox and he looked at each other for a moment then went their own ways. Afterwards he was born from a cockroach, from a lobster's eye, from a glass jug.]

Here, the protagonist Pon constantly returns to the moment *in statu nascendi* and is reborn repeatedly. This return of birth echoes the cyclical evolution found in the *Zhuangzi*, especially the idea of mankind returning to germs, which will eventually give birth to mankind again. Although there is a constant evolution of forms, there is no sense of progression or even the impression that all these repeated definitions of what Pon is indeed define him. Pon has dispersed, or expanded into so many different creatures such as an egg, a cod-fish, or a rhubarb leaf that any original structure or individual identity simply melts into the air. Pon's metamorphosis is a pure, random and purposeless process that takes joy in itself. For Michaux, there is never a reifiable or graspable thing as an end product: 'Formes? Quelles formes? C'est l'informe, son affaire à présent, c'est elle qu'il lui faudrait exprimer, s'il doit exprimer quelque chose' (1976b: 65). ('Forms? What forms? It is formlessness, its matter at hand which it must express, if something should be expressed at all.') The formlessness of all things shaping and deforming themselves shows nature to be 'ce pâté d'on ne sait quoi. [...] Mais d'objets non, point du tout' (Michaux 1929: 29) ('this pulp of we-don't-know-what. [...] But not of objects, not at all'). As in the *Zhuangzi*, nature is also non-teleological continuity for Michaux. Nature's strength lies precisely in the numerous rebirths and re-structurations that emerge through chance, similar to the fortuitous biology expounded by Jacques Monod (1970).

That transformation is nature also means that all forms and existences are transient. But this does not, for Michaux, mean that everything is illusory. On the contrary, this transience makes the experience of every specific moment of an existential state ever more intense, positive and real. From this affirmation of transience, we understand Michaux's thoroughly immanentist view of nature, for he accepts everything as it is and as it changes without seeking a *meta*-physical or *meta*-morphic (i.e. beyond matter and form) justification. More specifically, if we remember that the transformative flux in the *Zhuangzi* is affirmed even before death, and that ultimately all differences are experienced as a continuum, it will be easy to understand Michaux's statement 'je fus toutes choses' (1967a: 123). This sharing of oneself with cosmic entirety is further expounded (1967a: 125–26):

> [J]e me changeais toujours en animal, [...] mais je suis encore des choses, mais je suis des ensembles tellement factices, et de l'impalpable. [...]
>
> Et toujours, et sans cesse.
>
> Il y a tant d'animaux, tant de plantes, tant de minéraux. Et j'ai été déjà de tout et tant de fois.

> [I was always changing into animals, [...] but I am still other things; I am also composites of the most artificial kinds, and the intangible too. [...]
>
> And always, without ceasing.
>
> There are so many animals, so many plants, so many minerals. And I have already been all of them, many many times.]

One has always been, is, and will be everything. One's own body and any identity attached to it are simply layers and layers of 'shedded skins', in the *Zhuangzi*'s words (22.4), or as Michaux puts it (1967a: 187): 'pelures d'Êtres'. But at each peeling there is both a shuddering destruction and an ecstasy of the transitory moment (Michaux 1967a: 187):

Oh! anéantissement!
Oh! pelures d'Êtres!
Face impeccablement ravissante de la destruction!

[Oh! annihilation!
Oh! peelings of Beings!
The flawlessly ravishing face of destruction!]

When life has evolved through all nature's changes, there may be unassuageable anguish but also the intense sensation of spatial and cosmic elation (Michaux 1967a: 189–90):

Quand le miel devenu pierreux,
Les banquises perdant du sang, [...]
Le sable à la caresse rousse se retournant en plomb sur tous les amateurs de plage,
Les langues tièdes, [...] se changeant soit en couteaux, soit en durs cailloux, [...]
Quand l'*Épouvantable-Implacable* se débondant enfin, [...]
Oh! Malheur! Malheur!
[...]
Oh! Espace, Espace!

[When honey becomes stony,
and glaciers are losing blood, [...]
The sand with copper-red caresses are turning back into lead on all the impassionments of the beach,
Lukewarm tongues, [...] transforming into knives, or into hard pebbles, [...]
When the *Dread-Implacable* finally spills out, [...]
Oh! Misfortune! Misfortune! [...]
Oh! Space, Space!]

Through the unstoppable cosmic changes that erase the world until the past is annihilated, as honey becomes stone-like congealment and tongues become knives, the metamorphosis of nature manifests itself as this terrifying and implacable power that breaks out like tidal waves. Nature is incessant agony: the agon of different forces, the searing pain of forms distorting into other forms, the unhappiness of bleeding out one's identity and position in the world, the sensation of innumerable caresses that are scaldingly painful...and yet, and yet, nature goes on, just as the wave continues to billow in 'continuation', 'oscillation' and 'perpétuelle alternance' (Michaux 1961: 18). Nature is the wave — just like *phusis*, it changes *and* remains itself. Maybe this is why Michaux despairs before nature, for it is like the despair of an atom before infinity. But this is also how Michaux experiences nature in ways similar to the *Zhuangzi*: in continuity despite change, in oneness despite difference.

This flowing nature that connects everything has obvious Bergsonian overtones, especially as Michaux himself writes (1963: 185): 'L'élan est primordial, qui est à la fois appétit, lutte, désir.' In other words, metamorphosis and nature are also the drive of vital impulsion. Everything seems to stem from it, as Michaux uses the metaphor of music to describe its becoming: '*art de l'élan*', 'opération du devenir' (1963: 184–85). But Michaux, like the *Zhuangzi*, pushes the holistic aspect of the 'élan' further than Bergson, because for Michaux this force does not act upon matter, as Bergson believes, but is matter itself. In the infinite metamorphoses in Michaux's writings, there is no palpable form or matter to be grasped as an object, or oppositional *objectum*, by the flux of nature. The 'élan' for Michaux is simultaneously substance and energy, just as his own body can be the river and in the river. 'Je suis fleuve dans le fleuve qui passe' (Michaux 1966a: 369). The absolute immersion of the body in the cosmic energy field shows the 'élan' to be both cosmic and directly connected with the most intimate experiences (Michaux 1961: 42):

> Mon corps autour de moi avait fondu. Mon être m'apparaissait une substance informe, homogène, comme est une amibe. [...] Je ne me sentais pas rapetissé mais seulement indifférencié. Sur moi, sur mes frontières, avec une grande amplitude, des ondes, ou des lignes ondulantes, résistantes, d'énergie pleines. [...] Mais toujours sans impétuosité, sans méchanceté, [...] très patiemment, très flexueusement.
>
> [My body around me had melted. My being seemed to me a formless, homogeneous substance, like that of an amoeba. [...] I did not feel diminished, simply undifferentiated. Upon me, on my boundaries, in large expanses, there were waves, or undulating lines, tenacious, brim-full with energy. [...] But never with violence or wickedness, [...] always very patiently, very tortuously.]

The 'matter' of the body melts into a pulp and finally the only sensation is that of energy waves. As Michaux professes to feel 'undifferentiated', the substance of his body cannot be distinguished from the forces that are kneading it. The 'élan' of nature is him as well as makes him. The experience of biological interpenetration is so deeply rooted in Michaux that he declares that he feels the pulsation of the cosmos (1985: 120):

> Le martèlement d'un cœur, qui aurait été musical, un cœur venu aux arbres, [...] issu d'un grand cœur végétal (on eût dit planétaire), cœur participant à tout, retrouvé, enfin perçu, audible aux possédés de l'émotion souveraine, celle qui tout accompagne, qui emporte l'Univers.
>
> [The throbbing of a heart, which you could say was musical, a heart originating from trees, [...] emitted from a big botanic (we might have said planetary) heart, a heart taking part in everything, rediscovered, discerned at last, audible to those possessed by supreme emotion, the emotion that is accompanied by all, that prevails in the Universe.]

The planetary heartbeat coincides with Michaux's heartbeat, the vital blood pumped out being the fundamental source and force of life, which are also nature. Thus, Michaux's organic co-sentience with nature reveals the same hylozoistic cosmology that the *Zhuangzi* points to.

Although the ideas of heaven and fate, *qi* and continuity, 'Cruauté' and metamorphosis are different from and non-equivalent to each other, they show themselves to be able mutually to interlace through the broad semantic field of nature. Some deep-seated philosophies of nature are thus revealed to be the basis of these three bodies of thought. Although these texts often do not use the term 'nature', this is in effect a way to speak about nature without identifying it as a specific concept, or alienating it as something separable from culture and man.

This oblique way of speaking about nature by not speaking about nature shows, however, a meta-discursive problem that underlies all holistic natural philosophies: that the naming of nature should involve something that is differentiated from culture and man — an approach which already pre-supposes alienation. All three texts are in fact acutely aware of this difficulty and try to address it in various ways, not least by exploring these concepts of nature and culture.

Questions and meta-questions: the nature-culture relationship

Simply put, the difficulty of negotiating the nature-culture question lies in that the very difference between the understandings of nature and culture becomes the schism between them. The twentieth century has seen the rise of a few paradigmatic views: 'nature is culture', which is supported by much of twentieth-century cultural anthropology and cultural theory, such as poststructuralist feminism that negates the naturality of the female body by positing it as a thorough ideological construction. This view debunks the myth of nature — i.e. that nature is used to disguise and justify social norms of identity and morality — but it also makes the notion of nature disappear, for everything turns out to be 'constructed'. Besides this culturalist view, the view that 'culture is nature' has also been on the rise. This view affirms everything — from cyborgs to trees — as natural, or sees nature as the sole determinant of all thought and action, as in the biological determinism advocated by brain scientists (Damasio, E. O. Wilson). Although the claim that 'everything is nature' is hard to refute, it can be used in exploitative ways to justify the ethics of any technological or environmental enterprise. Finally, since the 1980s, a more holistic understanding of nature and culture, mainly propounded by anthropologists such as Bruno Latour and Philippe Descola, supports the view that instead of nature/culture, there is a nature-culture hybrid. This view makes a significant effort to go beyond the nature-culture dichotomy, but still leaves many questions unanswered. In fact, to think that the relationship between nature and culture constitutes a problem is already a problem itself, because if nature and culture are always already one, then what is there to solve and why need any discourse? But to deny that there is a problem cannot be a solution either, because even if there is no problem in material reality, a huge problem nevertheless exists in thought and discourse. As for Artaud, Michaux and the *Zhuangzi*, in fact they not only have a high awareness of the tension between nature and culture, but also address this tension in a holistic way, while recognizing the self-undermining nature of treating this problem as such.

The *Zhuangzi* admits the problem between heaven (nature) and man by pointing out their differences, especially in that man cannot control heaven whereas heaven controls man. 'There is man, that is of heaven; there is heaven, that is also of heaven. That man cannot have what heaven has, that is an inborn fact' (*ZZ*, 20.7). Man is posited as part of what heaven encompasses, the part being always smaller than the whole. Thus a boundary exists between nature and man, which seems to be clarified in this dialogue (*ZZ*, 17.7):

> 'What is called heaven? And what is called man?'

> The north sea Ruo replied: 'That oxen and horses have four feet is called heaven; to halter horses' heads, and pierce the noses of oxen, that is called man. Therefore it is said: "Do not use man to destroy heaven, do not use the purposeful to destroy fate [*ming* 命]".'

The difference between the heavenly and the human is presented as a tension between the inborn and artificial, the naturally-so and intentional. But this tension does not establish a dichotomy between nature and man, for the authors of the *Zhuangzi* clearly see the danger of any defining boundaries (*ZZ*, 6.1, Graham's translation, modified):

> To know what is heaven's doing and what is man's is the utmost in knowledge. [...] Nevertheless, there's a difficulty. Knowing must depend on something before it can be applied, but what it depends on is never fixed. How do I know if what I call 'heaven' is not man? How do I know if what I call 'man' is not heaven?

The profound scepticism expressed here shows that although the *Zhuangzi* asserts that heaven and man are indeed different and heaven is more powerful and important, it does not define what heaven and man are, and considers any attempt at definition futile. Not only is the opposition between nature and man questioned, the meta-question of debating the question of nature and man is also problematized. As the text further illustrates in a bold statement (*ZZ*, 23.18): 'The perfect man hates heaven, and hates what man thinks is heaven, and even more so the question of what heaven is or what man is!' The crux of the question is no longer about how to overcome the tension between nature and man, but about the very problem of making distinctions. Once the distinction between heaven and man is made, one is already trapped in its dialectic, even if one talks about oneness; for is not making distinctions itself a division of oneness — namely, distinguishing between making distinctions and not making distinctions? This is why the non-differentiating attitude seems to be a possible solution:

> The true men of antiquity [...] were one with what they liked and one with what they disliked, one when they were one and one when they were not one. When one they were of heaven's party, when not one they were of man's party. Someone in whom neither heaven nor man is victor over the other, this is what is meant by the true man (*ZZ*, 6.1, Graham's translation).

The state of balance and harmony between heaven and man, although apparently ideal, is nevertheless achieved through a dual relationship. Certainly, by stating that the true men are 'one even when not one', the text explicitly affirms that the genuinely monistic view does not see dualism as a problem. This seems paradoxically to mean that even when man is in conflict with nature he nevertheless is in harmony with nature; or, less self-contradictorily, that man can never really be in conflict with nature, and/or that nature is always already self-conflict (man being part of it). From these ambiguities, we see that the ideal state of balance is not really a solution. The *Zhuangzi* not only refuses to give straightforward answers, but also answers questions with more questions. Ultimately, rather than address the question of heaven and man, the *Zhuangzi* prefers to forget it and make it obsolete (25.3): 'For the sage, heaven has not yet begun to exist, man has not yet begun to exist, the beginning has not yet begun to begin, things have not yet begun to be.' This total oblivion is not a resignation of critical thought but an unselfconscious non-differentiation, an ideal state towards which people should orientate themselves. Although in actuality *absolute* oblivion may be non-achievable, the *Zhuangzi*'s authors nevertheless think it desirable for one to infinitely approach it.

So far the *Zhuangzi* has raised the issue of the duality between heaven and man, which reflects upon the meta-question behind it. This meta-discursive reflection will prove to be relevant to Artaud's and Michaux's treatment of the nature/culture divide. There is, however, another aspect of the *Zhuangzi* that is also very important for comparison: the re-understanding of the natural and artificial. The quotation above about haltering horses (*ZZ*, 17.7) seems to understand artifice as human intervention in the spontaneous course of existence, but from other passages engaging with the same theme, this interpretation is revealed as too simplistic. In a story about an ingenious carpenter who makes bellstands that are wondrous to behold, the carpenter explains his skill by saying that he 'observes the heavenly dispositions inborn in trees' and shapes their wood accordingly (*ZZ*, 19.11). This is why his bellstands are 'daimonic' (神) like heaven. Lafargue comments (in Girardot et al. 2001: 47) that this story shows that nature is 'part of human culture', for the carpenter's '"reverence for nature" did not express itself in admiration of trees as they exist in their natural habitat themselves, but rather in chopping down and carving up a "natural" tree to produce a luxury item'. Furthermore, besides being part of culture, nature is shown by the carpenter to not be an uncultured, raw state. The bellstands are no less natural than the trees they are made from; human craftsmanship and culture — when they follow natural disposition (as in *phusis*) — can be a continuation and enhancement of nature rather than damage. Artifice is not necessarily unnatural.

This understanding of naturalization through cultivation and vice versa justifies to a certain extent other parts of the *Zhuangzi* that refuse artificiality, such as the destructive actions of piercing oxen's noses and boring seven holes into Hundun, the embodiment of harmonious chaos (seen in chapter 3). Since these actions do not follow the natural dispositions of the beings which they aim to change, they are spurious and maim nature. But this explanation cannot totally justify other passages when trees are praised for being gnarled and useless for woodwork (*ZZ*, 4). Self-contradiction in the *Zhuangzi* cannot be explained away and should be accepted. This exploration of nature and artificiality proposes one possible understanding of one aspect of Zhuangzian thought, not a universally applicable justification of consistency.

If the *Zhuangzi* sheds light on the nature-culture problem by probing the conceptual origins of the opposition between heaven and man, namely, differentiation, and by showing that artifice and culture can advance rather than hurt nature, then these ideas reappear in Artaud and Michaux. This is prominent in their painful awareness of the split between nature-as-experienced and the modern ideology of nature as alienation, and in their refusal of the correlation between nature and regression, culture and development. In more detail, firstly, Artaud is haunted by the paradoxical recognition that while modern man increasingly separates himself from nature, he nevertheless can never begin to stand outside nature. Like the

Zhuangzi's authors, Artaud seeks the discursive origins of this difficult relationship and traces it back to a key moment in history: the appearance of Humanism (IX: 80):

> L'Humanisme de la Renaissance ne fut pas un agrandissement mais une diminution de l'homme, puisque l'Homme a cessé de s'élever jusqu'à la nature pour ramener la nature à sa taille à lui, et la considération exclusive de l'humain a fait perdre le Naturel.
>
> [Renaissance Humanism was not an expansion but a diminishment of man, for Man ceased to aspire to reach up to nature in order to bring nature in its full stature to himself, and the exclusive preoccupation with the human caused the loss of Naturality.]

Humanism is seen as a self-important anthropocentrism that reduced nature to man's small dimensions. In other words, Humanism made nature 'nature' in the sense of how it could meet human needs, hence the understanding of 'culture' and 'nature' in terms of the human and non-human. With the development of modern science and philosophy, nature further becomes an object of epistemological pursuit and control (Artaud VIII: 187–88, 198):

> Nous ne savons plus regarder la nature, sentir la vie dans sa totalité. [...] L'Europe a écartelé la nature avec ses sciences séparées. [...] Quand on lui parle de la Nature, elle demande de quelle Nature on veut aujourd'hui lui parler.
>
> [We no longer know how to see nature, how to feel life in its totality. [...] Europe has torn nature apart with its specialized sciences. [...] When you talk to Europe about Nature, she asks you which Nature you wish to talk about nowadays.]

Artaud is keen to point out that the problem of reifying and taxonomizing nature is on the level of discourse and epistemology, not in the order of concrete experience and existence. It is the dichotomist view of nature and culture that creates the dichotomy, not that the dichotomy first existed and a discourse had to be created to address it. This does not, however, mean that the problem is illusory, firstly because concepts are not unreal but only immaterial, secondly because conceptual problems guide actions, which then have concrete impact. This is why Artaud takes this question seriously and demands a re-understanding of nature (VIII: 194): 'Une idée géométrique, numérale, organique, harmonieuse, occulte, qui réconcilie l'homme avec la nature et avec la vie.' ('A geometrical, numeral, organic, harmonious and occult idea that reconciles man with nature and life.')

Now it seems that Artaud takes the same position of proposing holistic harmony as is seen in the *Zhuangzi* (6.1). But as the *Zhuangzi* demonstrates, this is a weak proposal because it remains on the superficial level of the problem created by the dualist view but does not inquire into the roots of the dualism itself. The holistic proposal therefore undermines itself, which Artaud realizes. He speaks with certainty that everything obeys nature, or 'Cruauté', even despite itself: 'Les choses obéissaient à une loi universelle cosmique' (XX: 118), the estrangement of nature in European thought becomes questionable. That is, if everything stems from nature, then is the emergence of this conceptual dichotomy also the natural path that European civilization had to follow? Is the advocation of holism itself a non-recognition of naturally-directed destiny? Clearly the questions Artaud faces are fundamentally the same questions raised in the *Zhuangzi*. Although Artaud does not recommend forgetting all distinctions as the *Zhuangzi* does, he does something similar: he rejects any definition of nature and truth, as well as any question about them: 'La vérité n'est pas une question de définition' (V: 111); 'pas de problème,/pas de question,/pas de solution,/pas de cosmos' (XIVii: 14).

In Michaux's case, nature is 'le Grand Inexpliqué' (1978a: 19), an irresoluble problem that culture — when it is assumed to be an external viewpoint from nature — can never penetrate. This is partly because the complexity of nature refuses any all-encompassing articulation through human language and knowledge; and more fundamentally because the autonomy of culture from nature cannot be established, while a monistic union of the two also remains problematic. To illustrate these points, firstly, there is an episode where a wise man talks about forty-nine explanations for why the sun goes dim, and professes that all explanations are necessary (1981a: 16–17):

> 'Aucune n'est la principale [explication]. Il faut connaître la totalité des quarante-neuf pour savoir pourquoi le soleil a cessé d'être brillant. Sinon, on ne le sait pas, on est un ignorant'.
>
> ['None of them is the major [explanation]. You have to know the entire forty-nine explanations to understand why the sun has stopped being bright. If not, you don't understand it at all, you are an uneducated person'.]

Here, Michaux humorously points out that one can try endlessly to grasp nature through epistemology, yet one would fail to find a theory of everything. Nature can be explained ad infinitum, which is also why it remains unexplained. Secondly, Michaux expresses the desire for monistic indifferentiation, so that culture and nature can be recuperated into each other. Michaux cites admiringly a Daoist story about a perfect sage who enters fire and stones and does not know it (1967b: 186), commenting that 'ce taoïste parfait, complètement effacé, ne rencontrait plus aucune différence nulle part' ('this perfect Taoist, completely self-effacing, no longer encountered any differentiation anywhere'). This is an ideal (though hardly achievable) state of unselfconsciousness, corresponding to Zhuangzian oblivion. But Michaux is also profoundly sceptical about such a healthy monism, for how do we know if oneness is not a convenient fiction? 'En te méfiant du multiple, n'oublie pas de te méfier de son contraire, de son trop facile contraire: l'un' (Michaux 1981b: 27). ('While distrusting the multiple, don't forget to also distrust its opposite, its all-too-easy opposite: the one.') As Noël says (in Michaux 2000: 12): 'Le Un est [...] une fiction qui passe pour une réalité parce que cela arrange tout le monde.' ('The One is [...] a fiction that is regarded as reality because that sorts out everyone.') Recalling the *Zhuangzi*'s question about distinguishing monism from duality, the distinction of which itself is a duality, Michaux's scepticism can be understood as the same disbelief in overcoming conceptual schisms by further conceptual differentiation.

Besides the difficulty in conceptualizing how nature is not alienated from culture, Michaux's thought also connects to the *Zhuangzi*'s re-understanding of nature and artifice. As discussed in chapter 2, simplicity can be extreme sophistication for Michaux and Artaud, and nature is a more cultivated state than culture. This issue is very important for the nature-based thought in all three texts and merits further discussion here. With Michaux, the moment of identification of the 'natural' is precisely the moment when artifice is revealed. But this 'artifice' is not necessarily understood as being different from the crude and original state (i.e. the state usually identified with nature), but can mean an artifice that is natural, like the bellstands of the *Zhuangzi*'s carpenter. For instance, Michaux narrates with thoughtful irony an incident during his travels in South America (1929: 177):

> Une jeune femme [...] venant de *Manaos*, entrant en ville ce matin avec nous, quand elle passa dans le Grand Parc, bien planté d'ailleurs, eut un soupir d'aise.
> 'Ah! enfin la nature!' dit-elle. Or elle venait de la forêt.

> [A young woman [...] who was from Manaos and entered the city with us this morning, when walking through the Grand Parc, which was indeed thickly cultivated, sighed with pleasure.
> 'Ah! Nature, finally!' she said. Yet she came from the forest.]

Although this anecdote seems unambiguous in meaning, it is in fact far more complex. At first, one may think that Michaux considers it ridiculous that the artificial preservation of a patch of greenery in an urban environment should strike a forest-dweller as natural. But Descola's remarks on the young woman in this passage inadvertently reveal that Michaux could be thinking otherwise:

> Pour cette citadine de l'Amazonie, la forêt n'est pas un reflet de la nature, mais un chaos inquiétant où elle ne se promène guère, rebelle à tout apprivoisement et impropre à susciter un plaisir esthétique (2005: 58).

> L'idée de sauvegarder la forêt dont les concitoyens pillaient les ressources ne l'avait jamais effleurée. Elle était préromantique, la pauvre, et avait en horreur la végétation débridée, les bêtes inquiétantes et les insectes par légions. Peut-être même s'était-elle étonnée du goût pervers dont témoignait le jeune poète européen pour ce tohu-bohu de plantes dont elle cherchait à se distancier (*Ibid.* 90).

> [For this dweller of Amazonia, the forest is not a reflection of nature, but a menacing chaos where she hardly strolls. It rebels against any domestication and can hardly evoke any aesthetic pleasure.]

> [The idea of preserving the forest whose resources her co-inhabitants plundered had never even occurred to her. She was pre-Romantic, poor thing, and abhorred unruly flora, intimidating animals and hordes of insects. She might even have been astonished by the perverse taste shown by this young poet from Europe for this hurly-burly of plants which she herself was trying to get away from.]

Descola very pertinently points out that the appreciation of wild nature as an aesthetic experience is a Romantic phenomenon. Michaux's intellectual context is no doubt post-Romantic, but Michaux is not definitely a Romantic aestheticist as Descola suggests. In fact, Michaux could be trying to retrieve precisely the young woman's pre-Romantic understanding of natural beauty as cultivated nature. Her surprising identification of an artificial park with nature could have shaken up the idea of raw nature and made Michaux rethink the entire question. So this anecdote could also be written in an ironic tone mocking European Romantic assumptions, and mocking readers who would think Michaux is a Romanticist. From other parts of Michaux's works, where he sees the childlike state as more developed than adulthood, where he writes that 'Il n'y a pas, en cette vie, de naturel vraiment naturel. Seulement de l'adaptation' (1975: 50), ('There is, in this life, no naturality that is truly natural. Only the adapted exists'), it is understood that Michaux is criticizing pointedly the Romantic connections between nature and unrefined primitiveness. Thus the anecdote above more likely indicates another view of artifice, one that is naturally-directed acculturation.

In this way, Michaux refuses to think of nature in terms of regression or the 'sauvage'. And this is the case for Artaud and the *Zhuangzi* too. For them, nature needs increasingly to advance towards integrity, not return to a transcendent and unchanging perfection, which is an essentialist illusion. As Artaud says (IX: 44): 'Comme elle [la nature] a *évolué* des hommes, elle a également *évolué* des rochers.' ('Just as nature has *evolved* human beings, she has equally *evolved* rocks.') Humanity and stones are both evolutions of nature, and are, as suggested, 'equally' evolved. The extremely complex system of Chinese medicine, which visualizes 380 acupoints (as Artaud believes) and numerous meridians, is seen by him as the reflection of a cultivated natural body (VIII: 198). On the *Zhuangzi*'s side, the appreciation for ingenious artisanal skills is always expressed by emphasizing how, unconsciously and naturally as if by basic instinct, a feat is performed (see *ZZ*, 3.1, 19.10). Ultimate skill and understanding are also ultimate simplicity and oblivion. The perfection of nature equates to the apogee of culture. This view overturns the conventional notions of nature and culture and is close in spirit to Castro's argument (1992) that nature is supernature and multiple natures, that the original state is in fact humanity (and in extension, culture), which is also universal. Animality developed from humanity instead, and through different bodies and physicalities, multiple natures are born. This reaffirms the limitations of the naturalist view that nature is continuous physicality whereas culture is discontinuous spiritualities. Neither nature nor culture is monolithic or universal and the attempt to determine either often ends up in discovering its alterity. This logic is precisely illustrated by Artaud's comments on anthropocentrism (VIII: 144):

> Plus l'homme se préoccupe de lui, plus ses préoccupations échappent en réalité à l'homme, [...] l'homme quand on le serre de près, cela aboutit toujours à trouver ce qui n'est pas l'homme.
>
> [The more human beings concern themselves with themselves, the more this preoccupation in fact separates them from their humanity [...]. When humanity is grasped after, this only ever leads precisely to what is not human.]

In sum, all three texts show an awareness of the nature-culture problem on the meta-discursive level, which means they can neither speak innocently nor unparadoxically about nature. Nature therefore remains a problem, and ethically needs to remain so. Nevertheless, these texts suggest new ways of rethinking the question, particularly in terms of naturalization as cultivation and multiple natures. These views are particularly significant for Artaud and Michaux, given their intellectual context, for their thought seems to be both before modern times and ahead of their time.

Conclusion

Through comparisons of different ideas and aspects related to nature, these texts have made it possible for an understanding of nature as fatalist but not determinist, nutritional but non-teleological, evolving but non-progressive. Moreover, the texts' treatment of the nature/culture divide shows that they do not embrace nature simplistically but reflect deeply on the emergence of the question of nature itself. These philosophies of nature relate closely to the concerns of non-logical rationality, indeterminate time and space and testify that nature is a keystone in the interpretation and appreciation of the three texts. Also, concepts as elusive as nature can be better understood when examined as an open field of ideas than when pinned down to a key term and definition. This open field then does not only exist in literature, but is permeable by ideas and theories from other disciplines, such as anthropology in this case, which shows that literary exegesis can potentially take recourse to anything, that comparative literature also means engaging with comparative disciplines.

From a rationality that is not rooted in human subjectivity, from non-anthropocentric time and space to nature as a cosmic principle and self-transforming life force, an underlying primary concern about human life attitude and conduct emerges. This involves the question of ethics, the topic of our next chapter.

Notes to Chapter 4

1. Another version of the anti-naturalist view is that Artaud understands nature as 'reality' and non-premeditation. As Brunel implies (1982: 116), Artaudian theatre is divorced from daily life and highly calculated, with actors like 'automatons' performing the 'geste scénique', not as 'un mouvement spontané, naturel' but as 'le produit d'une composition'.
2. See Trotet (1992: 294): 'accès à la sérénité [...] fusion avec la nature, ouverture aux flux naturels; ces caractères propres au taoïsme apparaîtront comme l'arrière-fond' (1992: 294).
3. These interpretations are represented by Ames (1986), Berkson (2005), and Chen (2009).
4. For instance, Wu (1982) recognizes the text's holistic approach to nature, in which nature is an organicist harmony between all beings. This view has also been related to the understanding of nature as spontaneity (see Tu 1989).
5. Graham (1986) and Poo (2005) have noted that what the *Zhuangzi* calls 'heaven', i.e. 'the power which is responsible for everything outside human control' (Graham 1986: 7), is also nature. This idea of nature as a non-humanly concerned force will be further examined in my study. Billeter holds a similar view by emphasizing the *Zhuangzi*'s strong fatalism.
6. See Descola (2005) for a detailed explanation of his schematization of different ontologies.

CHAPTER 5

Ethical Alternations: The Gift, Indifference, and Agency

The philosophical thought that Artaud, Michaux and the *Zhuangzi* have clarified and enriched so far now raises an urgent philosophical question: the question of ethics. If ethics is broadly understood as the actions of life and their principles, does it have a place in the thought of these texts? And can these texts say something important on the topic? At first these texts' relationship to ethics seems very precarious. If nature as fate and metamorphosis shows the predetermined, impersonal and non-teleological dimensions of life, then there is already a negation of personal agency, freedom and purpose. But can there be an ethics that is fatalist, unintentional and non-consequentialist? As usually understood, consequentialist ethics seeks to maximize the highest good: typically, happiness, or the flourishing of life, as in Aristotelian teleology, and the effects of human actions towards achieving it. But the views on nature in Artaud, Michaux and the *Zhuangzi* render the notions of choice and *telos* impossible, which means that ethics lies elsewhere. Also, these texts' cosmological views flag up a tension with ethics, for if cosmic time is preferred to the human, and indeterminate infinity to demarcative space, then does this imply an ethics that goes beyond the human (though not excluding it)? But whether ethics is exclusively human and social is itself a fundamental question that needs investigation. Furthermore, if these texts embrace a non-rationalist worldview in which reason and non-reason coexist, and epistemological claims cannot be made in terms of propositional truth but only according to particular perspectives, then how can an ethics that stems therefrom, if any, be guided by rational principles? Certainly, it cannot be deontological as represented by the Kantian view that the moral imperative is decided by reason and justice rather than the consequences of action. In contrast, Artaud, Michaux and the *Zhuangzi*'s non-rationality seems to propose an *an*-archic, antinomian and circumstantial ethics. All these questions about ethics show the urgent need for the topic. In brief, what would be an alternative ethics that is non-agential, non-teleological, unprincipled and even transhuman? Is it still an ethics at all or a non-ethics that is nevertheless ethical from a certain viewpoint? These enquiries not only open the question of ethics from a meta-ethical angle but also will show the primary texts' distinctive position within meta-ethics.

Preliminary reflections: what does ethics mean?

> Precisely because many moral philosophers had only a crude knowledge of moral *facta,* selected arbitrarily and abbreviated at random — for instance, as the morality of their surroundings, their class, [...] their *Zeitgeist,* [...] — precisely because they were poorly informed (and not particularly eager to learn more) about peoples, ages, and histories, they completely missed out on the genuine problems involved in morality, problems that only emerge from a comparison of many *different* moralities.
>
> — NIETZSCHE: *BGE,* V.186

In Nietzsche's view, the comparative perspective is crucial to a deeper understanding of ethics because cross-cultural knowledge dissolves conceptual limitations and impasses created in specific contexts, and reveals new food for thought as regards accepted norms. Therefore we may start thinking about ethics by comparing some key ideas about ethics in ancient Greek, Chinese, and South Asian cultures to open up the theoretical field and introduce some approaches to ethics alternative to those that typically arise in European philosophies.

From an etymological viewpoint, in both ancient Greek and classical Chinese contexts, thought about ethics involves the key terms *ethos* and *xing* 性, which both relate to naturalist and fatalist views of life. In Aristotle especially, *ethos* denotes character. '*Êthos* peut signifier le tempérament naturel d'une espèce animale ou d'un individu, mais aussi la manière habituelle d'être et de se comporter; quant au pluriel *êthê*, il désigne les mœurs d'un individu, d'une espèce, d'un peuple' (Vergnières 1995: v). ('*Ethos* may denote the natural disposition of an animal species or an individual being, but also the habitual way of existence and behaviour; as for the plural *êthê*, it indicates the customs of an individual, a species and a people.') *Ethos* is thus both an inbornness given a priori and 'something that can grow and change' (Darcus 1974: 394), as in the situation when one's thought and behaviour adapt and change according to the cultural and natural environment. In these aspects, *ethos* is very close to *phusis* and often used interchangeably in Aristotle, since they both denote a predetermined disposition as well as its flexibility and malleability. As Darcus observes (1974: 393), Pindar 'believed that a person's accustomed way of acting [i.e. *ethos*] [...] was dependent on the nature [i.e. *phua*] that he inherited at birth'. *Phua*, however, is in turn dependent on the 'δαίμων γενέθλιος' (Pindar: *Olympians* 13.104–05): the divine and spiritual 'destiny' (*daimon*) given to human beings unconditionally, as in various pre-Socratic texts such as Heraclitus, Hesiod, and Homer. In this way, one's *ethos* is decided by the *daimon* that is non-human, close to a *theos*, and is shaped as *phusis* develops. An ethics that stems from *ethos* is characterological, fatalist, and not completely human because it depends on innate tendencies that are fundamentally daimonic and non-human. This is why ethics in ancient Greek thought is often seen as virtue ethics, denoting the view that morality stems from being as it is naturally given and develops, rather than from deliberate action and its consequences. Thus, the 'ought' dimension — namely, the ethical obligation and prescription highlighted in modern thought by Hobbes and

Kant, and opposed to the descriptive 'is' dimension — is neither a necessary nor crucial concern in ethical thought.

Like *ethos*, the classical Chinese term *xing* 性, especially in the *Zhuangzi*, points to a naturalist, non-coercive understanding of goodness and virtue. Conventionally, *xing* carries various meanings such as 'natural inclination', and 'directionality of life'. But in addition, *xing* may also denote 'basic capacity' and 'instinct', which are characteristics seen as perfect in themselves and requiring no change. More specifically, firstly, *xing* is typically interpreted as a '"heavenly ordained" tendency, directionality, or potentiality of growth in the individual' (Hall and Ames 1995: 189). This is evidenced by statements such as: 'The *xing* of water is that if it is not mixed with other things it is clear, if it is not stirred it is calm, [...] this is the sign of heavenly integrity' (*ZZ*, 15.2). *Xing* here indicates a natural propensity that comes from heaven and is maintained without human intervention. Moreover, instead of non-intervention, deliberate change — even when intended for the better — is considered to corrupt and maim the integrity of *xing* (*ZZ*, 8.3):

> Ever since the three dynasties [i.e. the first three reigns in Chinese mythic history], everyone in the world has bartered their *xing* for other things. Petty men risk their bodies for profits, noble men risk theirs for reputation, [...] the sages risk theirs for the world.
>
> [...]
>
> In terms of maiming their life and injuring their *xing*, then even the moral exemplar Boyi is no different from the great Robber Zhi.[1]

This is clearly a protest that deliberately altering *xing* to achieve a certain end is unethical. At this point, the explanation of natural inclination for *xing* should be questioned: for not following one's dispositions does not necessarily 'injure' them, not manifesting or effectuating one's nature — as in 'the nature of wood is to float on water' — is not harming it. That *xing* can be 'injured' just as health and vitality can be maimed (Graham 1986: 10) shows that *xing* has to be, besides an ungraspable propensity and abstract property of life, something more basic and concrete. As the *Zhuangzi* states, '*xing* is the basic substance of life' (*ZZ*, 23.17); 'to desire and hate, to avoid and follow, these do not need to be taught, they are the *xing* of men' (*ZZ*, 29.3). *Xing* in these cases can be understood as 'instincts', or the basic fact of existence. By emphasizing that *xing* is followed and preserved rather than (ex-) changed for anything, the text's conception of goodness is rooted in existing-as-such, without any rationalization or obligation that is calculated towards a goodness beyond bare existence. Again, as in ancient Greek ethical thought, the normative and rationalizing functions of ethics are questioned whereas the naturalist, fatalist and existential dimensions are considered crucial to ethical life. Of course, here emerges the question of why preserving *xing* is ethical, because the goodness of *xing* is an arbitrary and self-justificatory, i.e. non-rational decision. This decision, however, is necessarily arbitrary because it stems from the self-justificatory insistence upon existence-as-such, not on existence as it should be. In other words, it needs nothing other than itself to justify itself, using a minimalist and self-identical logic like Frank Stella's 'What you see is what you see', but here being 'what you are is what you are'. As we will see, this tautological state of being-what-one-is is considered the ultimate in ethics in the *Zhuangzi* as well as in Artaud and Michaux.

The naturalist roots of Greek and Chinese ethical thought show that instead of being prescriptive and principled as in the debates of Enlightenment philosophy, ethics can be understood as descriptive and spontaneous. Furthermore, the givenness of *ethos* and *xing*, which depends on the non-human powers of *daimon* and heaven (*tian*), implies that ethics, even in human life, is not primarily controlled by human agency. This shows how the modern assumptions about ethics — that it is prescriptive, rational, agential, or human — cannot be taken for granted. There are now two more key concerns about ethics in modern European thought that need rethinking, the first being the view that ethics is socially engaged and about the self-other relationship. This view is a legacy of Hegel's master-slave dialectic that translates into the self-other opposition, and is represented by much twentieth-century French thought, from Sartre to Derrida and Lévinas, who respond to nineteenth-century philosophies that divide reality into individual consciousness and the world. The second concern is about the view that ethics should aim at the well-being and preservation of the human species. This view is deep-rooted and extends from advocates of environmental ethics, from Moore, to Hume, and back to Aristotle. These two issues are relevant to Artaud, Michaux and the *Zhuangzi*, and particularly so, because they are most significantly absent in these texts. How are we to understand this absence of the self-other dialectic and human-orientated concern? Again, a cross-cultural consideration would be helpful, especially through ideas about ethics that have emerged in anthropological studies.

To begin with, in regard to the self-other relationship in ethics, the common perception in many cultures, especially the European, is that actions for others are better than those for one's own benefit. Reflecting back on the nineteenth century which characterizes European modernity and colonialist mentality, the twentieth-century enterprise to re-address morality has been revolving around how to negotiate between the self and other without appropriating the other in various ways, be it colonial, cultural, or even epistemological (as we find in Lévinas). But this emphasis on the other can be challenged, which is precisely what Nietzsche sets out to do (*GM*: 2):

> People originally praised unegoistic actions and called them good from the perspective of those for whom [...] such actions were useful. Later people forgot how this praise began, and because unegoistic actions had, according to custom, always been praised as good, people then simply felt them as good, as if they were something inherently good.

The moral preferability of altruistic action over self-centred action is in fact a historically and culturally-specific value. This can be shown by the ethics of self-cultivation and self-realization in South Asian cultures. For example, in classical Hindu cosmology, 'the reincarnating self is composed of three qualities (literally 'strands' = *guṇas*)' (Bussanich 2010: 9), which are cosmic forces of lightness, energy and heaviness. These forces perpetually struggle and interact with each other, and action is born therefrom. The *Bhagavad Gītā* (3.5) states that even if one chooses not to act, 'nobody not even for a moment remains inactive' because the *guṇas* are always acting. The *guṇa*-self is thus the source of all ethically-related action and is the first concern of ethics (*Gītā* 18.40–47):

> The actions of priests, warriors, commoners and servants
> are apportioned by qualities [*guṇas*] born of their intrinsic being.
> [...]
> Each one achieves success by focusing on his own action (*svakarma*);
> [...]
> Better to do one's own duty (*svadharma*) imperfectly than to do another man's well;

The didactic message in these lines is that 'there is nothing higher than attaining the Self' (*Apastamba Dharmasiltra*: 153, cited in Dhand 2002: 353). The best ethics is about realizing and perfecting the self, not about the other. This is not, however, a version of egoism because one still acts altruistically, but it 'is not a rehearsed or practised kind of altruism; rather, one's altruism is the spontaneous and unprompted expression of one's mental and spiritual self-refinement' (Dhand 2002: 356). This form of ethics thus seems to be centripetal and has three layers: the battle between cosmic forces, the interaction between these forces and one's personal actions and choices, which then relate to one's position in society. The interhuman relationship is thrice removed from the crux of ethics, namely, the *guṇa*-self. This provides a good example of how an ethics without the other as major concern is possible.

Although the view that ethics is significantly concerned about the self-other relationship can be explained as a cultural construction, the view that ethics should improve the well-being of mankind and preserve human life seems to be much more universal and difficult to challenge. But even this view can be doubted, if we consider the understanding of murder in Tantric Buddhism. In studies of Padmasambhava (the guru who is said to have transmitted Vajrayāna Buddhism from India to Tibet), Wang (1975: 148) observes that 'Padma murdered two infants, a man, and a woman with the rationale that their karma from previous lives was bad and he was keeping it from becoming worse'. This is because in Tantric Buddhism, 'murder by a Great Yogi to stop an evil-doer is permissible'. It can even be said to be ethical, because the Yogi undertakes an act of evil that society dare not undertake and sullies himself for the sake of his victims, the assumption being that death is better for them than life. Although this justification of killing as ethical is highly debatable and radically detached from basic human needs and instincts, it shows how even ethical views normally seen as universally accepted are not really universal. It also leads to the question of whether ethics is necessarily human-centred or whether it could revolve around a greater cosmic scheme without particularly attending to the welfare of humans.

The ideas discussed above regarding ethics in different cultures, and their comparison with key views in European thought — which assert moral obligation, human agency, orientation towards the other, and human well-being — demonstrate that ethical values vary widely, and the problems and solutions posed by European moral philosophy since modern times are neither always prevalent nor universally applicable. This is not to say, however, that the alternative ways of thinking about ethics I have discussed are unproblematic in themselves or provide neat solutions (if possible) to problems in European thought. Non-occidental perspectives are not a refuge for failed or unsettled intellectual attempts of the West, but they are necessary elements for a broader, better informed view of many common topics, including ethics. Nietzsche is not this militantly comparatist for nothing, for bringing in alternative understandings opens up a wider conceptual field where ethics may be rethought in the absence of agency, social relationship and anthropocentrism — as will be found in Artaud, Michaux and the *Zhuangzi*. On the other hand, despite differences in views and practices, this comparative discussion has confirmed one commonality: that ethics is ubiquitous and necessary, no matter what form it takes. Even when the case seems to be non-ethics, like Padma's philosophically-motivated murder, we cannot define it as non-ethics because that presumes clear ethical boundaries, which are in themselves contentious and uncertain. Although, arguably, everything in ethics can be doubted, this does not mean ethics does not exist or can be refused *in toto*. This inevitability of ethics will show itself in the three primary texts, through a discussion that will be framed by three concepts in ethics: the gift, indifference, and agency. These concepts not only have a prominent place in contemporary ethical theory, but will also reflect different aspects of the texts' challenge to and re-understanding of ethical thought.

The Gift: Giving and taking without benevolence and gratitude

Since Mauss's seminal essay, the gift has been one of the most important and heavily debated notions in both ethical philosophy and anthropological theory. The reason the gift sparks off so much discussion is that it associates with two fundamental problems: economical exchange and the gift's impossible genuineness. These problems are seen to constitute the paradoxical nature of the gift that undermines its ethical value. If the gift is the keystone of exchange that links the cycles of 'l'obligation de donner' and 'l'obligation de recevoir' (Mauss 1923–24: 21), then it is never pure giving but tainted with the duty and expectation of return. The gift cannot be truly unselfish because the donor is not totally disinterested in return, and because the gift is not non-demanding and free but binds the recipient by economic or moral obligation. This makes the ethical value of the gift dubitable, and in much continental philosophy, ultimately the gift is ethical only when it effaces itself. Derrida is representative of this view, as he argues (1991: 29): 'Pour qu'il y ait don, il ne faut pas seulement que le donataire ou le donateur ne perçoive pas le don comme tel, n'en ait ni conscience ni mémoire, ni reconnaissance; il faut aussi qu'il l'oublie à l'instant.' ('For the gift to exist, it is not only necessary for the recipient or the donor not to perceive the gift as a gift, not to be conscious of it, nor remember it, nor recognize it; it is also necessary for him to forget it immediately.') Heim aptly remarks (2004: 36) that 'for Derrida, the paradox of the gift is that once it is perceived as such it is consumed in the cycle of obligation, return, debt, and counter-gift'. Therefore 'le don est [...] la figure même de l'impossible' (Derrida 1991: 19). The gift becomes something that 'exceeds any economy', and 'occurs in the absence, or in excess, of subjectivity' (Moore 2011: 3). But this is impossible, as the gift's different versions show — from Bataille's *la part maudite* and the Lacanian Real, to Deleuzian repetition and Levinasian alterity.

Insightful as these (post)structuralist views are in the context of reflecting upon the exchange logic and metaphysical closure of European cultures, they create an impasse in thinking about the gift. Along their lines of argument, either the ethics of the true gift forever lies beyond the thinkable and actualizable, or it oscillates between the dichotomies of give-and-take, self-and-other. These issues are framed around notions of authenticity and equality that demand giving to be purely disinterested in order to exist, and interhuman relationships to be reciprocal rather than hierarchical. But these conceptual frameworks are not the only ones available for understanding the gift. In fact, Mauss does not question the possibility of the gift from the standpoints of subjectivity and equality, because his interest is anthropological and he understands that these European philosophical notions apply poorly to non-Occidental cultures. This gives us a clue: an anthropological perspective that includes ways and conceptions of giving in different cultures may help to reformulate and expand the understanding of the gift and subjectivity, so that we need not affirm one at the cost of the other. For example, Heim's anthropological study of the practice of offering gifts to mendicants — usually religious practitioners such as monks and Brahmin priests — shows that giving in this context, termed *dāna*, 'does not and should not inspire gratitude from the recipient' (Heim 2004: 34). This is because the gift here is simultaneously a sacrifice, which embodies 'the sins of the donor, whom it rids of evil by transferring the dangerous and demeaning burden of death and impurity to the recipient' (Heesterman in Parry 1986: 459). Rather than acting without self-interest, the donor wishes to gain good karma; the donor is not in the position of being morally obliged to give: on the contrary, the recipient of the gift, who is in a spiritually superior position, bestows a favour on the donor. The gift is therefore a sign of 'esteem to religious elites', and is 'explicitly *not* based on altruism and compassion' (Heim 2004: 50). This alternative practice of gift-giving is even noted by Mauss in a footnote (1923–24: 94): 'L'obligation de rendre, nous avons trouvé peu de faits dans le droit hindou, sauf peut-être MANU, VIII, 213. Même le plus clair consiste dans la règle qui l'interdit.' ('In Hindu law we have found very little evidence of the obligation to give back, except perhaps in MANU VIII, 213. The clearest law is precisely established in the rule that forbids giving in return.') In other words, *dāna* is not about 'the give-and-take of human relations', but about 'one-way regard and respect' (Heim 2004: 54). We see that this kind of giving does not require non-recognition or pure disinterest, nor is concerned with exchange or reciprocity. Both the donor and recipient have an interest, but it is not the egoistical and exchange-driven interest that Derrida refers to, since their interest is in executing a religious duty to cultivate oneself towards greater perfection and fulfil the cosmic order. In this sense, either their interest in giving and receiving is ethical *per se,* or the meaning of what ethics involves is different. This example suffices to show that the ethics of gift can be more complex than the problems of exchange and subjectivity, as well as less paradoxical or impossible than the Derridean version. In fact, these ideas about *dāna* find notable echoes in the *Zhuangzi* and in Artaud, texts which also consider the gift as a crucial dimension of ethics, but not undermined by an impossibility of actualization, nor fraught with the binaries of self or other, exchange or altruism.

Although there is so far no critical examination of the notion of gift in the *Zhuangzi*, the text includes plenty of discussion about giving and receiving. These discussions revolve around two kinds of relationships: first, the non-equal and hierarchical relationship between heaven, the highest power, and everything else that is subordinate to it. In this relationship, the gift comes from heaven's part and embodies an absolute, one-way cosmic giving, understood as the unconditional acceptance by all beings of their life, forms and conditions of existence from heaven. Secondly, there is the relationship between humans, which should be modelled after the first cosmic relationship. In more detail, passages describing the first relationship repeatedly emphasize that heaven is the greatest donor, for it creates and nourishes all things equanimously, silently and unselfconsciously. As the text states (23.1):

> When the breath of spring rises, the hundred grasses are born. Then when autumn comes the ten thousand fruits ripen. Spring and autumn, how could they be so without obtaining anything in return? It is because the way of heaven already operates [within them].

Cosmic giving as exemplified here in the life and bounty brought about by spring and autumn is spontaneous and unreciprocated, and so naturally experienced that it is taken for granted. As a wise but crippled man says (*ZZ*, 5.3), 'there is nothing which heaven refuses to cover or earth to support'. Therefore, although he is despised in human society, he is never bothered because heaven's indiscriminating and constant nourishment enables him to continue living and learning. That things are born and grow, that the world is always already out there with all its resources that enable existence and its continuation, are by themselves the most solid evidence that heaven gives unreservedly, infinitely and ceaselessly. Needless to say, there can be no expectation of return as regards heaven's gift. 'To give to men but not forget about it, this is not the giving of heaven' (*ZZ*, 32.10), which means that heaven's giving is necessarily forgotten and should not be reciprocated. The cosmic gift, being inevitable and fundamental to existence, is simply being itself, which has to be taken for granted because it is not given out of benevolence but *for no reason*, since it needs no other justification than itself. The ethics of gift is grounded in the ethics of heaven, which is, as Wu puts it, simultaneously 'true morality' and 'non-morality' (1982: 66). It effectuates the greatest benevolence without being conceptualized as such. As the *Zhuangzi* lauds heaven for its virtue (6.8): 'Your bounty extends to myriad generations but it is not benevolence.'

Reflecting on this gift relationship between heaven and everything else, it is understood that giving takes place in an absolute, non-reciprocal and non-exchangeable way. Heaven's gift of existence is so impersonal and non-refusable that it cannot be considered a 'gift' although it is *in fact* a gift. In this aspect, heaven's gift is similar to the pure, unconscious and unrecognized gift that Derrida envisages, except that in the interhuman relationship, such a gift is impossible. In the *Zhuangzi*, however, this gift is possible and actualized, for it comes from the transhuman cosmic force of heaven. All that the recipient can do is to accept and acknowledge this gift of existence, without being able to reciprocate anything. Like the *dāna* in classical Hindu practices and beliefs, the cosmic gift in the *Zhuangzi* also requires a hierarchical and one-way relationship.

Besides this primary cosmic gift, the gift in interhuman relationships is also significantly present in the *Zhuangzi*. But, unlike the understanding in twentieth-century anthropological and philosophical theories, the gift between humans is seen here as a correlation to and consolidation of cosmic rather than social life. For instance, the sage, the mirror of cosmic order and the ideal man, models his ethics of giving and receiving according to the logic of heaven (*ZZ*, 5.5, Graham's translation, modified):

> For the sage, [...] morality is a way of trafficking, getting credit for his deeds is peddling. [...] Since he has nothing to lose, what use has he for morality? Since he does not treat things as commodities, what use has he for peddling? [...] Since he receives food from heaven, what use has he for man?

Morality and recognition, being social codes that bind people together, are seen as spurious by the sage because he accords with heaven's order and even in his relationship with other humans, he refuses to enter into any system of exchange, either concrete or ideological. Thus ideally, the human donor should also give without considering giving as a benevolent act, and take without regarding acceptance as making oneself beholden. The equanimity and impersonality of the cosmic gift should be reflected in the social gift, meaning that the identity of the recipient is no longer important. If a gift, for instance benevolent deeds, can be given to anyone and anything, then the donor is no longer excluded from being the recipient. The idea is that since heaven treats everything indifferently, then there is no reason that benevolence to others should be preferable to benevolence to oneself, since the self and other are the same. The non-discrimination between the donor and recipient is a remarkable aspect of the Zhuangzian notion of gift, since the gift transforms from a typical way of negotiating between and reinforcing the self-other dichotomy as a means to collapse their distinction. This point is well voiced in the following passage, where the sage Lao Dan challenges Confucius's advocation of benevolence (*ZZ*, 13.6):

> 'Are benevolence and duty the *xing* [性 'basic instincts', 'disposition'] of man?'
> Confucius said: 'Yes.' [...]
> 'May I ask what you mean by benevolence and duty?'
> 'To delight in harmony from your heart and love everyone impartially, that is the essence of benevolence and duty.'
> 'Ah! Your last words are dangerous! Is not loving everyone an aberration? Impartiality to all is nevertheless a partiality. [...] It is inherent in the stars to form ranks and patterns, in the birds and beasts to form their own groups. [...] If you seek after benevolence and duty so intently, [...] you will bring disorder to man's *xing*!'

Here, benevolent deeds and impartial love for others can be understood as a gift from the self to the other. They are idealized by Confucius, who makes them moral principles. But Lao Dan dismisses this idealization of the gift as overwrought, misleading, and deviant from man's natural dispositions, for giving benevolence and love to others should not stem from subjectivity but from an unconscious instinct. According to Billeter (2004: 40), for the *Zhuangzi*, the very codification of an ethical act or intent — even when the latter is morally sound — is itself an error because 'tout calcul est vain'. The conscious practice of trying to give impartial love in exactly the same way to everyone is already partial because of its deliberate and forced impartiality. Just in the sense that animals cannot be judged partial to their own species when they flock together because they cannot but stay with their own kind, the *xing* of man decides that humans do not and cannot love everyone equally. Paradoxically, true impartiality should involve a spontaneously occurring degree of partiality. But this is not a problem because the very notions of partiality, as well as self and other, would have disappeared. Consequently, the bond and opposition between the donor and recipient in the ethics of the gift are dissolved. The Zhuangzian gift, even in the human realm, has nothing particularly human about it, for it should reflect cosmic and natural order. The Zhuangzian gift can be free of the questions of obligation, exchange and subjectivity because it is not a product of human intention and society but a phenomenon inherent in the cosmic system. It thus implies that ethics more broadly speaking is not specifically human either. To consider these ideas further, we need to turn to Artaud's articulations of the gift, which run along similar lines.

In Artaud, just as in the *Zhuangzi*, reflections upon the gift centre on interhuman and human-cosmos relationships, with the former ultimately subsumed under the latter. For example, Artaud observes and reflects upon the Tarahumara people's practices and views of giving and receiving, and is struck by how different they are from the European conception of the gift, especially in that the Tarahumaras' gift involves no interhuman negotiation (IX: 99):

> Cette loi de réciprocité physique que nous appelons la charité, les Indiens la pratiquent naturellement, et sans aucune pitié. Ceux qui n'ont rien, [...] arrivent au soleil levant dans les maisons de ceux qui ont quelque chose. Immédiatement, la maîtresse de maison leur apporte tout ce qu'elle a. Personne ne regarde, ni celui qui donne, ni celui qui reçoit. Après avoir mangé, le mendiant s'en va sans remercier ni regarder personne. [...]
>
> Car donner à celui qui n'a rien n'est même pas pour eux un devoir, c'est une loi de réciprocité physique. [...] Leur attitude semble dire: 'En obéissant à la loi, c'est à toi-même que tu fais du bien, je n'ai donc pas à te remercier.'
>
> [This principle of physical reciprocity which we call benevolence, the Indians practise naturally, without any compassion. Those who have nothing, [...] come at daybreak to the houses of those who have something. Immediately, the house-mistress brings them everything she has. Nobody looks, neither the person who gives, nor the one who receives. After having eaten, the mendicant goes away without thanking or looking at anyone. [...]
>
> Giving to someone who has nothing is not even a duty for them, it is a principle of physical reciprocity. [...] Their attitude seems to say: 'When obeying this principle, you do good to yourself, therefore I have nothing to thank you for.']

The Tarahumaras practise charity so unselfconsciously and impersonally that giving could hardly be considered a charitable act any more. Artaud's expressions of 'pitié', 'réciprocité', 'devoir' — vocabulary from the European language of the gift that emphasizes exchange and moral obligation — are used subversively to show that the Tarahumaras' gift does not embody kindness or entail social bonds. Relating back to the *Zhuangzi*'s idea that cosmic giving is undemanding, impersonal, and taken for granted like the sun giving its light to the earth, the action of the Tarahumara housemistress who is the donor precisely illustrates the same kind of giving. She gives without compassion, that is, without any underlying contempt for a person in a less well-off situation; she offers all the food of the household to the mendicant without second thought, thus not egoistically thinking of her own possessions in the first place; she does not even look at the recipient, since her act of giving is not considered by herself as deserving any acknowledgement, and is so impersonal that she would have done the same thing to every mendicant at her door. As for the recipient, neither does he look at the donor nor acknowledge the gift. He receives the food as if it is his right to do so, and leaves without expressing gratitude. The mendicant here is like the Zhuangzian sage who understands that the ethics of gift is precisely in its non-exchangeability, unselfconsciousness and natural occurrence. The Tarahumara mendicant does not insult an act of spontaneous and impersonal giving by recognizing it as charity, precisely because giving is not a moral duty: 'donner [...] n'est même pas pour eux un devoir'. Giving is instead a cosmic law of interaction between bodies ('réciprocité physique'), it reflects what is already inherent in nature. Note how Artaud adds that the donor actually does herself rather than the recipient a favour because she fulfils the cosmic principle and completes a spontaneously ethical act. The donor's gift is to herself as well as to the mendicant, since she does not need to give in total disinterestedness for the gift to exist as such. But her interest is of a cosmic or religious nature, like the Zhuangzian sage's interest in reflecting the ways of heaven, and the South Asian donor's interest in receiving good karma. The Tarahumara donor's interest lies in accordance with cosmic principles and fully integrating into their cosmology. In this case, both the donor and recipient benefit from the gift, so the distinctions between self and other, interest and altruism are blurred.

The first gift relationship between humans in fact goes beyond the human and moral dimension and reveals the second kind of gift relationship: that between the human and divine. The divine here does not refer to any god, as Artaud notes: 'le mot "Dieu" n'existe pas dans leur [Tarahumara] langue', but 'un principe transcendant de la Nature' exists (IX: 83). This principle is for the Tarahumaras, as Artaud believes, the highest cosmological power. The gift in this second relationship is therefore from the divine to humans, and it appears notably in Artaud's writings about the Peyotl. Although some have remarked that Artaud's fascination with the Peyotl is related to his long-term obsession with mystic and drug-induced trances that return the body to a primitive and purer state,[2] nobody has explicitly pointed out that Artaud sees the Peyotl as an incarnation of the divine gift, which is then given to human Peyotl-hunters and eaters. Artaud takes great pains to describe the process of the Peyotl rituals, which include the stages of Peyotl hunting, Peyotl gathering and food preparation, ritual dancing and Peyotl consumption. The details of the initiating dance of the Tarahumara Peyotl-eaters are meticulously executed and show how the Tarahumaras respect the Peyotl:

> Le Prêtre [...] tira de son sein un sachet et versa dans les mains des Indiens une sorte de poudre blanche [i.e. pulverized Peyotl] qu'ils absorbèrent immédiatement.
>
> Après quoi ils se mirent à danser. [...] Les deux servants se courbèrent contre

> la terre où ils furent l'un en face de l'autre comme deux boules inanimées. (Artaud 2004: 1685–86).
>
> [The Priest [...] took out from his bosom a small bag and poured into the Indians' hands a kind of white powder which they immediately consumed. After this they started dancing. [...] The two servants contorted themselves on the ground where they were positioned facing each other like two inert balls.]

If Artaud's account and understanding of the Peyotl are compared with anthropological studies of Peyotl rituals in Mexican tribal cultures, we see that despite his mystic ecstasies and hallucinations, his descriptions and understanding are generally accurate. Anthropologists such as Lumholtz, who wrote records about the Tarahumaras' ritual celebration of the Peyotl's divine healing powers (1902), or Myerhoff, who joined and described the Peyotl hunt (1974), and Stewart (1987) all affirm that the Peyotl is treated as a being with will, in the figure of a protector. Le Clézio's proposition (1965) that the Tarahumara episode is Artaud's fantasy is therefore quite doubtful: being physically present in the Mexican tribes was important for Artaud, because through this experience he came into contact with a distinctly different notion of gift represented by the Peyotl. The central idea in the Peyotl rituals is that the Peyotl is a divine personality who gives itself as a gift to its hunters and eaters. Upon consumption of the Peyotl the eaters receive the *mana,* or spiritual power that protects and gives good luck as well as vitality: 'On prend tout le jus d'un fruit jusqu'à la source de la vie' (Artaud 2004: 1680). ('All the juice of one fruit down to the very source of life is imbibed.') By letting itself be hunted and eaten, the Peyotl gives its spiritual and vital power to its eaters, and enacts both a sacrifice and divine gift. The Peyotl, 'saluted in the same way as a man' (Stewart 1987: 17), occupies the position of the benevolent donor who gives a one-way gift. The only thing the recipients, the Peyotl-eaters can do is to show respect to this divine gift through rituals and accept the invigoration and other hallucinogenic sensations that Peyotl consumption entails. 'Quand ses adeptes ont obtenu par l'accomplissement religieux du Rite que Ciguri [i.e. the Tarahumara name for the Peyotl] veuille entrer en eux' (Artaud 2004: 1685), ('Only when its followers have obtained [it] through the religious performance of the Ritual will Ciguri want to enter them',) then the Tarahumaras start their 'metempsychotic' experiences of crying and dancing frenetically. In this gift relationship, the same aspects of non-exchange and hierarchy that characterize the *Zhuangzi*'s notion of cosmic gift exist. Parallel to the interhuman relationship of the gift with the Tarahumara housemistress and mendicant, this gift between the human and divine is also gratuitous and not constructed on moral codes but happens by natural principles, namely, the Peyotl's spontaneous self-sacrifice in its role of protector and healer.

In both gift relationships described by Artaud, the gift is fundamentally a reflection and embodiment of the cosmological relationship between man and the higher order of the world. This shows that the ethics of the gift is, for Artaud as for the *Zhuangzi*, cosmic rather than social. If giving can happen without the self-other distinction or reciprocity, spontaneously and unconditionally like a natural phenomenon, then it can be affirmed as supremely ethical rather than a self-effacing ethical contradiction. An ethics of giving is therefore not only possible, but also crucial to maintaining cosmic order, since everything starts by predetermined giving-and-receiving — existence, for example. The implication is that ethics is the starting point rather than the end goal. Ethics is returned from the imperative to the indicative, a theme that underlies the entirety of views on ethics in these texts.

Indifference and meta-ethics

The concept of the gift already shows how ethics can be cosmological and non-social. The notion of indifference, however, finds other expressions of ethics in the *Zhuangzi* and Michaux. These two texts recurrently feature indifference, but rather than seeing indifference as ethically negative, can it be a positive and ethical indifference? At first it is surprising that indifference could be so perceived, since it implies 'an absence of interest, care, or intention [...and] suggests neutrality regarding good and evil, or lack of an active quality' (Scott 2007: 3). This seems to contradict the ethical attitude, usually understood as concern for the best life and engaging with life's responsibilities. This is evidenced from the ancient Greeks' reflections on *eudaimonia* and the ideal life to Kantian deontological responsibility and Bernard Williams's affirmation that emotions and moral judgements are inseparable (Williams 1999: 207). But the indifference that is present in the *Zhuangzi* and Michaux is far from insensibility and irresponsibility, lying rather in expressions of the desire for self-perfection and detachment, an imperturbable state of mind similar to Epicurean and Pyrrhonian *ataraxia*, or emotional invulnerability, which then leads to an oceanic feeling of greatness that transcends good and evil. This particular kind of philosophical indifference turns out to be a life attitude that occupies a vital position in Zhuangzian and Michauldian ethics.

With the *Zhuangzi*, indifference is seen as a distinctive quality of heaven and fate, which is also something that man can aspire to and embody. Heavenly indifference manifests itself in many aspects, the most important of which is an amorality that is 'beyond good and evil'. For example, heaven's impersonal and indiscriminating way of giving as argued above is also an indifferent act that cannot be measured by exclusively human conceptions and evaluations of morality. Heaven 'is lofty without intending to be so, perfect without benevolence and duty, orderly without accomplishments and reputation, [...] indifferent and calm in infinity yet all good things follow it' (*ZZ*, 15.1). Heaven's indifference therefore characterizes good qualities that are greater than human morality, with this greatness exceeding the moral vocabulary of man: heaven's way is great but 'not named; great arguments are not spoken; great benevolence is not benevolent; great honesty is not humble; great courage is not fierce' (*ZZ*, 2.10). In other words, cosmic indifference is *meta*-ethical, in both the meta-normative and meta-discursive senses, for the deeds of heaven, or nature, take place in a way that is so impersonal and taken for granted that they are indifferent: whatever good they do cannot be seen as 'moral', whatever bad they do cannot be seen as 'evil'. Life is given unconditionally but also taken away inexorably, nature carries on with its operations and cycles of time regardless of how individual existences suffer or disappear. As Scott observes (2007: 28), 'indifference characterizes all impersonal inevitabilities'.

The question now is why this indifference manifested by the cosmic system should be considered ethical, since there is no adequate human conception or language of goodness and badness that can justify it. The *Zhuangzi* seems to affirm this indifference on the basis of its absolute totality, understood as the undifferentiating encompassment of everything — e.g. the greatest kindness and the greatest cruelty — by the universe. The *coincidentia oppositorum* in Zhuangzian trivialism reappears here as the intrinsic virtue of natural order. But this affirmation of maximum totality as ethical perfection is an arbitrary decision. Given Zhuangzian trivialism, however, it is impossible to argue against this decision because trivialism already affirms everything. What the cosmic ethics of indifference entails is, for the *Zhuangzi*, a corresponding ethics of indifference in human beings. In this way, indifference would not be intimidating and overwhelming to man but a source of wisdom and tranquillity, as the figure of the sage shows (*ZZ*, 6.1):

> His mind forgets, his expression is calm, [...] he is chilly like autumn, warm like spring, his joy and anger go through the four seasons and fit with things without any definite limits. This is why when the sage wages war, he may destroy countries but he will not lose people's hearts; he may benefit the myriad things but that is not love for men.

The sage is a micro-version of heaven. He acts but remains as indifferent as natural phenomena. His emotions are like the changes of weather and seasons and do not reflect his personal will — in fact, he does not have any will as such. When heavenly indifference is transposed to the exemplary man, it becomes an imperturbable and invulnerable state of being. In Huang's view (2010: 1059), the sage loves 'so naturally, spontaneously, and effortlessly' that he 'forgets' he loves. But more importantly, he also loves *indifferently*, that is, without any particular conscious attachment (*ZZ*, 25.2):

> The sage loves others, and people label him with names for it. But if they do not tell him, he will not know that he loves others. Whether he knows it or not, whether he is told of it or not, his love for others remains constant, [...] for it is his *xing*.

Love, commonly perceived as a most intimate and intentional emotion, is portrayed here like a natural instinct (*xing*) that cannot help but exist. The sage's love is indifferent and detached because it is like heaven's unselfconscious giving, neither specifically directed towards any object (or recipient), nor desiring return. On the other hand, however, the sage's ethics includes destructive aspects simultaneously with its caring aspects. As stated in the above quotation 6.1, sages can also hate, be angry, and wage war. This is not surprising because if the sage reflects the indifference of cosmic order, then his ethics is also the trivialist oneness that encompasses opposites. Moral distinctions established by tradition and society are typically dismissed in the *Zhuangzi*. So the Zhuangzian sage does not seek recognition, nor is disgusted by immorality (*ZZ*, 17.4):

> The great man [...] does not fight for goods or wealth, nor does he particularly refuse or give them away; [...] he does not despise the greedy and corrupt, though his actions are different from the worldly. [...] For he knows that right and wrong cannot be separated.

The sage, like nature, exists in a non-judgmental way. He treats the noble on equal terms with the low, can make profits but stays detached, and understands that goodness and badness depend upon each other to exist. His ethics is of a trivialist and meta-ethical nature, since it negates nothing and sees morality from a viewpoint outside its norms and evaluations. Here one may object that despite the sage's trivialist indifference, he still behaves in a certain way rather than any way. Although the *Zhuangzi* does not explicitly explain this, its emphasis on the spontaneity of the sage's actions suggests that they stem from his natural dispositions, which are fully realized because he attains an omnicentric perspective on all things and values. Therefore the sage's behaviour does not reflect individual choice but inherent auto-regulating natural principles.

If the *Zhuangzi*'s ethics of indifference includes surpassing moral codes and values in both cosmic and human realms, then it naturally follows that this kind of ethics is non-social and focuses on self-cultivation and self-realization rather than changing the external world. This view is supported by the text, for instance when it says that men become heavenly 'by forgetting other men' (23.19). The implication is that by forgetting one's social image and obligations one becomes ethical in the cosmic sense. The culture of reclusion, which became an important lifestyle for certain unconventional and career-frustrated Chinese intellectuals in the first few centuries CE, has its roots in the *Zhuangzi*'s representation of hermits. These hermits may live in society without becoming social, for they are indifferent to social perception and do not try to improve the world but perfect themselves first. The *Zhuangzi* warns that 'clear perception does not mean seeing others but seeing oneself', and 'he who is suited by what suits others fails to suit himself with what is suitable to himself' (*ZZ*, 8.3). Trying to influence others before achieving self-cultivation and self-knowledge only brings more disorder to the world; catering to the tastes of society in terms of behaviour will injure one's inborn instincts and characteristics. A good example the text offers is Confucius, who spends years trying to teach others moral principles, yet never succeeds in improving others. The sage Lao Dan then tells him that he cannot morally transform the world without first letting himself transform with the cosmic processes (*ZZ*, 14.7). Indifference to society therefore does not show insensibility but a conception of ethics that is, as in the Hindu ethics discussed above, centripetally directed towards the inner self rather than centrifugally orientated towards others. This is not, however, a reinforcement of the self-other opposition, for the other is not seen as a dichotomous alterity but *externality* — that is, what is more superficial when compared to the interiority of self, but not discontinuous from the self. As the text says (*ZZ*, 31.4): 'If you do not perfect your own person but make demands on others, is that not superficial?' For these reasons, the *Zhuangzi*'s indifference to the social dimension of ethics has been seen as apolitical throughout the centuries. But as an ethical attitude, this refusal of politics is nonetheless radical, because it does not perpetuate power relationships by entering into their network to try to re-negotiate them, but refuses power *in toto*. In Billeter's words (2004: 95): 'Il n'y a pas de *bon* pouvoir chez lui [*Zhuangzi*].'

Although the idea of indifference in the *Zhuangzi* means unconcernedness about moral judgments, social perception and power, paradoxically, indifference is brought about through the great concern for cosmic order, which is not indifferent itself. This paradox will be better understood when we see how the *Zhuangzi*'s ideas may shed light on Michaux's articulations of indifference. Michaux's works often engage with the experience of an overwhelming and annihilating grandeur of the cosmos that translates into a transhuman ethics similar to the *Zhuangzi*'s heavenly indifference. For example, Michaux is obsessed with the sea, as well as with the oceanic mystic feeling that the sea and other powerful natural phenomena trigger in him. Certainly, one way to understand this obsession is to recognize the sea as one of the most recurrent poetic clichés, which also ties in closely with the fluidity of Michaux's language, the Heraclitean image of incessant flux, and the formlessness of life. A different approach to understanding the sea in Michaux, however, can be made by thinking about it as the embodiment of the indifference of cosmic ethics. This is evidenced by Michaux's return to the sea again and again, awed and overwhelmed by its vastness, wonderstruck by its change, pensive and melancholy when contemplating its indifference to time and its travellers. In *Ecuador* (1929: 190–91), Michaux writes:

> L'Océan. Bien sûr, tout le monde y a passé, les Phéniciens, les Chinois; les galères romaines y étaient, le *Mauretania,* il y a une heure. Oui, mais il ne garde pas la trace. Cette putain est toujours vierge.
>
> Il y a dans la monotonie une vertu bien méconnue, la répétition d'une chose vaut n'importe quelle variété de choses, elle a une grandeur très spéciale et qui vient sans doute de ce que la parole ne peut que difficilement l'exprimer.

> [The Ocean. Certainly, everyone has traversed it: the Phoenicians, the Chinese; the Roman galleys were there, the *Mauretania*, an hour ago. Yes, but no trace is left on it. This whore is always virgin.
>
> In monotony there is a virtue that is hardly recognized: the repetition of a single thing is as good as no matter what variety of different things; repetition has a very particular greatness that originates undoubtedly from that something which words can express only with difficulty.]

Here, Michaux marvels that all the events, temporal and spatial changes that came to pass on the ocean have left no imprint on it. The ocean is more ancient than history but fresher than anything else, having endured throughout the centuries in fundamentally the same form whereas the Phoenicians, Chinese and Romans who traversed it have long disappeared. The waves repeat themselves incessantly, yet by repetition they renew themselves. Repetition then becomes a virtue that maintains the sea's vitality. The startling juxtaposition of 'putain' and 'vierge' accentuates the feeling of exasperation and helplessness on the part of humans: the sea is free from the deterioration and moral evaluations that humans suffer. Measured against the sea's quasi-eternity, human life and its significance are minimal. This infinite endurance and intemporality of the sea in fact make the perfect image of indifference. The sea's strength and vitality precisely lie in remaining indifferent and unaffected, despite the upheavals of human civilization.

What then is the ethical significance of this oceanic indifference according to Michaux? It is already implied in the above quotation: by ceaselessly repeating and renewing itself, the sea always preserves itself as it is ('toujours vierge') and lets nothing add to or subtract from it. 'La mer résoud toute difficulté', Michaux says

(1929: 31), it is the paradigm of self-perfection. And self-perfection is the biggest obsession in Michaux's quest for ethics. He sees the sphere as the symbol of divinity for its perfection (1978b: 112): 'Dieu est boule. Dieu est. Il est naturel. Il doit être. La perfection est. C'est lui'; and he declares that his relationship with others ultimately aims at self-perfection (1929: 103): 'Une fois pour toutes, voici: Les hommes qui n'aident pas à mon perfectionnement: Zéro.' ('Once for all, this: The people who do not help me reach my perfection: Zero.') In the *Zhuangzi* we already find this affirmation of self-cultivation as an ethical act per se, and in fact, as anthropologists Jain and Kripal (2009: 204) demonstrate in their study of Jain quietism, ethics can be about 'becoming more perfect' rather than action'. The Jain tradition that upholds quietism as supreme ethics, for example, shows that action towards improving the world is not necessary a part of all ethical philosophies. For Michaux, therefore, the sea's indifference to human ephemerality manifests an ethics of self-perfection that humans may aspire to. Paradoxically, ultimate indifference comes only after fulfilling the desire for it — although this 'desire' is not a desire in the conventionally-accepted sense of 'wanting to have', but is 'wanting not to care about any kind of having'. Despite starting from self-perfection, one finally arrives at the disappearance of identity in cosmic impersonality, experiencing 'la divine perfection de la continuation de l'Être à travers le temps, continuation qui est [...] belle à s'évanouir' (Michaux 1964: 78) ('the divine perfection of the continuity of Being through time, a continuity that is...so breathtakingly beautiful). In its continuation with everything, the self becomes indifferent to itself and dissolves. In this way, the correspondence between the sea and the individual in Michaux subverts the Romantic poetic vision of the sea as self-reflection and reinforcement.

The *Zhuangzi* offers the view that ethics is cosmic rather than social, and that nonhuman existences such as natural phenomena are exemplary embodiments of philosophical indifference. These ideas, when used to reflect upon Michaux's predilection for the sea as the perfect indifferent existence, bring out the understanding that for Michaux also, ethics is concerned with integrating in the entire natural order rather than acting as an agent in the network of society. Michaux values indifference because it returns him, as a locus of sensations, to the primordial experience of *un*differentiatedly existing in the world. He is recurrently wonderstruck at the indifferent immensity and eternity of the universe: 'L'affaire de l'univers [...] semble en effet cohérente, mais pour peu de temps et elle redégringole vite dans l'abîme indifférent' (1966a: 337). ('The events of the universe [...] indeed seem to be coherent, but only for a short time and they quickly fall back into the indifferent abyss.') Experiencing this abyssal universe is both frightening and ecstatic. One often loses all selfconsciousness and melts into a pure experience of the instant, similar to drowning in the sea:

> Je savais encore des choses de mon corps, mais je ne l'occupais plus, ou si peu, et comptant pour si peu, dans ce grandiose présent, qu'extasié je voyais vivre avec une majesté pharaonique (1964: 78).
>
> [I was still somewhat aware of my body, but I no longer occupied it, or so minutely — it amounting to so very little — that I, in this magnificent present, in an ecstasy, saw what it is truly to live, with pharaoh-like majesty.]

These experiences affirm Michaux's belief that man is above all a cosmic rather than social being, which explains why he makes an ethical claim based on cosmology when he writes didactically that one must hold onto one's fundamental cosmic roots:

> Cependant n'oublie pas que c'est au monde, au monde entier que tu es né, que tu dois naître, à sa vastitude.
>
> À l'infini ton immense, dure, indifférente parenté (1981b: 28).
>
> [Meanwhile don't forget that it is to the world, to the whole world that you are born, that you should be born, to its vastness.
>
> Ad infinitum may your immeasurable, difficult and indifferent genealogy be.]

Infinity, vastness, entirety — all these impersonal traits of the cosmos are, in Michaux's view, people's natural affinities, i.e. 'parenté'. It seems that human life would do best to model itself after the unselfconscious existence of the sea, the sky and stars — given that this can be considered an ethics. Like the Zhuangzian sages who model themselves after the meta-ethics of heaven and become impersonal like natural phenomena, Michaux also wants ultimately to become an eternal, perfect and indifferent existence like the 'monde entier', or the eternal virgin of the sea.

Michaux's preferences in both literary creation and life attitude attest to his appreciation of the indifference of nature. He reflects upon his own literary and artistic activities and concludes that only an indifferent writer who dispenses with the attachment between his person and work can make remarkable creations. 'L'indifférence étant l'état d'inspiration se retrouve dans l'œuvre achevée. L'indifférence qui est à la racine est aussi dans le fruit' (2000: 155). ('As the state of inspiration, indifference lies in the finished work. Indifference which is at the root but also in the fruit.') Meaningfully, Michaux uses a plant metaphor for indifference, thus emphasizing the vegetal, natural and un-self-aware character of artistic creation in an inspired and impersonal state. Noël's insightful remark that Michaux's literary quest is about 'comment écrire sans être un écrivain' (in Michaux 2000: 11) ('how to write without being a writer') reveals Michaux's authorial indifference. Ideally, it seems, writing should be as auto-poietic and unintentional as the growth of plants, there being no 'consanguineous' bond analogous to the parent-child relationship that ties the author to his work. This annihilation of self-awareness, which is essentially an indifference to oneself that matches the indifference of the universe, is also featured in the life attitude that Michaux professes to admire. Michaux has, firstly, an express horror of any kind of entanglement that would jeopardize his indifferent mind-set: 'Hélas, mille fois hélas pour les naissances, dit le Maître de Ho. C'est un enlacement, qui est un entrelacement' (1945: 68). ('Alas! A thousand-fold alas for new births! says the Master of Ho. It is an entanglement, it is an intertanglement.') And he professes (1972: 195): 'Je ne suis pas très doué pour la dépendance.' Instead of a quagmire of bondages, life should be a detached and imperturbable state. Michaux gives various examples of this: the Hindu sage who treats all externality like smoke and is only less indifferent to the world than the cow (1967b: 83, 22): 'Il ne s'occupe pas des autres, mais de *son* salut. [...] Quant à son indifférence vis-à-vis du monde extérieur, là encore [la vache] est supérieure à l'Hindou'; ('He does not worry about others, but about his own deliverance. [...]

As for his indifference towards the exterior world, indeed only the cow surpasses the Hindu in that matter'); and Plume, the classic anti-hero, who, when charged wrongly with his wife's inexplicable murder, goes on sleeping (1978b: 140):

> — L'exécution aura lieu demain. Accusé, avez-vous quelque chose à ajouter?
> — Excusez-moi, dit-il [Plume], je n'ai pas suivi l'affaire. Et il se rendormit.
>
> ['The execution will be tomorrow. Defendant, do you wish to add anything?'
> 'I beg your pardon', he said, 'I haven't followed the case'. And he was back in sleep.]

These examples of indifference in human life point to an existence that, in the *Zhuangzi*'s words (7.5), is like 'a clod of earth', invulnerable as a stone to whatever happens to itself and its surroundings. It is an ethical attitude for Michaux since it could reveal what he instinctually considers the ultimate goodness: 'une sorte d'état pré-personnel, un état "d'avant existence" infiniment archaïque' (Michaux 1972: 168). This view of ethical indifference is akin to ancient Greek philosophies of *ataraxia* ('freedom from disturbance'), exemplified by Pyrrho, who believed that the ideal and most ethical human life would be like 'that of jellyfish' or pigs, with pure sensory reactions and no reasoning (Warren 2002: 124). For 'it is better not to have to go through a process of thought and argument in order to free oneself from the surrounding *pragmata* since that [...] denotes a failure to rid oneself of the necessity to base everything on arguments or theories' (*Ibid.*). Pyrrhonian *ataraxia* well explains Michauldian and Zhuangzian indifference, for it is also an undifferentiated, non-specifically human life without rationalizing principles. A self-contradiction, however, exists here: is not indifference a conclusion arrived at through reasoning about the non-necessity of reasoning? And if one is truly indifferent, one would be indifferent to indifference rather than see it as a desirable state. But this non-indifference to indifference of Michaux's also reveals much about his thought and oeuvre, since often, despite his acclamations to imperturbability and perfect evasion of the ties of this world and existence, he is anything *but* indifferent. How to come to terms with always having to depend on something in order to exist? How *can* one come to terms with it? By refusing food (as his autobiography professes)? — wrapping food up in little parcels, these invaders of his body — for burial? Why must one endure the burden of one's own body — *despite* being able to experience it in fragments, in a pulp, in atomized sensory points? But no, even the lightest body, dispersing like wind, would still gasp from suffering with its dying breath. This is one of the important lessons Michaux learned in his experience in *Epreuves, exorcismes 1940–1944*. Is it precisely because of his hypersensitivity to pain — a neuroticism of existence that would feel grazed even by the touch of a butterfly's wing — that Michaux yearns for indifference and impersonality? And yet, could this hypersensitivity and yearning of indifference have taught Michaux to endure so well that he no longer feels enduring is enduring — that he *does* experience, from time to time, moments of the indifferent state that he admires? Unlike the *Zhuangzi*'s sages, it is in this state of paradox and not being able to come to terms with what one has already come to terms with, that Michauldian indifference is played out.

In fact, indifference is the counterpart in ethics to trivialism in logic, which makes us better understand why the paradox of indifference should occur in Michaux, and to a lesser extent in the *Zhuangzi*. It is important to point out this paradox but there is no need to explain it away. Some difference, however, still exists between indifference to life in reality and indifference to indifference. The former deals with concrete existences, actions and relationships, while the latter is conceptual self-reflection. In other words, the desirability of an ethics and whether this ethics advocates desire or not are different issues: one is meta-ethical evaluation, the other is ethical preference. But precisely because of this paradoxical preference for indifference, although such an ethics clearly transcends the human, seeming to be non-ethical, it remains ethical in the sense that it does not tear down life and action through sceptical questions about what are the bases for ethical decisions. The *Zhuangzi* and Michaux do not discuss how to calculate and arbitrate the best ethical choices; their ethical exemplars simply act in the way most appropriate to themselves, as naturally as a fish swims without being taught how to swim.

The problem of agency

Having discussed how an unintentional but gift-giving and indifferent ethics is possible in the three texts, we now turn to the question of agency, which logically follows the previous analyses, since they already undermine the notions of agent and subject. Firstly, the crucial problem of the possibility of the gift is that there is somebody or something that gives intentionally, consciously, agentially. The comparison of the *Zhuangzi* and Artaud regarding the gift showed that there is no need for the *human* agent who gives, since on the most fundamental level, heaven or nature brings about the unconditional gift of existence. But this does not solve the problem of there being an agent at all, for heaven and cosmic forces can be understood as agents too, which tends towards a theistic understanding that substitutes the human agent with a superhuman one. This issue needs to be addressed because the three texts precisely do not understand cosmic order as an agent with some form of subjectivity or intentionality. Secondly, agency is also an inevitable question that the notion of cosmic indifference raises. An indifferent life is as light and random as seafoam floating and dispersing, but how can this be realized while there is consciousness of one's own actions and of one's own body? If cosmic order is accepted indifferently and impersonally, how is this different from a totally determinist life that rules out the possibility of ethics, since nothing can be changed for better or worse? Is it possible that both fatalism and a naturalist ethics can coexist, and that the body can be lived affirmatively instead of helplessly?

Because discussions of agency usually involve linguistic considerations of the grammatical subject, we may start by thinking about how agency is reflected by the linguistic medium. Here, comparative linguistic analysis is particularly relevant to considering the problems of the agential implication of the verb, notably the difference between the existential and copulative uses of 'to be'; the grammatical subject and the notion of subjectless action; and the middle voice and its philosophical implications. These problems arise from the linguistic constitution of the idea of agency. Our questions are whether agency exists apart from human and theistic agency, and whether agency necessarily involves subjectivity. In much of European thought, agency depends upon rational choice and intention to exist. This unavoidably posits a subject that thinks and acts as well as an object that is acted upon, and presupposes that only beings who have subjectivity, such as humans and gods, can be agents. Such a subjective, rational and human agency is, however, significantly absent in Artaud, Michaux and the *Zhuangzi*. Does this mean that these texts attribute agency to a theistic power, namely, that nature and cosmic order are understood as divine agents with subjectivity? Or is there an agency that is neither human nor theist, and which can be effectuated without subjectivity? If so, the notion of agency is either expanded or abandoned. Since the three texts support the idea of an impersonal, amoral and unselfconscious cosmic order, a theistic agent cannot be affirmed. So what about the second possibility? In fact, the idea of the subjective agent is to a large extent rooted in the grammatical construction of the verb predicate, especially the verb 'to be'. In the modern understanding, 'to be' has two main functions: serving as a copula that links the grammatical subject and its predicate, and as a predicate itself asserting the existence of the subject. But the existential use of 'to be' is, as many scholars have pointed out (Kahn 2009, Graham 1986, John Stuart Mill 1843), a deviation from the earlier copulative use and confusingly asserts being as an abstract entity per se, 'which is not to be anything definite at all' (Kahn 2009: 4). Aristotle gives an example as support (cited in Kahn 2009: 47): 'Homer is something (say, a poet). Does it follow that he is? No, for the "is" is predicated accidentally of Homer; for it is because he is a poet, and not per se, that the "is" is predicated of Homer'. Thus the statement X is Y only shows the relationship between X and Y, but asserts neither the existence of X nor of Y. In other words, the grammatical subject of 'to be' is not necessarily a *de facto* subject or an agent of the act of existence.

If we now consider the problem of withdrawing the subjective and theistic understanding of agency by thinking the impersonal 'there is something' instead of 'something/someone makes something happen', the subjective and agential force of 'something' in the first sentence is clearly reduced, for 'there is something' can be easily rephrased as 'something is somewhere/something else'. As Kahn shows (2009: 113), in ancient Greek, the verb 'to be': *esti,* has the same copulative function in '*Esti polis Efyri myxoi Argeos*' ('there is a city Ephyre in the corner of Argos') and 'Ephyre is a city' (*Efyri polis esti*). Although *esti* has an existential implication in the first sentence, that relates to the interpretation and metaphysics of the verb *esti*, which is a matter different from though not unrelated to *esti*'s syntactical meaning and function: '*to be* is *to be something/ somewhere*' (Kahn 2009: 4). Turning to 'there is' — as in Heidegger's *Es gibt*, which re-understands Being not as some ultimate being, but Being *as such*, so that we can say 'It gives, there is Being' (*Being and Time*: 212), or Lévinas's *il y a* (1981: 105) which denotes 'évènements impersonnels' but is also 'présence de l'absence' — the problem for them seems to be that there is still a proxy *Es* or *il* acting instead of the theological subject. But the crux of this problem is elsewhere, for it stems from the overlap of the copulative and existential, or grammatical and metaphysical uses of 'to be'. As Smith explains, by using *Es gibt*, 'instead of getting lost in the traditional term Being with its metaphysical baggage, we merely say, "There is/It gives" instead of "Being is"' (Smith 2007: 213). Nevertheless, ultimately 'we are still stuck waiting for It to "do" something or other. It may be true that in the idea *It gives* we have a concept that does not think It as the ground of beings, as did metaphysics. Nor do we think It as itself a being. Perhaps that means we have avoided metaphysics. But we are most certainly still thinking It as ultimate *aitia*, cause, ground, *arche*, even if It is a total *Abgrund*' (Smith 2007: 214). How can this lingering of the subjective agent be avoided? There could be two ways of rethinking the problem. First, a commonly accepted approach is to point out that the problem of the subject is determined by language, especially the grammar of Indo-European languages where the grammatical subject is usually attributed agency by the verb predicate. Except for avalent verbs that have neither subject nor object, such as 'piove' in Italian and '[it] rains' in English where an impersonal expletive pronoun is necessary, verbs predicate the subject and establish the link between subject and agency, so philosophical arguments that use these linguistic structures cannot escape from this link, as is illustrated by Nietzsche's claim that (*TI*: III.5) 'we are not getting rid of God because we still believe in grammar'. If we change, however, to a language that does not rely fundamentally on the verb, linguistically-restricted metaphysical problems could disappear. For example, in classical Chinese, the verb *you* 有 — meaning 'there is', '[the world] has' ('the world' functioning only as an expletive), 'to exist', 'to happen' — is a subjectless verb. That is, *you* predicates nothing. The linguist Harbsmeier thus identifies (2006: 1) *you as* an 'intransitive verb with neither an explicit nor an implicit omitted subject'. In a typical sentence like '*you tian*' 有天, 'there is/ [...] has heaven', *you* neither posits an agent or subject, nor indicates how the thing or action mentioned in the sentence — in this case, heaven — came about. And because *you* is intransitive here, heaven is not an object either. The whole sentence is both subjectless and objectless, neither active nor passive. So for a statement such as '[the world] has (*you*) X', 'the Chinese [language] cannot treat *you* as a predicate' (Graham 1986: 356). Thus, what we understand in '[the world] has (*you*) the myriad things' is that the world, or nature, is not posited as a subject or agent. Although the myriad things are unconditionally given by nature, nature is not understood as a subjective donor, because it is neither a metaphysical nor grammatical subject.

Now emerges the second concern about the grammatical subject, subjectless action, and the agent of action. These three can exist independently of each other, as the example of *you* above shows. We may find another linguistic phenomenon to show that the agent can be separated from the grammatical subject, which appears notably in Sanskrit, for instance in this sentence:

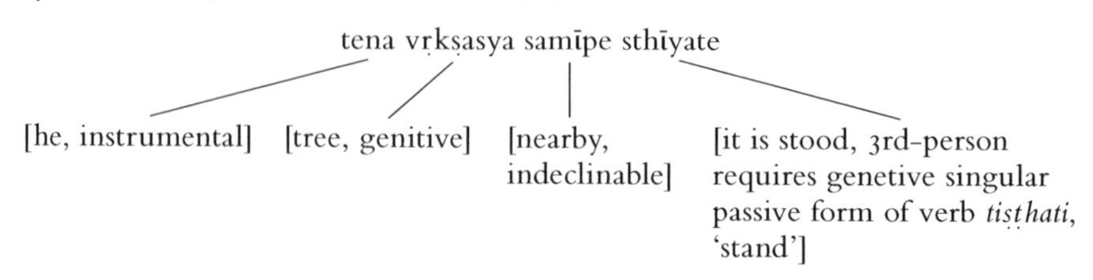

Literally translated, the sentence is 'by him near the tree it is stood', meaning 'he stands near the tree'. The intransitive verb *tiṣṭhati* takes the impersonal third-person singular form in the passive, and the whole sentence has no subject, not even an implied omitted one, since *sthīyate* requires none. There is however the agent of action, 'he', for in Sanskrit the instrumental case can attribute agency. Thus the grammatical subject is not identical with the agent. The fact that grammatically, there is zero subject does not mean there is no corresponding agent in reality; and vice versa, that a grammatical subject exists does not mean it definitely refers to an agent in reality, for example in the case of expletive pronouns. The separation of the grammatical subject from the main verb or action and/or the agent in reality that is referred to shows that the meaning of a sentence can exceed its grammatical structure.

This leads us to the second approach to the problem of the lingering subjective agent, which is opposite to the first approach: i.e. thinking that the problem lies more in the argument and use of language than in grammatical restrictions. So far the first approach involves the view that philosophical arguments are restricted by their linguistic medium, thus an alternative language without certain restrictive structures could open up new philosophical insights. This approach is revealing but also limited, for it has just been shown that the overall meaning of language — taking into account what it refers to both explicitly and implicitly, its context of use and its speaker's intent — exceeds its grammatical meaning. Thus Wittgenstein's argument that meaning and words are defined by 'how they are used' rather than by their syntax and referentiality precisely explains this second approach. If the problem is in understanding the use of language rather than grammatical structures, we can reconsider whether phrases like *Es gibt* and *il y a* really denote, even subtly, an agent or subject. In idiomatic usage, these expressions simply show the occurrence of something in an impersonal and unexplained way. In this aspect, although they syntactically use proxy subjects *Es* and *il*, they are semantically close to *you* in Chinese: they also indicate subjectless action or naturally-occurring happening. Therefore, the grammatical restriction of German and French in *Es gibt* and *il y a* does not need to be taken semantically when we use these expressions to understand philosophically how actions do not necessarily stem from a subject.

In fact, this kind of non-subjective action indicated by 'there is', *you*, or *il y a*, which happens rather than is brought about, can be seen as either a negation of agency — if agency is understood as necessarily subjective and purposeful, or an expansion of the notion of agency to include the non-subjective. These negative and expansive aspects can be combined in a *coincidentia oppositorum*: agency is expanded infinitely so that any particular subjective agency is dissolved, since expanded agency potentially includes all acts and happenings. This is not only a philosophical interpretation, it also has some reflections in grammar, most notably the middle voice, which is my third point in examining the relationship between agency and linguistic construction. As Scott expounds (1989: 752):

> [The middle voice] is able to articulate nonreflexive enactments that are not "for" themselves or "for" something else. As a formation it does not need to suggest intention outside of its movement or a movement toward another. It does not suggest action by which the subject becomes other to itself'.

For instance, in Sanskrit the middle voice (*ātmanepada*) of '"die" (*mriyate*) we translate as "dying occurs (of itself)". Or in the case of "born" (*ayate*), "birthing occurs (of itself)"' (Scott 1989: 746). In modern Greek we have verbs in the middle voice that show 'an intrinsic change or a major alteration' resulting from a certain process (Manney 1992: 214), e.g.: '*ehelisomai*' (X develops), '*aposintithemai*' (X decomposes). These verb forms show 'non-agentive natural events' (Manney 1992: 214). Besides showing action or occurrences that happen unintentionally and impersonally, the middle voice can also mix active and passive meanings by making its grammatical subject both the agent and recipient of action. This is Benveniste's argument (1971: 149): where 'the subject is the centre as well as the agent of the process; he achieves something which is being achieved in him'. Examples can be found in the *parasmaipada* and *ātmanepada* verbs in Sanskrit, which generally indicate the active and middle voices. *Parasmaipada* denotes action for others whereas *ātmanepada* denotes action for oneself or spontaneously occurring action. Thus *yajati* ('sacrifice') means 'one sacrifices for the sake of somebody else', while *yajate* means 'one sacrifices for oneself'. Although most modern European languages do not retain the middle voice, the self-reflexive construction such as 'elle se lave' shows in the same way how the subject both acts and is acted upon. The philosophical implications of the middle voice and self-reflexivity are that actions can happen without being caused by any agential or intentional force, and that there are actions in which the agent and recipient of action coincide.

Although language structures involving the verb predicate and grammatical subject greatly influenced the understanding of agency as subjective in European thought, through comparative linguistics certain misleading connections between subject, agent, and action can be clarified. It is simplistic, however, to embrace either faith in grammar or an ideal alternative to grammar, because meaning and understanding exceed grammar but nonetheless depend upon it to exist. Therefore, both approaches to rethinking agency — using an alternative language to rethink philosophical concepts, and better understanding the meaning of language-in-use despite certain debilitating structures — are necessary. In the light of these ideas, especially the expansion and dissolution of agency, the non-necessity for an agent when an action happens, and the combination and blurring of agent and recipient, the (non-)agency in ethics in Artaud, Michaux and the *Zhuangzi* may be better understood.

Agency and fate

Given their fatalist views in the *Zhuangzi* and Artaud, ethical action cannot stem from an individual subject with free will. This does not, however, render ethical action impossible. In fact, both texts assert that fate does not reduce particular beings to passive objects of subjugation. The *Zhuangzi*'s rigorous fatalist dimension has been recognized: 'nothing is as good [...] as following orders (obeying fate), and this is what makes it so difficult' (Billeter in Slingerland 2003: 208). The text provides evidence for this by stating: 'The commandments from which there is no escape between heaven and earth [...]. The important thing is to fulfil what is ordained for you; and the hardest thing to do is precisely to fulfil one's own fate' (*ZZ*, 4.3). The *Zhuangzi* does not have a naïve idealist belief that one can live without predetermination or circumstantial constraints. Being forced into life, into a particular family and society, in short, all that is unconditionally given at birth, are the 'commandments' one cannot refuse. The text, however, exhorts people to submit to these commandments rather than struggle against them. What is ethical seems to be the coincidence of individual actions and fate. This is emphasized in a passage about a dying sage (*ZZ*, 6.5)

> 'Something presses on my death, but if I refuse to listen to it then it would be defiance, for what fault does that something have? [...] That which made me live well is also that by which I die well. [...] Now if once and for all I see heaven and earth as a great furnace, transformation as a great smelting, why should I object to whatever I will become?'

The sage talks about death and bodily transformation so affirmatively that accepting death is no longer seen as coming to terms with any negativity. There is no negativity in fate, no need for reconciliation or resignation, since the absolute affirmation of fate reflects trivialism on the ethical level, and demands a wholehearted embrace of fate on the individual's part. Zhuangzian fate is not, despite its absolute necessity, a rigid top-down force. It is partly constituted and finally realized by each particular life. The sage's embrace of fate precisely allows the sense of relief and freedom to emerge. This way of liberation by affirming fate is close to the Nietzschean *amor fati*, which is willing exactly what nature, or fate, compels one to do. Nietzsche summarizes this in the subtitle of *Ecce homo* as: 'Wie man wird, was man ist' ('You shall become the person you are'), which takes Rousseau's autobiographical naturalism of the self returning to 'la vérité de la nature' (*Confessions*, I) and redirects it in an anti-individualist sense of fulfilling cosmic law. The best thing for the individual to do is absolute affirmation: 'All in all and on the whole: some day I wish to be only a Yes-sayer' (*GS*: 276). When personal volition and action completely coincide with what is ordained, for Nietzsche as well as the *Zhuangzi*, 'it is not necessary to deliberate or even to make a decision' (Solomon 2002: 81), for fate and freedom become identical. The total embodiment of fate in life makes the particular being both agent and patient, or this *coincidentia oppositorum* can be seen as a dissolution of the active and passive. This is the same logic as that of the middle voice's implications for re-understanding agency. Thus the *Zhuangzi* differs from Nietzsche in that the willing of fate is not even seen as an agential force of the individual but part of the entire active-passive fluid of life. It is also important to note that what Zhuangzian *amor fati* says about ethics on the individual level is not only expanding and/or dissolving agency and subjectivity. There is no sense in advocating fulfilling fate if one will definitely fulfil it in *any* case. To will and act out fate means that one can *not* do so. The *Zhuangzi* sees the refusal of fate as the sure path to self-destruction, for it 'distances you from your instincts and destroys your nature' (*ZZ*, 25.6). On the other hand, considering that 'nothing conquers heaven' (*ZZ*, 6.6) and everything is fate, contradictorily, it seems that refusing fate is ultimately fated too. This is an irresolvable self-contradiction. It may, however, be more understandable if we think that ethics involves what is desirable, not what is logical. Even a trivialist who affirms everything can still have preferences, because affirming everything does not equate to finding everything equally desirable, and having preferences cannot be proved to be non-trivialist either (since for a trivialist, non-trivialism cannot exist). The *Zhuangzi* expresses the desirability of fate, but it is not concerned about justifying this desirability.

If the individual being is an active-passive participant in the actualization of its fate, then on the cosmic level, the question of whether fate is a theistic agent is easily answered. There is no fate external to the particular participant's action, and if the participant is both active and passive, fate is also so. Moreover, fate as the natural principle has an inexplicable and numinous dimension, but it is not an agent enforcing moral codes or having personal concerns about the world. Since it is indifferent, non-subjective and naturally-occurring, it cannot be attributed agency if agency stems from subjectivity. If, however, efficiency in action suffices to make something agential, then impersonal cosmic principles can be regarded as agents too. A passage about the inexplicable *dao* shows the idea of a supremely effective force from which actions spring, but which is not an intentional agent (*ZZ*, 6.3):

> As for the *dao*, it is something of reality [...] but does nothing purposefully. [...] It can be embodied but not seen. It is its own root. [...] The sun and moon embodied it and they shine constantly throughout the ages; [...] Pengzu [a man of legendary longevity] embodied it and lived long.

The *dao* is not defined but the way it works is shown. It can bring about beneficent things, such as the regular light of the sun and moon, and extreme longevity. But this happens not on purpose, for the *dao* is unintentional and not a concrete thing that can be pinpointed as a subject. On the other hand, the ethical value of the good actions of beings that embody the *dao* does not fundamentally lie in these particular beings but in the *dao* embodied in them. This suggests that the myriad existences are like empty vessels that can receive the *dao*, and that the *dao*'s ethical value seems to be something external to all existences but which can be given to anything once it is embodied. Ethics seems to become a gift in itself, although it does no giving. In both ways, it is hardly possible to identify an agent in the conventional sense: the being embodying the *dao* is not an ethical agent because what makes it ethical has nothing to do with it; the *dao* is not an ethical agent because it does good deeds without any consciousness or intention. Ethical action here — e.g. the shining of the sun, or Pengzu's act of living long — is subjectless action; whereas the agents of action — e.g. the sun and Pengzu — are not understood in the subject position but as mediums: *through* them the *dao*'s ethics is realized. If we recall the separation of subject, agent and action examined above, the sun and Pengzu would correspond to the instrumental case denoting the agent. Thus we have a good example of an ethics that resides in *relationship* instead of any particular thing or agent. Significantly, this relational ethics is not based on social relationships but on cosmic ones. Agency is minimized in the particular but maximized in the macrocosmic, for it is diffused in a non-subjective, non-anthropocentric and infinite network of relationships.

The *Zhuangzi*'s ideas of subjectless ethical action, non-theistic fate and *amor fati* reappear in Artaud's thought. Artaud is also a thinker of necessity rather than of freedom, as demonstrated in chapter three in the inevitable principle of 'Cruauté'. But is 'Cruauté' an agent? And is 'soumission à la nécessité' resignation on the human being's part (IV: 158)? Seen earlier, 'Cruauté' is not the substitute of an agentive god figure, since it represents natural principles. Even when Artaud mentions a divine figure that appears in the creator's role, agency is totally denied to it (IV: 122): 'Le dieu caché quand il crée obéit à la nécessité cruelle de la création qui lui est imposée à lui-même, et il ne peut pas ne pas créer.' ('The hidden god when creating obeys the cruel necessity of the creation, which he imposes on himself, thus he cannot not create.') The god-creator here has no free will, no choice in creating or not. He is also subordinated to 'Cruauté' and has no more freedom than the beings he creates. Nevertheless, does 'Cruauté' have a subjective agency alternative and superior to the theological one? Artaud gives a precise answer: there exists 'au-dessus des dieux la loi inconsciente [...] de la Nature' (VII: 265). 'Cruauté' is nature, it has no subjectivity, is unconscious, 'désintéressé, supérieurement humain, [...] sans attaches égoïstes' (VII: 308). Like the naturally-occurring fate in the *Zhuangzi*, Artaud's idea of necessity is impersonal but nonetheless effective. Operating in everything, even 'les dieux', this necessity is an immanent principle like the *dao*, embodied in concrete existences. 'La matière quand elle est bonne [...] s'accomplit jusqu'à ce que son être soit satisfait, son être corps de sa moralité, je dis *moralité* interne au milieu des exigences' (XVIII: 107). ('When matter is good it completes itself to the point when its being is satisfied, its being is the body of its morality, I say *morality* internally existing within constraints.') Artaud believes that morality is an inherent quality that emerges from necessity ('exigences'), and matter that embodies the principles of necessity is naturally orientated towards completing its inherent moral quality. Using the *Zhuangzi* to think about this 'morality', ethical value exists also in the relationships between the cosmic principle, its medium of embodiment, and its subsequent realization. Grossman remarks that (2004: 18) 'la Cruauté incarne un [...] *lien vivant'*. Although she reads 'Cruauté' as a principle of movement that 'defigures' forms and destroys categories, her observation can also be read as a recognition of the relational and embodying aspects of 'Cruauté'.

The ethics of 'Cruauté' lies in cosmic relationships and embodiment rather than divine agency. Its embodiment in human life is especially important for Artaud, for although humans bear the burden of necessity, Artaud thinks that we should bear it willingly. Firstly, it is well noted that Artaud abhors the notion of individual free will, as in his depreciation of Sartre and in his recurrent attacks on the ideology of freedom:

> La liberté n'est plus qu'un poncif plus insupportable que l'esclavage (I: 11);
>
> Liberté, liberté, liberté, liberté.
> Brûler l'être de la liberté.
> Il n'y en a pas. [...]
> Et je crois que pour être libre je dois d'abord me déclarer prisonnier
> (XII: 152).
>
> [Freedom is nothing more than a cliché that's even more unbearable than slavery.
>
> Freedom, freedom, freedom, freedom.
> Burn the existence of freedom.
> There is no freedom. [...]
> And I believe that to be free I should first proclaim myself prisoner.]

Asserting free will is, for Artaud, turning a blind eye to necessity and cosmic laws. Ethics cannot stem from a free agent, because the latter does not exist (XVII: 166): 'Il n'y a jamais eu de morale que le besoin et la nécessité.' ('There has never been any ethics other than want and necessity.') In the typical paradoxical language of Christian mysticism claiming that truth comes after surrendering individual will, Artaud says that only after one fully accepts being a prisoner can one become free. But Artaud's understanding of the supreme power of 'Cruauté' is non-theistic, so how are we to understand his paradox of freedom? One understanding could be that of Zhuangzian *amor fati* that absolutely affirms fate and eliminates the alienation of personal volition from necessity. Each particular being becomes as free as the principle of necessity itself, auto-regulating and auto-poietic of its own actions. If freedom is understood as absolute autonomy and non-constraint of the individual subject, Artaud will have none of it. But if freedom means the state of active-and-passive in the particular being embodying natural principles, which becomes the *radix ipsius* of all actions, then Artaud embraces it as an infinitely greater freedom. The textual evidence supporting this view is found as follows:

> La Force de la *Nature* est la Loi, et cette Loi est la *Nature des choses* qui de toute façon fait la Loi, qu'on l'accepte ou qu'on le nie. Et c'est Nous, aussi, qui avons fait la Loi et sommes que nous le veuillons ou non les responsables et les complices de la Loi.
> C'EST AINSI et IL N'Y a Rien A FAIRE.
> Le nier c'est nous nier nous-même (VII: 287–88).
>
> [The Strength of *Nature* is the Law, and this Law is the *Nature of things* which upholds the Law by all means, regardless of whether you accept it or deny it. And We are the ones, moreover, who have made the Law and, whether we like it or not, we are accountable for and complicit with the Law.
> IT IS SO and NOTHING CAN BE DONE.
> To deny it is to deny ourselves.]

Natural principle is in the nature of things. We embody this nature and thus partly constitute the natural principle, therefore we should coincide with the principle rather than deny it.

> L'effort est une cruauté, l'existence par l'effort est une cruauté (IV: 160).
>
> Il ne suffit pas d'accuser le destin, il faut agir en fait à la main et au moule (XX: 454).
>
> [Effort is a form of cruelty, to exist] by effort is a form of cruelty.]
>
> [It is not enough to blame fate; we must act by putting our hand to the plough.]

The existence of necessity does not mean one should not act and wait passively for things to happen. Existence demands effort, which is also necessity. The effort to embody and act the cosmic law could lead to the greater freedom that is 'libre de moi' (XII: 100).

In sum, both the *Zhuangzi* and Artaud find an inherent ethics in the cosmic order of fate itself. This ethics is relational and involves an infinitely diffused, non-exclusively human agency, or efficiency, which is impersonal and unselfconscious. Humans can become ethical agents only in this expanded sense of agency. More accurately, humans are ethical mediums by embodying invisible laws. The body, however, is the most substantial and self-conscious basis for human existence, for it inevitably acts and feels, thus giving one the sense of agential power. How we live our bodies as vessels of cosmic order therefore merits more examination. This will be further explored in the connection between agency and the body in the *Zhuangzi* and Michaux, since for them, the body is the crucial site for ethics, although it is not an intentional agent.

Agency and the body

Many commentaries on the *Zhuangzi* have singled out the body as the primary site of self-cultivation and regulation in ethics, so it seems that the text fully affirms bodily agency.[3] The idea of any individual bodily agency is, however, questionable, even if the body is simultaneously asserted as the ethical site par excellence. For the *Zhuangzi*, the universe is constituted by the one pervasive cosmic breath (*qi*), which moves spontaneously and transforms unpredictably. The body is a congelation of *qi* and moves in the same unprincipled, unselfconscious and non-teleological way. By embodying the principle of *qi*, the body is ethical. But the body also brings about acute self-awareness. How can we live our body in a spontaneous way without the effort or desire to control it? Let us first consider some examples of the spontaneous body in the *Zhuangzi*. As in this advice on body cultivation (*ZZ*, 11.4):

> You have only to act naturally without deliberation and things will transform by themselves. Smash your form, spit out your hearing and eyesight, forget things and their borders, and join the great continuity in the vast cosmic breath. Undo your intentions, [...] be blank, [...] and be in undifferentiated chaos.

Body cultivation is directed towards a formless, oblivious and indistinguishable body that merges of its own accord with the changes of cosmic forces. This fusion with the 'undifferentiated chaos' is an outcome of forgetting one's sensorial and cognitive functions. The body becomes a piece of malleable matter in the auto-generating process of cosmic transformation. In this state, bodily actions do not need to be controlled by intention, or subjectivity, but flow from the self-changing process of life force that automatically adjusts to circumstances and bodily conditions. As an ingenious swimmer describes how swimming is a naturally-occurring action for him (*ZZ*, 19.10):

> 'I grew up with my nature, and let things come to completion with fate. I enter the water with its swirls and come out with its reflux, following along the way the water goes and not thinking about myself. This is how I stay afloat.'

The swimmer 'forgets the water' (*ZZ*, 19.4) and becomes part of its flow. Precisely because he completely yields to the water and does not treat his own body as an *objectum*, he swims effortlessly. Brian Bruya (2010) calls this the 'flow experience', which shows a body unconscious of goals, or an 'autotelic' body for which actions are 'intrinsically rewarding' (Jochim in Ames 1998: 63). Other real-life examples could be the body of a musician immersed in performing, or of someone sunk in vivid imagination and oblivious of himself and his surroundings. The *Zhuangzi* values above all spontaneity in the body, as is demonstrated by many criticisms.

But in addition, spontaneity is valued because it is an exemplary embodiment of cosmic ethics.

Owing to the autotelic ways of living the body, the body's agential power is called into question. The distanciation between the body and the agency of bodily actions is in fact rooted in the question of whether 'I have my body' or 'I am my body'. The split between these two views represents two major philosophical outlooks in Western thought, which are, in Žižek's view (2004), the Cartesian and the phenomenological views. Although this problem does not emerge in the *Zhuangzi*'s context, the text shows some insights that can be used to approach this question. As in this dialogue (22.4):

> Shun asked Cheng: 'Is it possible to find and possess the *dao*?'
>
> 'You do not even possess your body, how could you possibly possess the *dao*!'
>
> 'If I do not possess my own body, then who does?'
>
> 'It is a form lent to you by heaven and earth. [...] You do not possess your nature and fate, they are orientations lent by heaven and earth. You do not possess your offspring, they are cast-off skins lent by Heaven and earth. [...] All these are the workings of the powerful *qi*, [...] how could they be possessed?'

In Kohn's words (in Littlejohn and Dippmann 2011: 170), 'here it is made very clear that the body is part of a larger entity that we have no possession or control over'. Although I live my body, I do not have it. As an existence I am fully embodied, but this embodiment is not monitored by my subjectivity. Moreover, my body is 'a form lent' to me, which means it does not constitute my identity, for I am not my body either. The answer to the Cartesian and phenomenological questions on the subject and body is clear: I neither have nor am my body. And for the *Zhuangzi*, this 'I' stands for no metaphysical self, since 'I' only denotes a certain position, being 'blank' and 'undifferentiated' (*ZZ*, 11.4). Thus, my body is neither object nor subject; it is not a subjective agent but a medium through which actions take place. Its agential power lies in the workings of a field of connections and not on any entity.

Michaux's thought on body and ethical agency seems at first very different from the *Zhuangzi* because Michaux's expressions give the impression of accentuating the individuality and self-consciousness of the body. As is well known, the body is of primary importance to Michaux. Given Michaux's meticulous and obsessive observations of bodily sensations and changes in his drug writings, and his fantasies about the body torn into fragments, or being run over by a truck (Michaux 1949: 70), we understand that bodily suffering is, for Michaux, the acutest evidence of physio-psychic existence: 'Quand je ne souffre pas, me trouvant entre deux périodes de souffrance, je vis comme si je ne vivais pas' (1949: 110). ('When I am not suffering, finding myself between two phases of suffering, I live as if I were not living.') The body is Michaux's most intimate space of experience, the most concrete affirmation of being alive. But do these views affirm the body as a subjective agent? Upon closer examination of Michaux's images of the body, one striking example is that of an atomistic cell, an amoebic existence (1949: 110), an ephemeral bubble in currents of water (1973: 130), or a floating and weightless object ready to dissipate at a gust of wind (1978b: 41). These images characterize a body that lacks active will, agency, and self-command. Athough Michaux's body sometimes suffers terrible fragmentation and discomfort, both in reality and imagination, his pain is often observed impersonally rather than felt personally. For example, he uses 'il' to refer to himself when talking about the feeling of fragmentation after drug intake (1961: 181): 'Après l'injection de mescaline, de L.S.D. 25, de psilocybine, [...] Il ne peut plus en éprouver la variété, la masse, la présence.' ('After injections of mescaline, L.S.D. 25, and psilocybin, [...] he could no longer feel differences, quantity or presence.') Although it is Michaux's body, it is extracted from him, and melts away into an absence without any unity of action or thought. In addition to this loss of any substantial and coherent experience of the body, in *Infini turbulent* Michaux professes a loss of consciousness and feels like being in a dream where one sees oneself killed (1964: 10):

> On a perdu la conscience de ses points d'appui, de ses membres et organes, et des régions de son corps, lequel ne compte plus, fluide au milieu de fluides. On a perdu sa demeure.
>
> [One has lost the consciousness of one's supporting points, of one's limbs and organs, and the sections of one's own body, which do not matter any more, being liquid amongst liquids. One has lost one's abode.]

Michaux's somatic experiences seem to be intimate, but are in fact remote, for an infinite distance separates him from his body. This is also the main cause of his rage and despair when it comes to bodily pain. It would have been better if he could suffer in and as his own body, yet he only suffers *via* his body (or is it really his any more?). If the *Zhuangzi*'s idea that one neither has nor is the body is transferred to Michaux's distantiated corporeal experience, we may say that for Michaux also, his body is neither an object of possession and control, nor a constituent of identity. The main point that Michaux makes is that these bodily sensations are experienced, but this does not reveal anything about possessing or being the body. In fact, the body and its experience become so impersonal that Michaux considers the body a site of energetic interactions rather than subjective feelings (1964: 181): '[Il] n'est plus un corps, n'est plus évocable, n'est plus sien, n'est plus qu'un lieu.' ('It is no longer a body, it can no longer be called forth, it is no longer his body, it is nothing more than a place.') Consequently, the relationship between the body-as-site and consciousness is that of interdependence rather than identity, for body and consciousness are distanced to a certain degree from each other yet function on the condition of each other's existence. On the one hand there is panpsychic cosmic consciousness that is embodied; on the other hand the body-as-site is a medium through which this consciousness emerges. Because the body operates in a network of cosmic relationships and principles, it is no longer a definite form but extends into its multiple relationships and their interactions. In this way, the Michauldian body can be experienced impersonally, and cannot be agential in the sense of consciously and rationally choosing its actions.

But how can we read ethics into such a body? If the *Zhuangzi* sees ethical value in the spontaneous non-teleological body, does Michaux see the impersonal and unmonitored body as ethical too? To start with, Michaux does not show any dislike of such a body. In fact he embraces it and professes to prefer living like a sleepwalker or daydreamer rather than a rational Cartesian. For instance, he highly appreciates 'la rêverie':

> Rêverie du rêveur devenu plus semblable à un fluide qu'à un homme, torrent plein d'éclaboussements et d'éclairs.
>
> *Un champ de forces, voilà le rêve vigile*; [...] rêverie à quoi pourtant je dois tant, je dois presque tout (1969: 202, 232).
>
> [The reverie of the dreamer has become more like a liquid than a man, a torrent full of splashes and sparks.
>
> *A field of energies, that's the wakeful dream*; [...] the reverie, to which I nonetheless owe so much, to which I owe almost everything.]

On another occasion, when Michaux accidentally discovers that some drugs switched off his normal consciousness and gave him a sudden revelation of the 'inconscience journalière' (1966b: 11), he is enraptured to think that the deep 'mechanisms' of the body and mind exist unconsciously. This unconsciousness is, for Michaux (1966b: 9), a part of bodily existence that is 'le méconnu, l'insoupçonné, l'incroyable, l'énorme normal'. It is always present but put into a slumber or suppressed by normal vigilance. Michaux's view here echoes the parapsychologist Méheust's description of the body's latent physiopsychic powers that surface during hypnosis (1999: 141):

> Pendant le jour les étoiles sont invisibles, bien que leur lumière parvienne à nos yeux; mais elles redeviennent visibles après le coucher du soleil. De même, le sens interne demeure actif, mais de façon imperceptible, pendant la veille; il ne se manifeste que pendant la transe.
>
> [During daytime stars are invisible, although their light reaches our eyes; but they become visible again after sunset. In the same way, the inner understanding remains active in the waking state, but imperceptibly; it is only manifested in the state of trance.]

Hypnosis does not, in Méheust's view, add anything to the somnambulist's existing physiopsychic capacities, but sets into motion what is normally invisible and repressed by the controlling ego. This view coincides surprisingly with Michaux's view on the body's hidden and unselfconscious powers and operations, for cannot the abnormal physiopsychic states which Michaux describes and experiences be read as moments of somnambulism, or as the unveiling of a deep unconscious knowledge that parallels that of somnambulists? According to parapsychologic studies, somnambulism is typically manifested in extraordinary abilities like clairvoyance and claircognizance. As Méheust further expounds (1999: 21–24), the activation of these abilities reveals the raw state of the somnambulist's existence, a holistic 'lucidité' of perceiving the whole field of surroundings without self-awareness, an 'excès de l'homme sur lui-même'. Michaux's account of his abnormal states in fact fits very well with the cases Méheust describes.

> Ma conscience n'arrive pas à s'emparer de ce que je vois, mon œil distingue, mais mon intellect laisse le tout ensemble, tarde à individualiser l'un après l'autre les éléments du spectacle (Michaux 1966b: 73).

> [...]
> À un point comme celui-là, l'esprit, recueillant "soi" et "non-soi" pareillement, se trouve dans un monisme de fait (1966b: 125).
> Je serais probablement hypnotisable (1975: 77).
>
> [It is beyond my consciousness to grasp what I see; my eye discerns, but my intellect puts aside the whole, and takes time to consider separately the elements of the spectacle one after another.
> [...]
> At such a moment, the spirit, gathering together the 'self' as well as the 'non-self', exists in a de facto monism.
> Probably I could be hypnotized.]

Michaux experiences his body in an extra-mundane, more holistic and radical (understood as 'from the root') reality. He seems to become immersed in an indefinitely large extent of his body that is normally out of reach. Instead of making the body dysfunctional, the cessation of analytical thought and desire for self-control mark the emergence of a profound bodily spontaneity. The Zhuangzian autotelic experience is therefore relevant to understanding Michaux. For it is precisely in this hypnotic and impersonal state of 'abandonment' that Michaux finds his 'demeure' (1975: 88): 'L'abandon, pour moi, meilleur que les actes. Y demeurer.' ('Abandonment is for me better than actions. Just stay there.') Michaux is like the ingenious swimmer who swims effortlessly by yielding instead of striving. These instances of experiencing the larger-than-self body is for Michaux an insight into cosmic integration, which is an intrinsic goodness, as shown in my discussion of indifference (e.g. 'c'est au monde [...] entier que tu es né, que tu *dois* naître' [my italics]). The body merges with and dissolves in infinite space, but is simultaneously most fully oneself (Michaux 1976a: 89):

> Le nuage d'être se condense
> se replie
> Cosmos-Univers
> cosmos de l'univers du 'soi'.
>
> [The cloud of being condenses
> bends back upon itself
> Cosmos-Universe
> cosmos of the universe of the 'self'.]

Despite all the bodily pain and 'revolting' ugliness of life (1966b: III), thanks to the discovery of this cosmic body, Michaux asserts (1976a: 71): 'J'existais en hauteur. Je n'avais pas vécu en vain.' ('I existed in elation. I had not lived in vain.')

To answer, now, the questions about the body and agency in Michaux and the *Zhuangzi*, the texts do not affirm the body as a subjective atomistic agent, but see ethical value in an impersonal, autopoietic and limitlessly diffused body. This notion of the body corresponds to relational ethics, for the body is no longer a unit or entity, but a site of vast potentiality for actions, a connection between connections. Throughout this exploration of agency in the three texts, it is understood that Artaud, Michaux and the *Zhuangzi* offer a rethinking of ethical action by showing how action can be effectuated without subjectivity, and how each particular subjectivity can be infinitely distributed through the whole cosmic system so that it is minimized to almost zero. If ethical agency exists, it would not depend on an individual agent but exists in the interactions of cosmic relationships.

Conclusion

Through the concepts of the gift, indifference and agency, the three texts outline an ethics that is active but not subjective, experienced rather than constructed, relational instead of agential. Remarkably, these texts assert an ethics that is neither exclusively human nor rational, neither normative nor consequentialist. Undeniably, it has its own problematic aspects too. Firstly, it is more meta-ethical than ethical since it goes beyond all norms and definitions; secondly, it is paradoxical in its return of ethics from the imperative to the indicative, as in the self-contradictions of 'you ought to be what you are', or 'better be indifferent than attached'; thirdly, the assertion of cosmic integration as intrinsically good and ethical is arbitrary, for this goodness cannot be justified. Nevertheless, as has repeatedly been shown, Artaud, Michaux and the *Zhuangzi* are not arguing for consistent systems of thought. In fact, they rarely argue at all, for their primary concern is expression, not propositions and persuasion. Although the ethical views they articulate are non-normative, these views are not meta-ethical in the sense of suspending all action because of the lack of ethical criteria. Judging what is ethical is no longer important, since this kind of ethics is non-rational. In regard to its paradox of prescribing ethics in the indicative, this may be understood as a blurring of the 'ought' and 'is' distinction in ethics rather than a logical contradiction. In fact, this paradox manifests the trivialist inclusiveness of opposites, and combines 'is' and 'ought' without eliminating either. This is why there is ethics rather than non-ethics in the three texts, because they do not give up preferences for action and say 'anything goes'. Finally, the arbitrariness of the goodness in cosmic immersion is not a big drawback, for does not the vast majority of ethical philosophy presume arbitrarily what is good — be it happiness, truth, the flourishing of life, one's duty to a higher order, or the preservation of the human species? As Moore points out in his *Principia Ethica*, goodness 'is indefinable' (§13). When asserting 'something is good', we must always resort to something other than 'goodness' to justify goodness, which says nothing about the intrinsic value of goodness itself. Therefore, simply pointing out goodness without defining or justifying it does not automatically invalidate a view on ethics. The main significance of the three texts' views on ethics is their deep rethinking of the conceptual frameworks of ethical thought, not their logical inconsistencies. This rethinking is, of course, only possible when incorporating their heterodox views on rationality, cosmology and nature. The dialogues between these texts thus conclude by envisaging an ethics that includes trivialist stances, naturalist spontaneity, and the cosmic infinitization of ethical relationships.

Notes to Chapter 5

1. Boyi is the legendary exemplar of virtue in early China because he starved himself to death in protest against the new Zhou dynasty and ruler, remaining loyal to the former ruler of the Shang

dynasty despite the fact that he was cruel and violent. Robber Zhi is, in contrast, the legendary rebel of the Warring States period who chose to be a robber despite his noble birth, and outraged society by his violence and non-conformism. He was often depreciated by his contemporaries as an extremely immoral person, and so the *Zhuangzi*'s setting up a parallel between Boyi and Robber Zhi is shocking.

2. See Barber (1993: 82) and Boon (2002).
3. For this view see Kohn (2009), Schipper (1982) and Robinet (1996).

EPILOGUE

We have now come to the end of this dialogue between Artaud, Michaux and the *Zhuangzi*, but in fact the dialogue has just begun. The interaction of these texts created by the comparative frameworks of rationality, cosmology and ethics has revealed that many more possibilities for dialogue with other writers, texts, and perspectives exist. Imagining intercultural and cross-temporal encounters between literatures and thought is always more than imagination, for it can create a new way of understanding as well as a new understanding. In other words, the fictionalization of the space of literature can bring about real effects in interpretation. In the case of this study, new light is shed on some neglected aspects of Artaud, Michaux and the *Zhuangzi*, in particular, their sense of surrationalist epistemology, a holistic interest in scientific thought that is inspired by literary imagination, and a spontaneous ethics that nevertheless needs cultivation. That these texts have much to say about philosophical concepts also shows that they have much philosophical thrust, for they offer ideas that can be clarified and developed further into serious philosophical arguments that have implications beyond the texts themselves. Indeed, in this aspect, the texts show themselves to be capable of participating in contemporary debates of philosophical issues and contributing to them in their own way. The fact that they interact with contemporary theories such as paraconsistency and the anthropology of nature, and coincide with the recent tendency of relational thinking as exemplified by Bourriaud's relational aesthetics (1998) and Latour's (1996) hybrid actants proves their contemporary relevance. They thus offer from the side of literature another means to gain knowledge about these theoretical debates to their readers, who may not be au fait with trends in contemporary philosophical thought. Nevertheless, they do not simply reflect existing views and approaches in theory and philosophy. They possess something more compared to philosophy properly speaking: their free form and expression have infinite potentiality in inspiring thought. The argumentative and logical form that philosophy usually takes is much more restrictive than literature and art, since it is necessarily concerned with justification and causal explanations. Thus philosophy can miss out on interesting and thought-provoking ideas that do not agree with the overall system of argument, or cannot be philosophically formalized. Artaud, Michaux and the *Zhuangzi*, in contrast, do not have these formal limitations because they are not concerned with self-justification but with expression and performativity, which explains their pouring-out of unbridled ideas and words, however wild, absurd or self-contradictory. As Artaud says (V: 242), the thinker cannot fear words, for 'ceux d'ailleurs qui ont peur des mots, sont les mêmes qui ont peur des actes, c'est pourquoi rien n'est jamais fait' ('moreover, those who fear words are also those who fear actions, this is why nothing ever gets done'). The evocative power of these texts gives space to the readers to seek and formulate their own answers and thoughts, which shows how literature can also be approached as philosophy — sometimes in more effective ways than philosophy itself, as Danto asserts (1983: 2). This also accounts for prioritizing the interpretation of ideas and their metaphysical implications over the scrutiny of literary texture, for these texts' stylistic and aesthetic value needs no more assertion whereas their philosophical status is much more debated. In this way, the texture and aesthetics of these texts can be analysed within frameworks of metaphysics instead of more conventional literary criticism that reveals the intricacies of linguistic expressions or re-stages the effects of poetic imagery. This does not suggest, however, that full-fledged theoretical systems can be extrapolated from these texts, since the elusive richness of their thought is irreducible to any final say such as a theory of everything, or even a systematic and self-consistent theory of a particular topic. But refusing a theory of everything can precisely be a strength, for indeterminateness keeps thought alive, as supported by Michaux's view (1963: 52) that 'c'est de réponses que l'homme meurt'.

This book also started with the purpose of discovering a way of studying comparative literature via the case study of reading Artaud, Michaux and the *Zhuangzi* together. Now the study itself already proves the feasibility of a comparative project between different cultures, languages, times and spaces. The comparability between the texts has not been predetermined, but emerged simultaneously with the interpretation of texts through their interactions. More precisely, comparative literature was made possible through specific sites where ideas connect, the role of simply comparing similarities and differences being relatively small. In this sense, comparatism is not so much a method to be defined as one that can be created, depending on the particular conditions of each specific comparison and the critic's chosen perspectives. More importantly, through the creation of this method, new dimensions of thought in the texts are revealed — especially in regard to Artaud's and Michaux's works, which, when introduced to the alterity of the *Zhuangzi*, show their inherent alterity to any self-enclosed tradition of thought as well as their intrinsic potentiality of connecting with or absorbing any thought mode. A prominent example of this is how, when the *Zhuangzi*'s omniperspectivism is read into Artaud's preference for the multiplicity of viewpoints and the allowance of contradiction, Artaud is shown to be much more radical than a straightforward and conventional relativist, for he turns out to be affinitive to trivialism.

Comparative criticism thus takes place as the transformation of its compared elements through the attempt to think alterity, since ultimately, comparison is one way of manifesting the heterogeneity and elasticity of thought, which is potentially open to any otherness. This transformation through alterity not only applies to the difference of the texts and themes that are compared, but also to the interpretative methods used in comparative criticism, for the latter is in fact a method of using diverse methods. As evidenced by this book's borrowing from ideas through comparative analyses of language, anthropological theory, and mathematical philosophy, comparative literary criticism not only designs comparison between texts but also carries out comparison and interaction between methods. Methodological eclecticism is, in fact, a natural outcome of the interdisciplinary nature of comparison. Just as comparative linguistics can reveal certain grammatical problems and their semantic implications better or more easily than studying a language within itself, comparative literature can reveal the space between and connecting different literatures in meaningful ways. I therefore hope that this study has further confirmed the importance of comparison and provided more food for thought for the growing field of interdisciplinary and comparative studies.

BIBLIOGRAPHY

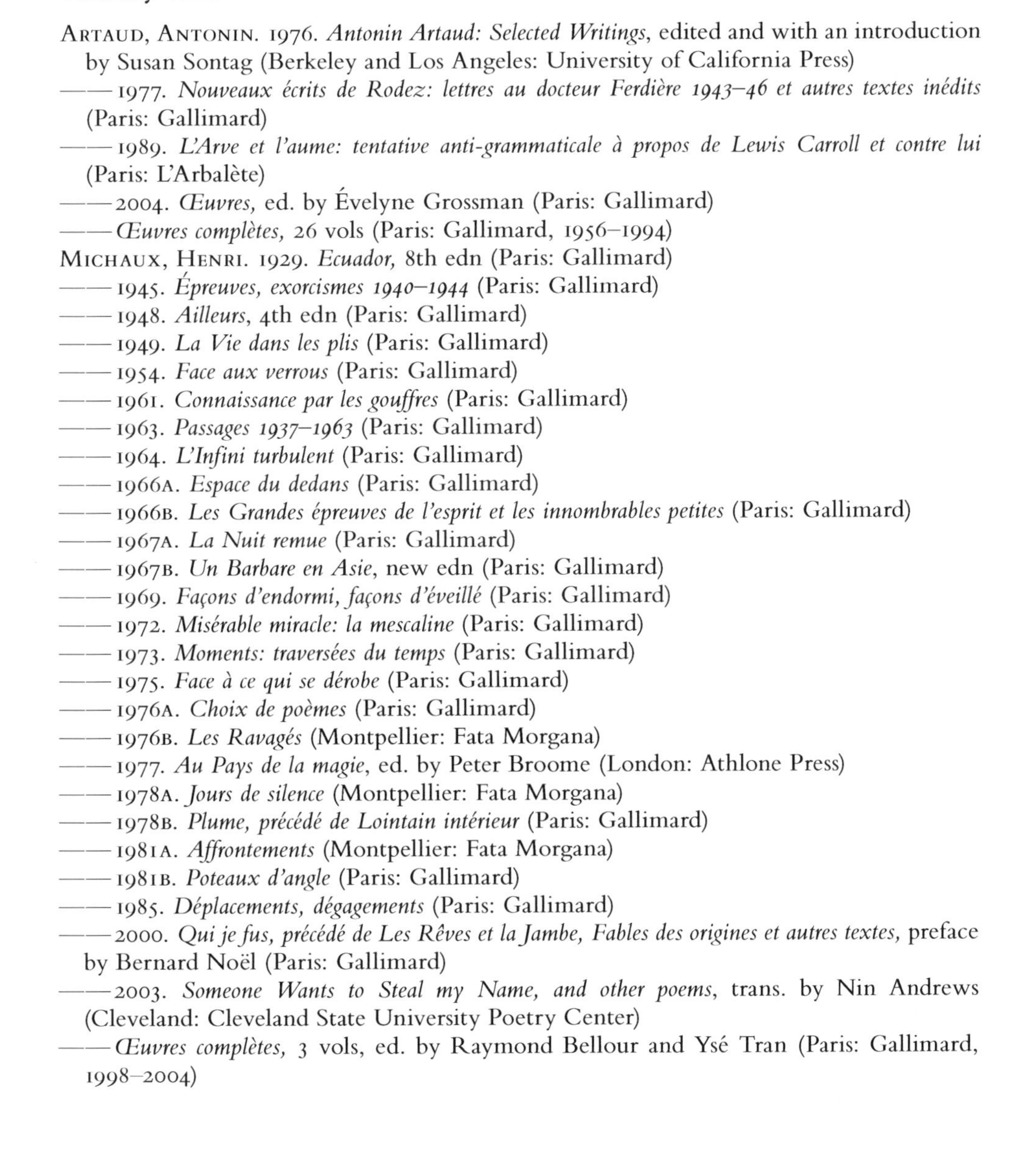

Primary texts

Artaud, Antonin. 1976. *Antonin Artaud: Selected Writings*, edited and with an introduction by Susan Sontag (Berkeley and Los Angeles: University of California Press)

—— 1977. *Nouveaux écrits de Rodez: lettres au docteur Ferdière 1943–46 et autres textes inédits* (Paris: Gallimard)

—— 1989. *L'Arve et l'aume: tentative anti-grammaticale à propos de Lewis Carroll et contre lui* (Paris: L'Arbalète)

—— 2004. *Œuvres*, ed. by Évelyne Grossman (Paris: Gallimard)

—— *Œuvres complètes*, 26 vols (Paris: Gallimard, 1956–1994)

Michaux, Henri. 1929. *Ecuador*, 8th edn (Paris: Gallimard)

—— 1945. *Épreuves, exorcismes 1940–1944* (Paris: Gallimard)

—— 1948. *Ailleurs*, 4th edn (Paris: Gallimard)

—— 1949. *La Vie dans les plis* (Paris: Gallimard)

—— 1954. *Face aux verrous* (Paris: Gallimard)

—— 1961. *Connaissance par les gouffres* (Paris: Gallimard)

—— 1963. *Passages 1937–1963* (Paris: Gallimard)

—— 1964. *L'Infini turbulent* (Paris: Gallimard)

—— 1966a. *Espace du dedans* (Paris: Gallimard)

—— 1966b. *Les Grandes épreuves de l'esprit et les innombrables petites* (Paris: Gallimard)

—— 1967a. *La Nuit remue* (Paris: Gallimard)

—— 1967b. *Un Barbare en Asie*, new edn (Paris: Gallimard)

—— 1969. *Façons d'endormi, façons d'éveillé* (Paris: Gallimard)

—— 1972. *Misérable miracle: la mescaline* (Paris: Gallimard)

—— 1973. *Moments: traversées du temps* (Paris: Gallimard)

—— 1975. *Face à ce qui se dérobe* (Paris: Gallimard)

—— 1976a. *Choix de poèmes* (Paris: Gallimard)

—— 1976b. *Les Ravagés* (Montpellier: Fata Morgana)

—— 1977. *Au Pays de la magie*, ed. by Peter Broome (London: Athlone Press)

—— 1978a. *Jours de silence* (Montpellier: Fata Morgana)

—— 1978b. *Plume, précédé de Lointain intérieur* (Paris: Gallimard)

—— 1981a. *Affrontements* (Montpellier: Fata Morgana)

—— 1981b. *Poteaux d'angle* (Paris: Gallimard)

—— 1985. *Déplacements, dégagements* (Paris: Gallimard)

—— 2000. *Qui je fus, précédé de Les Rêves et la Jambe, Fables des origines et autres textes*, preface by Bernard Noël (Paris: Gallimard)

—— 2003. *Someone Wants to Steal my Name, and other poems*, trans. by Nin Andrews (Cleveland: Cleveland State University Poetry Center)

—— *Œuvres complètes*, 3 vols, ed. by Raymond Bellour and Ysé Tran (Paris: Gallimard, 1998–2004)

Editions and translations of the Zhuangzi

CHEN, GUYING. (ed.). 2009. *Zhuangzi jinzhu jinshi,* 2 vols, 2nd edn (Beijing: Zhonghua Press)
GRAHAM, ANGUS C. (trans.). 1981. *Chuang-Tzu: the Inner Chapters*, repr. 2001 (Indianapolis and Cambridge: Hackett)
WATSON, BURTON. (trans.) 1968. *The complete works of Chuang Tzu* (New York: University of Columbia Press)

Secondary references

AARON, RICHARD. 1971. *Knowing and the Function of Reason* (Oxford: Clarendon Press)
ADORNO, THEODOR and MAX HORKHEIMER. 1995. *The Dialectic of Enlightenment*, trans. by John Cummings (London: Verso)
AKLUJKAR, ASHOK. 2005. *Sanskrit: An Easy Introduction to an Enchanting Language*, 2 vols (Richmond, B. C.: Svādhyāya Publications)
AMES, ROGER T. 1986. 'Taoism and the Nature of Nature', *Environmental Ethics*, Vol. 8: 317–50
——(ed.). 1998. *Wandering at Ease in the 'Zhuangzi'* (Albany: Suny Press)
ARISTOTLE. 350 BCE. *Physics*, trans. by R. P. Hardie and R. K. Gaye, The Internet Classics Archive e-book <http://classics.mit.edu/Aristotle/physics.html> [accessed 7 February 2015]
ATTEBERRY, JEFFREY. 2000. 'Reading Forgiveness and Forgiving Reading: Antonin Artaud's "Correspondance avec Jacques Rivière"', *MLN*, Vol. 115, No. 4: 714–40
AYER, A. J. 1956. *The Problem of Knowledge* (London and New York: Macmillan)
AZÉRAD, HUGO. 2002. 'Investigative Spaces in the Poetry of Pierre Reverdy, Jules Supervielle, and Henri Michaux', *Comparative Literature and Culture* 4.3: 1–11
AZZOUNI, JODY. 2006. *Tracking Reason: Proof, Consequence, and Truth* (New York and Oxford: OUP)
BADOUX, LAURENT. 1963. *La Pensée de Henri Michaux: Esquisse d'un itinéraire spirituel* (Zurich: Juris)
BACHELARD, GASTON. 1936. 'Le Surrationalisme', *Inquisitions*, 1: 1–4
BARBER, STEPHEN. 1993. *Antonin Artaud: Blows and Bombs* (London: Faber and Faber)
——2005. *The Screaming Body* (London: Creation)
BARRETT, NATHANIEL F. 2011. '*Wuwei* and Flow: Comparative Reflections on Spirituality, Transcendence, and Skill in the *Zhuangzi*', *Philosophy East and West,* Vol. 61, No. 4: 679-706
BÉGUELIN, MARIANNE. 1974. *Henri Michaux: esclave et démiurge* (Lausanne: L'âge d'homme)
BENVENISTE, ÉMILE. 1971. *Problems in General Linguistics*, trans. by Mary Elisabeth Meek (Coral Gables: University of Miami Press)
BERGSON, HENRI. 2007. *L'Évolution créatrice*, critical edn (Paris: Presses universitaires de France)
BERKOWITZ, ALAN J. 2000. *Patterns of Disengagement: The Practice and Portrayal of Reclusion in Early Medieval China* (California: Stanford University Press)
BERKSON, MARK A. 2005. 'Conceptions of Self/No-Self and Modes of Connection: Comparative Soteriological Structures in Classical Chinese Thought', *Journal of Religious Ethics,* Vol. 33, No. 2: 293–331
BERMEL, ALBERT. 1977. *Artaud's Theatre of Cruelty* (New York: Taplinger Pub. Co.)
BERTO, FRANCESCO. 2007. *How to Sell a Contradiction: The Logic and Metaphysics of Inconsistency* (London: College Publications)
Bhagavad Gītā, e-book at <http://www.sanskritweb.net/sansdocs/gita-big.pdf> [accessed 7 February 2015]
BILIMORIA, PURUSHOTTAMA, JOSEPH PRABHU and RENUKA SHARMA. (eds). 2007. *Indian Ethics: Classical Traditions and Contemporary Challenges,* vol. 1 (Aldershot: Ashgate)

BILLETER, JEAN-FRANÇOIS. 2002. *Leçons sur Tchouang-tseu* (Paris: Allia)
——2004. *Études sur Tchouang-tseu* (Paris: Allia)
BLANCHOT, MAURICE. 1969. *L'Entretien infini* (Paris: Gallimard)
BLOCH, ERNST. 1990. *The Heritage of Our Times*, trans. by Neville and Stephen Plaice (Oxford: Polity)
BLOCH, OLIVIER (ed.). 2000. *Philosophies de la nature: actes du colloque tenu à l'Université de Paris I, Panthéon Sorbonne* (Paris: Publications de la Sorbonne)
BOLDT-IRONS, LESLIE ANNE. 1996. 'Anarchy and Androgyny in Artaud's *Héliogabale ou L'Anarchiste Couronné*', *The Modern Language Review*, vol. 91, No. 4: 866–77
BONARDEL, FRANÇOISE. 1987. *Antonin Artaud, ou, La fidélité à l'infini* (Paris: Balland)
BOON, MARCUS. 2002. *The Road of Excess: A History of Writers on Drugs* (Cambridge Massachusetts: Harvard University Press)
BOURRIAUD, NICHOLAS. 1998. *Esthétique relationnelle* (Dijon: Presses du réel)
BOWIE, MALCOLM. 1973. *Henri Michaux: A Study of his Literary Works* (Oxford: Clarendon)
BRÉCHON, ROBERT. 1959. *Michaux* (Paris: Gallimard)
——1987. 'Vers la sérénité', in *Europe* 698/699 (Paris: Les Éditions Denoël), pp26–31
——2005. *Henri Michaux: la poésie comme destin* (Croissy-Beaubourg: Aden)
BROGNIET, ERIC. (ed.). 1996. *Les* Ailleurs *d'Henri Michaux,* Actes du colloque Namur, October 1995 (Namur: Revue de la Maison de la Poésie)
BROWN, LLEWELLYN. 2007. *L'Esthétique du pli dans l'œuvre de Henri Michaux* (Caen: Lettres modernes Minard)
BROWN, STEPHEN. 2008. *Moral Virtue and Nature* (London: Continuum)
BRUCHEZ, JACQUES. 2007. *Henri Michaux et Aldous Huxley: deux expériences* (Genève: Slatkine érudition)
BRUN, ANNE. 1999. *Henri Michaux ou le corps halluciné* (Paris: Sanofi-Synthélabo)
BRUNEL, PIERRE 1982. *Théâtre et cruauté: ou Dionysos profané* (Paris: Librairie des Méridiens)
BRUYA, BRIAN. (ed.). 2010. *Effortless Attention: A New Perspective in the Cognitive Science of Attention and Action* (Cambridge, Mass. and London: MIT Press)
BUSSANICH, JOHN. 2010. 'Ethics in Ancient India', in J. Hardy et al. (eds), *Grundlagen der Antiken Ethik/Foundations of Ancient Ethics* (V & R Unipress Gmbh), <http://www.academia.edu/247836/Ethics_in_Ancient_India> [accessed 7 February 2015]
CAHN, STEVEN M. 1967. *Fate, Logic, and Time* (New Haven: Yale University Press)
CAI, ZONG-QI. 2002. *Configurations of Comparative Poetics: Three Perspectives on Western and Chinese Literary Criticism* (Honolulu: University of Hawai'i Press)
CALLICOTT, J. BAIRD and ROGER T. AMES. (eds). 1989. *Nature in Asian Traditions of Thought* (Albany: SUNY Press)
CANALES, JIMENA. 2005. 'Einstein, Bergson, and the Experiment that failed', *MLN,* Vol. 120, No. 5: 1168–91
CARR, KAREN L. and PHILIP J. IVANHOE. 2010. *The Sense of Antirationalism: the religious thought of Zhuangzi and Kierkegaard*, 2nd edn (S. L.: Createspace)
CARRIER, JAMES G. 1995. *Occidentalism: Images of the West* (Oxford: Clarendon Press)
CASANOVA, PASCALE. 1999. *La République mondiale des letters* (Paris: Seuil)
CHAMAYOU, ANNE. 2001. 'Des fourmis et des hommes: pour une "histoire naturelle" de la Chine, selon Henri Michaux', in Christian Morzewski and Linsen Qian (eds), *Les Écrivains français du XXe siècle et la Chine* (Artois: Presses universitaires de Nankin), pp. 161–74
CHAN, ADRIAN. 2009. *Orientalism in Sinology* (Bethesda: Academica Press)
CHANG, WONSUK. 2009. 'Reflections on Time and Related Ideas in the *Yijing*', *Philosophy East and West*, Vol. 59, No. 2: 216–29
CLARKE, J. J. 2000. *The Tao of the West: Western transformations of Taoist thought* (London: Routledge)

Coutinho, Steve. 2004. *Zhuangzi and Early Chinese philosophy* (USA: Ashgate)
Cua, Antonio S. 1977. 'Forgetting Morality: Reflections on a theme in Chuang Tzu', *Journal of Chinese Philosophy*, 4(4): 305–28
Cusa, Nicholas de. 1990. *On Learned Ignorance*, trans. by Jasper Hopkins, 2nd edn (Minneapolis: The Arthur J. Banning Press)
Dainton, Barry. 2010. *Time and Space*, 2nd edn (Durham: Acumen)
Danto, Arthur C. 1965. *Nietzsche as Philosopher* (New York: Macmillan)
—— 1983. 'Art, Philosophy, and the Philosophy of Art', *Humanities*, Vol. 4, No. 1: 1–2
Darcus, Shirley. 1974. '"Daimon" as a Force Shaping "Ethos" in Heraclitus', *Phoenix*, Vol. 28, No. 4: 390–407
Davidson, Donald. 2004. *Problems of Rationality* (Oxford: Clarendon Press)
D'Avray, D. L. 2010. *Rationalities in History: A Weberian Essay in Comparison* (Cambridge: CUP)
Defoort, Carine, and Ge Zhaoguang. 2005. 'Editors' Introduction', *Contemporary Chinese Thought*, 37.1
De Man, Paul. 1979. *Allegories of Reading: Figural Language in Rousseau, Nietzsche, Rilke, and Proust* (New Haven: Yale University Press)
Deleuze, Gilles. 1969. *Logique du sens* (Paris: Minuit)
Deleuze, Gilles and Félix Guattari. 1972. *L'Anti-Oedipe* (Paris: Minuit)
—— 1980. *Mille plateaux* (Paris: Minuit)
Demaitre, Ann. 1972. 'The Theater of Cruelty and Alchemy: Artaud and Le Grand Œuvre', *Journal of the History of Ideas*, Vol. 33, No. 2: 237–50
Derrida, Jacques. 1965. 'La Parole soufflée', in Derrida, *L'écriture et la différence* (Paris: Seuil, 1967), pp. 253–92.
—— 1967. *L'Écriture et la différence* (Paris: Seuil)
—— 1991. *Donner le temps: la fausse monnaie* (Paris: Galilée)
Descola, Philippe. 2002. 'L'Anthropologie de la nature', in *Annales. Histoire, Sciences Sociales*, 57th year, No. 1: 9–25
——2005. *Par-delà nature et culture* (Paris: Gallimard)
Dessons, Gérard. 1993. *Méthodes et savoirs chez Henri Michaux* (Poitiers: UFR de langues et littératures)
Deutsch, Eliot. (ed.). 1991. *Culture and Modernity: East-West Philosophic Perspectives* (Honolulu: University of Hawaii Press)
Dhand, Arti. 2002. 'The Dharma of Ethics, the Ethics of Dharma: Quizzing the Ideals of Hinduism', *The Journal of Religious Ethics*, Vol. 30, No. 3: 347–72
Dumoulié, Camille. 1992. *Nietzsche et Artaud: pour une éthique de la cruauté* (Paris: Presses universitaires de France)
—— 1996. *Antonin Artaud* (Paris: Seuil)
Eliade, Mircea. 1967. 'Cosmogonic Myth and Sacred History', *Religious Studies*, Vol. 2, No. 2: 171–83
—— 1987. *The Sacred and the Profane: the nature of religion*, trans. by Willard R. Trask (San Diego: Harcourt Brace)
Eno, Robert. 1991. 'Creating Nature: Juist and Taoist approaches', in Kidder Smith (ed.), *Chuang Tzu, Rationality, Interpretation* (Breckinridge: Bowdoin College), p95
Eoyang, Eugene Chen. 2007. *Two-way Mirrors: Cross-Cultural Studies in Glocalisation* (UK: Lexington books)
Esslin, Martin. 1976. *Artaud* (London: Calder)
Europe: revue littéraire mensuelle, No. 698/699: *Henri Michaux*, 1987 (Paris: Les Éditions Denoël)
Europe: revue littéraire mensuelle, No. 873/874: *Antonin Artaud*, 2002 (Paris: Les Éditions Denoël)

Evans-Pritchard, E. E. 1937. *Witchcraft, Oracles and Magic among the Azande* (Oxford: Clarendon Press)
Feng, Youlan. 1983. *History of Chinese philosophy/Zhongguo zhexue shi*, 2 vols (Chongqing: Chongqing Press)
Fintz, Claude. 1999. 'Sagesse de Michaux: entre posture et imposture', in Pierre Grouix and Jean-Michel Maulpoix (eds), *Henri Michaux: corps et savoir* (Paris: ENS éditions Fontenay/Saint-Cloud), pp. 173–90
——2004. *Henri Michaux — 'homme-bombe'* (Grenoble: ELLUG)
Forsdick, Charles. 2004. *Victor Segalen and the Aesthetics of Diversity* (Oxford: OUP)
Foucault, Michel. 1972. *Histoire de la folie à l'âge classique: Suivi de Mon corps, ce papier, ce feu et La folie, l'absence d'œuvre* (Paris: Gallimard)
Froese, Katrin. 2012. *Nietzsche, Heidegger, and Daoist Thought* (Albany: SUNY Press)
Garelick, Herbert M. 1971. *Modes of Irrationality* (The Hague: Martinus Nijhoff)
Garelli, Jacques. 1982. *Artaud et la question du lieu* (Paris: J. Corti)
Girardot, N. J. 1983. *Myth and Meaning in Early Taoism: the theme of Chaos (hun-tun)* (Berkeley/ London: University of California Press)
Girardot, Norman, James Miller and Xiaogan Liu. (eds). 2001. *Daoism and Ecology* (USA: Harvard University Press)
Glicksberg, Charles. 1970. *Modern Literary Perspectivism* (Dallas: Southern Methodist University Press)
Gongsun, Long. 2010. *The Gongsunlongzi*, edited and annotated by Yujiang Wu and Xingyu Wu (Shanghai: Shanghai Guji Press)
Goosen, Gideon. 2008. *Spacetime and Theology in Dialogue* (Wisconsin: Marquette University Press)
Gourgouris, Stathis. 2003. *Does Literature Think? — Literature as Theory for an Antimythical Era* (Stanford: Stanford University Press)
Graham, Angus C. 1978. *Later Mohist Logic, Ethics and Science* (Hong Kong: The Chinese University Press)
—— 1985. *Reason and Spontaneity* (London: Curzon)
—— 1986. *Studies in Chinese Philosophy and Philosophical Literature* (Albany: SUNY Press)
Granet, Marcel. 1934. *La Pensée chinoise* (Paris: La Renaissance du Livre)
Graziani, Romain. 2006. *Fictions philosophiques du Tchouang-tseu* (Paris: Gallimard)
Grossman, Évelyne. 1996. *Artaud/Joyce: le corps et le texte* (Paris: Nathan)
——2004. *La Défiguration: Artaud-Beckett-Michaux* (Paris: Minuit)
Grouix, Pierre and Jean-Michel Maulpoix. (eds). 1999. *Henri Michaux: corps et savoir* (Paris: ENS éditions Fontenay/Saint-Cloud)
Hadot, Pierre. 2006. *The Veil of Isis: An Essay on the History of the Idea of Nature*, trans. by Michael Chase (Cambridge, Mass. and London: Belknap)
Hales, Steven D. and Welshon, Rex. 2000. *Nietzsche's Perspectivism* (Urbana: University of Illinois Press)
Hall, David. 1989. 'On Seeking a Change of Environment', in J. Baird Callicott and Roger T. Ames. (eds), *Nature in Asian Traditions of Thought* (Albany: SUNY Press), pp. 99–112
Hall, David L. and Roger T. Ames. 1995. *Anticipating China: Thinking through the narratives of Chinese and Western culture* (Albany: SUNY Press)
Halpern, Anne-Elisabeth. 1998. *Henri Michaux: le laboratoire du poète* (Paris: S. Arslan)
Halpern, Anne-Elisabeth et al. (eds). 1996. *Quelques orients d'Henri Michaux* (Paris: Findakly)
Hamdan, Dima. 2002. *Victor Segalen et Henri Michaux* (Fasano: Presses de l'Université de Paris- Sorbonne)
Hansen, Chad. 1983a. 'A Tao of Tao in Chuang-tzu', in Victor H. Mair (ed.), *Experimental Essays on Chuang-tzu* (Honolulu: University of Hawaii Press), pp. 24–55

——1983B. *Language and Logic in ancient China* (Ann Arbor: University of Michigan)

——1991. 'Should the Ancient Masters Value Reason?', in Henry Rosemont (ed.), *Chinese Texts and Philosophical Contexts* (La Salle: Open Court), pp. 179–209

HARBSMEIER, CHRISTOPH. 1992. *An Annotated Anthology of Comments on Zhuangzi, Serica Osloensia,* 2 vols (Oslo: University of Oslo)

——1995. 'Some Notions of Time and of History in China and in the West', in Chun-chieh Huang and Erik Zuercher (eds), *Time and Space in Chinese culture* (Leiden: Brill), pp. 49–71

——2006. 'Syntactic versus Semantic Notions of Subjectlessness in Classical Chinese Grammar', <http://crlao.ehess.fr/docannexe.php?id=405> [accessed 16 May 2012]

HARDY, J. ET AL. (eds). 2010. *Grundlagen der Antiken Ethik/Foundations of Ancient Ethics* (V & R Unipress Gmbh)

HEIDEGGER, MARTIN. 1962. *Being and Time*, trans. by John MacQuarrie and Edward Robinson (London: SCM Press)

HEIM, MARIA. 2004. *Theories of the Gift in South Asia: Hindu, Buddhist, and Jain reflections on Dāna* (New York and London: Routledge)

HEESTERMAN, J. C. 1964. 'Brahmin, Ritual and Renouncer', *Wien. Z. Kunde Süd-Ostasiens* 8: 1–31

HENDERSON, JOHN B. 1984. *The Development and Decline of Chinese Cosmology* (New York: Columbia University Press)

HUANG, CHUN-CHIEH and ERIK ZUERCHER. (eds). 1995. *Time and Space in Chinese culture* (Leiden: Brill)

HUANG, YONG. 2010. 'Respecting Different Ways of Life: A Daoist Ethics of Virtue in the *Zhuangzi*', *The Journal of Asian Studies,* Vol. 69, No. 4: 1049–69

JACOBS, CAROL. 1977. 'The Assimilating Harmony: A Reading of Antonin Artaud's *Héliogabale*', *SubStance*, Vol. 6, No. 17: 115–38

JAIN, ANDREA R. and JEFFREY J. KRIPAL. 2009. 'Quietism and Karma: Non-Action as Non-Ethics in Jain Asceticism', *Common Knowledge*, Vol. 15, Issue 2: 197–207

JAMES, WILLIAM. 1976. *Essays in Radical Empiricism* (Cambridge, Massachusetts: Harvard University Press)

JOCHIM, CHRIS. 1998. 'Just Say No to No Self in Zhuangzi', in Roger T Ames (ed.), *Wandering at Ease in the* Zhuangzi (Albany: Suny Press), pp. 35–7498Johnson, Barbara. 1978. 'The Critical Difference', *Diacritics,* Vol. 8, No. 2: 2–9

JOSÉ, BENARDETE. 1964. *Infinity: An Essay in Metaphysics* (Oxford: Clarendon Press)

JULLIEN, FRANÇOIS. 1998. *Un Sage est sans idée* (Paris: Seuil)

——2007. *Vital Nourishment: Departing from Happiness*, trans. by Arthur Goldhammer (New York/London: MIT Press)

KABAY, PAUL DOUGLAS. 2008. 'A Defense of Trivialism' (unpublished doctoral thesis, University of Melbourne)

KAHN, CHARLES H. 1999. *Plato and the Socratic dialogue: The philosophical use of a literary form*, 3rd edn (Cambridge: CUP)

——2009. *Essays on Being* (Oxford: OUP)

KEIGHTLEY, DAVID N. 2000. *The Ancestral Landscape: Time, space, and community in late Shang China* (Berkeley: University of California Press)

KIFFER, ANA PAULA. 2002. 'Les Corps de la faim', in *Europe: revue littéraire mensuelle*, No. 873/874: *Antonin Artaud* (Paris: Les Éditions Denoël), pp. 133–40

KING, R.A.H. and DENNIS SCHILLING (eds). 2011. *How Should One Live? Comparing ethics in ancient China and Greco-Roman antiquity* (Berlin/Boston: Walter de Gruyter)

KLOSSOWSKI, PIERRE. 1969. *Nietzsche et le cercle vicieux* (Paris: Mercure de France)

——1992. *Sade my Neighbour*, trans. by Alphonso Lingis (London: Quartet)

KNAPP, STEVEN and WALTER BENN MICHAELS. 1982. 'Against Theory', *Critical Inquiry*, Vol. 8, No. 4: 723–42

Kohn, Livia. 1992. *Early Chinese Mysticism: Philosophy and soteriology in the Taoist tradition* (Princeton: Princeton University Press)

——2009. *Readings in Daoist Mysticism* (Dunedin: Three Pines Press)

——2011. 'Body and Identity', in Ronnie Littlejohn and Jeffrey Dippmann (eds), *Riding the Wind with Liezi* (Albany: SUNY), pp. 168–72

Kohn, Livia and Yoshinobu Sakade (eds). 1989. *Taoist Meditation and Longevity Techniques* (Ann Arbor: University of Michigan)

Kristeva, Julia. 1980. *Pouvoirs de l'horreur: essai sur l'abjection* (Paris: Seuil)

Kuçuradi, Ioanna (ed.). 1995. *The Concept of Knowledge (*Dordrecht, Boston and London: Kluwer)

Kürtös, Karl. 2009. *Henri Michaux et le visuel* (Bern and Oxford: Peter Lang)

Lafargue, Michael. 2001. ''Nature' as Part of Human Culture in Daoism', in Norman Girardot, James Miller and Xiaogan Liu. (eds), *Daoism and ecology* (USA: Harvard University Press), pp. 46–55

Lamberth, David. 1999. *William James and the Metaphysics of Experience* (Cambridge: CUP)

Lanz, Henry. 1926. 'The Irrationality of Reasoning', *The Philosophical Review,* Vol. 35, No. 4: 340–59

Latour, Bruno. 1991. *Nous n'avons jamais été modernes. Essai d'anthropologie symétrique* (Paris: Éditions la Découverte)

——1996. 'On Actor-network Theory: A few clarifications plus more than a few complications', *Soziale Welt*, vol. 47: pp. 369–81

Laügt, Élodie. 2008. *L'Orient du signe: rêves et dérives chez Victor Segalen, Henri Michaux et Émile Cioran* (Bern: Peter Lang)

Le Clezio, J. M. G. 1965. *Le Rêve mexicain ou la Pensée interrompue* (Paris: Gallimard; Collection Folio/essais), p. 274

Lenk, Hans and Gregor Paul (eds). 1993. *Epistemological Issues in Classical Chinese Philosophy* (Albany: SUNY Press)

Levi, Jean. 2010. *Le Petit monde du* Tchouang-tseu (Paris: Philippe Picquier)

Lévinas, Emmanuel. 1981. *De l'existence à l'existant* (Paris: J. Vrin)

Lévy-Bruhl, Lucien. 1931. *La Mentalité primitive* (Oxford: Clarendon Press)

Li, Lieyan. 1988. *Shikong xueshuo shi* (Hubei: Hubei Renmin Press)

Li, Xiaofan Amy. 2015. 'Temporality in the Construction of Comparative Interpretation', *Comparative Critical Studies*, 12 (Edinburgh University Press)

Littlejohn, Ronnie and Jeffrey Dippmann (eds). 2011. *Riding the Wind with Liezi* (Albany: SUNY)

Liu, Xiaogan. 1994. *Classifying the 'Zhuangzi' Chapters* (Ann Arbor: University of Michigan)

Lumholtz, Carl. 1902. *Unknown Mexico: A Record of Five Years' Exploration Among the Tribes of the Western Sierra Madre* (New York: Charles Scribner's Sons)

Lupke, Christopher (ed.). 2005. *The Magnitude of* Ming*: Command, Allotment, and Fate in Chinese Culture* (Honolulu: University of Hawai'i Press)

MacIntyre, Alasdair. 1991. 'Incommensurability, Truth, and the Conversation between Confucians and Aristotelians about the Virtues', in Eliot Deutsch (ed.), *Culture and Modernity: East-West Philosophic Perspectives* (Honolulu: University of Hawaii Press), pp. 104–22.

Mair, Victor H. (ed.). 1983. *Experimental Essays on Chuang-tzu* (Honolulu: University of Hawaii Press)

Manney, Linda. 1992. 'States, Results, and the Active/Passive/Middle Continuum in Modern Greek', *Journal of Modern Greek Studies*, Vol. 10, No. 2: 205–33

Margel, Serge. 2008. *Aliénation: Antonin Artaud, les généalogies hybrides* (Paris: Galilée)

Marks, Joel and Roger T. Ames (eds). 1995. *Emotions in Asian Thought (Albany:* SUNY Press)

MARTIN, JEAN-PIERRE. 1994. *Henri Michaux: écritures de soi, expatriations* (Paris: J. Corti)
MAULPOIX, JEAN-MICHEL. 1984. *Michaux: passager clandestin* (Seyssel: Champ Vallon)
MAUSS, MARCEL. 1923–24. 'Essai sur le don', released as e-book in 2001, <http://www.uqac.uquebec.ca/zone30/Classiques_des_sciences_sociales/index.html>, [accessed 20 Oct 2012]
MELNICK, ARTHUR. 1989. *Space, Time, and Thought in Kant* (Dordrecht, Boston and London: Kluwer)
MÉHEUST, BERTRAND. 1999. *Somnambulisme et médiumnité: tome 1: Le Défi du magnétisme animal* (Le Plessis-Robinson: Institut Synthélabo)
MÈREDIEU, FLORENCE DE. 1992. *Antonin Artaud: Voyages* (Paris: Blusson)
——2006. *La Chine d'Antonin Artaud; Le Japon d'Antonin Artaud* (Paris: Blusson)
— *2008. Antonin Artaud: portraits et gris-gris* (Paris: Blusson)
MICHAEL, THOMAS. 2005. *The Pristine Dao: Metaphysics in early Daoist discourse* (Albany: SUNY Press)
MILL, JOHN STUART. 1843. *A System of Logic: Ratiocinative and Inductive* (London: Parker)
MILNER, MAX. 2000. *L'Imaginaire des drogues: de Thomas de Quincey à Henri Michaux* (Paris: Gallimard)
MINKOWSKI, EUGÈNE. 1970. *Lived time,* trans. by Nancy Metzel (USA: Northwestern University Press)
MOELLEGAARD, ESKE. 2003. 'Zhuangzi's Religious Ethics', *Journal of the American Academy of Religion*, Vol. 71, No. 2: 347–70
——2007. *An Introduction to Daoist Thought: Action, Language, and Ethics in Zhuangzi* (New York: Routledge)
MOORE, GEORGE EDWARD. 1903. *Principia ethica,* e-book on Fair Use Repository <http://fair-use.org/g-e-moore/principia-ethica> [accessed 7 February 2015]
MOORE, GERALD. 2011. *Politics of the Gift* (Edinburgh: Edinburgh University Press)
MORFEE, ADRIAN. 2005. *Antonin Artaud's Writing Bodies* (Oxford: Clarendon)
MORZEWSKI, CHRISTIAN and LINSEN QIAN. (eds). 2001. *Les Écrivains français du XXe siècle et la Chine* (Artois: Presses universitaires de Nankin)
MUNRO, DONALD J. (ed.). 1985. *Individualism and Holism: Studies in Confucian and Taoist values* (Ann Arbor: University of Michigan)
MYERHOFF, BARBARA G. 1974. *Peyote Hunt: The Sacred Journey of the Huichol Indians* (Ithaca, Cornell University Press)
NÆSS, A. 1989. *Ecology, Community, Lifestyle*, trans. and ed. D. Rothenberg (Cambridge: CUP)
NEUMANN, ERICH. 1989. *The Place of Creation,* trans. by Hildegard Nagel, Rolfe et al. (New Jersey: Princeton University Press)
NIETZSCHE, F. 2003. *Beyond Good and Evil*, trans. by Helen Zimmern, e-book at Gutenberg project <http://www.gutenberg.org/catalog/world/readfile?fk_files=3275478&pageno=1> [accessed 7 February 2015]
——2009. *On the Genealogy of Morals,* trans. by Ian Johnston, e-book at <http://www2.southeastern.edu/Academics/Faculty/jbell/nietzschegenealogy.pdf> [accessed 7 February 2015]
——1909. *The Birth of Tragedy*, trans. by A. Haussmann, e-book at Archive.org <http://archive.org/stream/thebirthoftragedoonietuoft/thebirthoftragedoonietuoft_djvu.txt> [accessed 7 February 2015]
——2001. *The Gay Science*, ed. by Bernard Williams, trans. by Josefine Nauckhoff (Cambridge: CUP)
——1998. *Twilight of the Idols,* trans. by Duncan Large (New York: OUP)
NORTON, B. 1991. *Toward Unity among Environmentalists* (New York: Oxford University Press)
PALUMBO-LIU, DAVID. 1992. 'The Utopias of Discourse: On the Impossibility of Chinese Comparative Literature', *Chinese Literature: Essays, Articles, Reviews (CLEAR)*, Vol. 14: 165–76

PARISH, NINA. 2007. *Henri Michaux: Experimentation with Signs* (Amsterdam/New York: Rodopi)

PARKINSON, GAVIN. 2008. *Surrealism, Art, and Modern Science: Relativity, Quantum Mechanics, Epistemology* (New Haven and London: Yale University Press)

PARRY, JONATHAN. 1986. 'The Gift, the Indian Gift and the 'Indian Gift'', *Man*, New Series, Vol. 21, No. 3: 453–73

PENOT-LACASSAGNE, OLIVIER. (ed.). 2005. *Artaud en revues* (Lausanne: L'âge d'homme)

——2007. *Vies et morts d'Antonin Artaud* (Saint-Cyr-sur-Loire: C. Pirot)

PEYRÉ, YVES. 1996. 'Permanence de l'ailleurs', in Eric Brogniet (ed.), *Les* Ailleurs *d'Henri Michaux,* Actes du colloque Namur, October 1995 (Namur: Revue de la Maison de la Poésie), pp. 28–45

PINDAR. 1999. *Olympians,* ed. by Diane Arnson Svarlien, e-book at Perseus Digital Library <http://www.perseus.tufts.edu/hopper/text?doc=Perseus:text:1999.01.0162> [accessed 7 October 2015]

POO, MU-CHOU. 2005. 'How to Steer through Life', in Christopher Lupke (ed.), *The Magnitude of* Ming*: Command, Allotment, and Fate in Chinese Culture* (Honolulu: University of Hawai'i Press), pp. 107–28

PLEYNET, MARCELIN. 1973. 'La Matière pense', in Sollers (ed.), *Artaud* (Paris: Union générale d'éditions), pp. 135–50

PRIEST, GRAHAM. 2006. *In Contradiction: A Study of the Transconsistent* (Oxford: Clarendon Press)

——2008. *An Introduction to Non-Classical Logic* (Cambridge: CUP)

PUETT, MICHAEL. 2005. 'Following the Commands of Heaven', in Christopher Lupke (ed.). *The Magnitude of* Ming*: Command, Allotment, and Fate in Chinese Culture* (Honolulu: University of Hawai'i Press), pp. 49–69

QIAN, ZHAOMING. 2003. *Ezra Pound and China* (Ann Arbor: University of Michigan Press)

QIAO, QINGJU. 2006. 'Western Discourse and Shadows in the Legitimacy Crisis of Chinese Philosophy', *Contemporary Chinese Thought*, 37.3: 69–76

RAPHALS, LISA. 1992. *Knowing Words: Wisdom and Cunning in the Classical Traditions of China and Greece* (Ithaca: Cornell University Press)

REDING, JEAN-PAUL. 2004. *Comparative Essays in Early Greek and Chinese Rationality* (Franham: Ashgate)

REGNAUT, MAURICE. 1975. *Sur Adamov, Artaud, Brecht, Genet, Gorki, Racine, Weiss* (Paris: P. J. Oswald)

REU, WIM DE. 2006. 'Right Words Seem Wrong: Neglected Paradoxes in Early Chinese Texts', *Philosophy East and West*, Vol. 56, No. 2: 281–300

RIGAUD-DRAYTON, MARGARET. 2005. *Henri Michaux: Poetry, Painting, and the Universal Sign* (Oxford: Clarendon Press)

ROBINET, ISABELLE. 1995. 'Un, deux, trois — Les différentes modalités de l'Un et sa dynamique', *Cahiers d'Extrême-Asie*, Vol. 8: 175–220.

——1996. 'Une lecture du *Zhuangzi*', *Études chinoises,* vol. XV, nos. 1–2: 109–58

ROETZ, HEINER. 2010. 'On Nature and Culture in Zhou China', in Han Ulrich Vogel and Gunter Dux (eds), *Concepts of Nature: a Chinese-European Cross-Cultural Perspective* (Leiden: Brill), pp. 198–219

ROGOZINSKI, JACOB. 2011. *Guérir la vie: la passion d'Antonin Artaud* (Paris: Éditions du cerf)

ROSEMONT, HENRY. (ed.). 1991. *Chinese Texts and Philosophical Contexts* (La Salle: Open Court)

ROSKER, JANA. 2008. *Searching for the Way: Theory of Knowledge in Pre-Modern and Modern China* (Hong Kong: The Chinese University Press)

ROTH, HAROLD. 1999. *Original Tao: Inward Training and the Foundations of Taoist Mysticism* (New York and Chichester: Columbia University Press)

ROUSSEAU, JEAN-JACQUES. 1782. *Les Confessions,* new edn, 1841 (Paris: Charpentier)

ROUTH, H. V. 2005. 'The Future of Comparative Literature', *The Modern Language Review,* 100: 5- 18

SASSO, ROBERT. 1978. *Georges Bataille: le système du non-savoir* (Paris: Minuit)

SHANG, GE LING. 2006. *Liberation as Affirmation: The Religiosity of Zhuangzi and Nietzsche* (Albany: SUNY Press)

SCARPETTA, GUY. 1973. 'La Dialectique change de matière', in Sollers (ed.), *Artaud* (Paris: Union générale d'éditions), pp. 263–97

SCHIPPER, KRISTOFER. 1982. *Le Corps taoiste: corps physique, corps social* (Paris: Fayard)

—— 1995. 'The Inner World of the Lao-tzu chung ching', in Chun-chieh Huang and Erik Zuercher. (eds), *Time and Space in Chinese culture* (Leiden: Brill), pp. 114–31

SCHWARTZ, BENJAMIN I. 1985. *The World of Thought in Ancient China* (Cambridge, Mass.: Harvard University Press)

SCOTT, CHARLES E. 1989. 'The Middle Voice of Metaphysics', *The Review of Metaphysics,* Vol. 42, No. 4: 743–64

——2007. *Living with Indifference* (Bloomington: Indiana University Press)

SEGALEN, VICTOR. 1911. *Essai sur l'exotisme,* 1978 edn (Montpellier: Fata Morgana)

SÉRIS, DELPHINE. 1999. 'Les Meidosems: l'entreprise paradoxale du portrait', in Pierre Grouix and Jean-Michel Maulpoix (eds), *Henri Michaux: corps et savoir* (Paris: ENS éditions Fontenay/Saint-Cloud), pp. 81–102

SHANKMAN, STEVEN and STEPHEN DURRANT. 2000. *The Siren and the Sage: Knowledge and Wisdom in Ancient Greece and China* (London: Cassell)

SHIH, SHU-MEI. 2001. *The Lure of the Modern: Writing Modernism in Semicolonial China, 1917-1937* (Berkeley and London: University of California Press)

SLINGERLAND, EDWARD G. 2003. *Effortless Action: Wu-Wei as Conceptual Metaphor and Spiritual Ideal in Early China* (Oxford: OUP)

SMADJA, ROBERT. 1988. *Poétique du corps* (Berne: Lang)

——2010. *De la littérature à la philosophie du sujet* (Paris: L'Harmattan)

SMITH, GREGORY B. 2007. *Martin Heidegger: Paths Taken, Paths Opened* (Plymouth: Rowman and Littlefield)

SOLES. DEBORAH H. and DAVID E. SOLES. 1998. 'Fish Traps and Rabbit Snares: Zhuangzi on Judgement, Truth and Knowledge', *Asian Philosophy: An International Journal of the Philosophical Traditions of the East,* 8:3: 149–64

SOLLERS, PHILIPPE. 1971. *L'Écriture de l'expérience des limites* (Paris: Seuil)

——(ed.). 1973. *Artaud,* conference at Cerisy-la-Salle, 1972 (Paris: Union générale d'éditions)

SOLOMON, ROBERT C. 2002. 'Nietzsche on Fatalism and 'Free Will'', *Journal of Nietzsche Studies,* No. 23: 63–87

SONTAG, SUSAN. 1961. *Against Interpretation* (New York: Octagon)

—— 1976. *À la rencontre d'Artaud,* trans. by Gérard H. Durand (Paris: Christian Bourgois)

STEWART. OMER. 1987. *Peyote Religion: A History* (University of Oklahoma Press)

SUBER, PETER. 1998. 'Infinite Reflections', *St John's Review,* XLIV, 2: 1–59

TAMOGAMI, KENJIRÔ. 1996. 'Michaux et Tchouang-tseu: L'infini et l'écriture de "l'homme sans nom"', in Anne-Elisabeth Halpern et al. (eds), *Quelques orients d'Henri Michaux* (Paris: Findakly), pp. 117–38

TAYLOR, RICHARD. 1962. 'Fatalism', *Philosophical Review,* 71: 56–66

THAPAR, ROMILA. 2005. 'Cyclic and Linear Time in Early India', in *Museum International,* No. 227, Vol. 57, No. 3: 19–31

THIHER, ALLEN. 1988. 'A Theory of Literature or Recent Literature as Theory', *Contemporary literature,* 29.3: 337–50

TRAUZETTEL, ROLF. 1999. 'A Sophism by the Ancient Philosopher Gongsun Long', *Journal of Chinese Philosophy,* 26: I: 21–35

Trotet, François. 1992. *Henri Michaux, ou, La sagesse du vide* (Paris: Albin Michel)

Trotignon, Pierre. 2000. 'Une difficulté dans la théorie bergsonienne de la nature', in Olivier Bloch (ed.), *Philosophies de la nature: actes du colloque tenu à l'université de Paris I, Panthéon Sorbonne* (Paris: Publications de la Sorbonne), pp. 401–12

Tu, Wei-ming. 1989. 'The Continuity of Being: Chinese Visions of Nature', in J. Baird Callicott and Roger T. Ames (eds), 1989. *Nature in Asian Traditions of Thought* (Albany: SUNY Press), pp. 67–78

Tzara, Tristan. 1978. *Lampisteries: précédées des Sept manifestes Dada* (Paris: Pauvert)

Van Norden, Bryan W. 2007. *Virtue Ethics and Consequentialism in Early Chinese Philosophy* (Cambridge: CUP)

Venturi, Robert. 1966. *Complexity and Contradiction in Architecture* (New York: MOMA Press)

Verger, Romain. 2004. *Onirocosmos* (Paris: Presses Sorbonne nouvelle)

Vergnières, Solange. 1995. *Éthique et politique chez Aristote: physis, ēthos, nomos* (Paris: Presses universitaires de France)

Vicari, Justin. 2012. *Mad Muses and the Early Surrealists* (North Carolina and London: McFarland and Company)

Vidieu-Larrère, Francine. 2001. *Lecture de l'imaginaire des œuvres dernières de Antonin Artaud* (Paris: Lettres modernes Minard)

Virmaux, Alain. 1970. *Artaud et le théâtre* (Paris: Seghers)

Viveiros de Castro, Eduardo. 1992. *From the Enemy's Point of View: Humanity and Divinity in an Amazonian Society,* trans. by Catherine v. Howard (Chicago & London: University of Chicago Press)

—— 1998. 'Cosmological Deixis and Amerindian Perspectivism', *The Journal of the Royal Anthropological Institute*, Vol. 4, No. 3: 469–88

Viveiros de Castro, Eduardo and Antonia Walford. 2011. 'Zeno and the Art of Anthropology: Of Lies, Beliefs, Paradoxes, and Other Truths', *Common Knowledge*, Vol. 17, Issue 1: 128–45

Vogel, Han Ulrich and Gunter Dux (eds). *Concepts of Nature: A Chinese-European Cross-Cultural Perspective* (Leiden: Brill)

Wang, Ning. 1997. 'Orientalism versus Occidentalism?', *New Literary History,* Vol. 28, No. 1: 57–67

Wang, Sally A. 1975. 'Can Man Go Beyond Ethics?: The System of Padmasambhava', *The Journal of Religious Ethics*, Vol. 3, No. 1: 141–55

Wang, Youru. 2003. *Linguistic Strategies in Daoist Zhuangzi and Chan Buddhism: the other way of speaking* (London: Routledge Curzon)

Warren, James. 2002. *Epicurus and Democritean Ethics* (Cambridge: CUP)

Watteau, Patrick. 2011. *Antonin Artaud: 'foudre du tact personnel'* (Paris: Presses universitaires de Vincennes)

Weingarten, Romain and Ruby Cohn. 1963. 'Re-Read Artaud', *The Tulane Drama Review*, Vol. 8, No. 2: 74–84

Weisstein, Eric W. 'Aleph-1.' From MathWorld — A Wolfram Web Resource. <http://mathworld.wolfram.com/Aleph-1.html> [accessed 7 February 2015]

Wertheim, Margaret. 1999. *The Pearly Gates of Cyberspace: a history of space from Dante to the internet* (London: Virago)

Westfahl, Gary, George Slusser, and David Leiby. (eds). 2002. *Worlds Enough and Time: Explorations of time in science fiction and fantasy* (Connecticut and London: Greenwood Press)

Whitehead, A. N. 1920. *The Concept of Nature* (Cambridge: CUP)

Williams, Bernard. 1999. *Problems of the Self* (Cambridge: CUP)

Wittgenstein, Ludwig. 1922. *Tractatus logico-philosophicus*, trans. by C. K. Ogden, released as e- book in 2010 at the Gutenberg Project: <www.gutenberg.org/files/5740/5740-pdf.pdf> [accessed 7 February 2015]

WU, KUANG-MING. 1982. *Chuang tzu: World philosopher at Play* (New York: Crossroad Pub. Co.)

—— 1995. 'Spatiotemporal Interpenetration in Chinese Thinking', in Chun-chieh Huang and Erik Zuercher (eds), *Time and Space in Chinese culture* (Leiden: Brill), pp. 17–48

YE, HAIYAN. 1979. *Zhuangzi yuzhoulun shitan* (Taibei: Chia Hsin Foundation)

YE, SHUXIAN. 1997. *Zhuangzi de wenhua jiexi* (Wuhan: Hubei Renmin Press)

YEARLEY, LEE. 1983. 'The Perfected Person in the Radical *Chuang Tzu*', in Victor Mair (ed.), *Experimental Essays on the Chuang Tzu* (Honolulu: University of Hawaii Press), pp. 125–39

YEH, MICHELLE. 1983. 'The Deconstructive Way: A comparative study of Derrida and Chuang Tzu', *Journal of Chinese Philosophy,* 10 (2): 95–126

ZANGHI, FILIPPO. 2002. *Un Hérétique de l'espace* (Lausanne: Archipel)

ZHANG, DAINIAN. 2002. *Key Concepts in Chinese Philosophy,* trans. and ed. by Edmund Ryden (New Haven and London: Yale University Press)

ZHANG, LONGXI. 1992. *The Tao and the Logos: Literary Hermeneutics, East and West* (Durham and London: Duke University Press)

—— 1998. *Mighty Opposites: From Dichotomies to Differences in the Comparative Study of China* (Stanford: Stanford University Press)

ZIPORYN, BROOK. 2000. *Evil and/or/as the Good* (Cambridge, Massachusetts and London: Harvard University Press)

ŽIŽEK, SLAVOJ. 2004. *Organs without Bodies: Deleuze and Consequences* (New York and London: Routledge)

INDEX

Printed in Great Britain
by Amazon